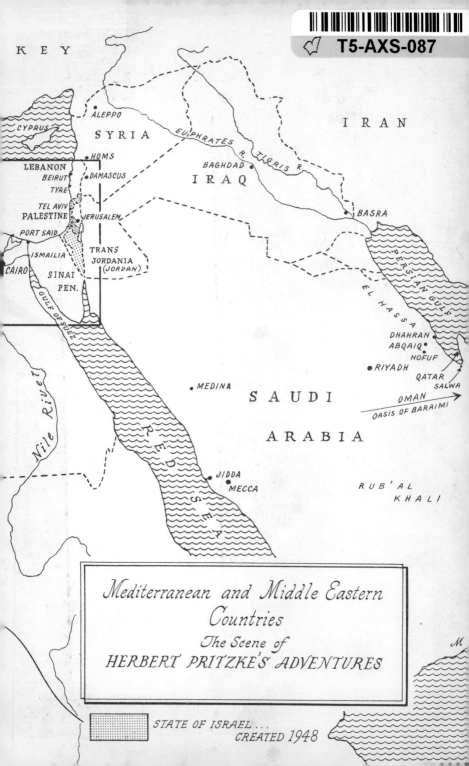

BEDOUIN DOCTOR

HERBERT PRITZKE

Bedouin Doctor

TRANSLATED FROM THE GERMAN BY

RICHARD GRAVES

E. P. Dutton & Company, Incorporated

NEW YORK, 1957

LIBRARY OF CONGRESS CATALOG CARD NUMBER: 57–8996

TABLE OF CONTENTS

ILLUSTRATIONS

BEDOUIN DOCTOR

Chapter I

ESCAPE

"MAKING a getaway?"

I felt a hand on my shoulder and nearly crumpled up with fear. I'm no hero by nature, but for days past I had been vowing never to show that I was frightened, whatever might befall, never to turn pale and never in any circumstances to give myself away.

The hand lay on my shoulder as if, by its pressure, its owner wanted to force me into a confession. Without looking up, I knew that it was the hand of the man in the next bed. I had been looking at him with suspicious scrutiny and wondering if he were really asleep, or peeping at me through half-closed eyelids. I sat with an air of boredom on the edge of my bed, putting my cap into the pocket of my overcoat and taking out from under the pillow a kitchen knife which I had had some trouble to acquire and which I was now hiding in the lining of my coat. As long as I was busy doing these things I had been able to keep my eye on my neighbor. There was nothing to fear from my other companions who were playing skat, reading, lying around on their beds or standing in groups talking. They took no interest in what a comrade might be doing by his bed. Anyhow, the light in the dormitory was not strong enough to enable them to see what was going on in an ill-lit corner.

Under my mattress I had hidden a tent pole. It was nearly seven feet long and I was taking it with me as a weapon to use when I escaped. It was made of hardwood and had an iron point and, if I were attacked by man or beast, it would serve me much better than the kitchen knife. I had been in a panic lest one of the skat players should look in my direction while I was drawing it out, or my neighbor be awakened by the noise. One could hardly help noticing an object of that length when I pulled it out and pointed it upward. Luckily the skat players were laughing at some crack at that moment and the men who were lying on their beds looked sleepily toward the laughing group, while my neighbor, flat on his back, went on sleeping. In a few seconds I had gotten the tent pole out and had pushed it through the low, open window by my bed. I gave a sigh of relief and was just going to stand up when I felt the hand on my shoulder. I thought to myself, there's another man who wants to earn a hundred cigarettes for giving away his comrade to the intelligence officer. A hundred cigarettes was the usual reward for information about preparations for escape or actual attempts. This fellow probably belonged to the group of POW's who were always spying for the English and getting privileges for their services.

Don't talk rubbish, man," I cried, I noticed that my neighbor had a friendly grin on his face and now realized that he had been observing me all the time. I went on, "Who the devil has played the corny old trick on me of putting a pole into my bed? I suppose he expected me to bruise myself against it." My attempt to talk myself out of this awkward situation fell rather flat.

"Don't talk like that to an old hand," said he, turning toward me and propping his head on his hand.

"My dear fellow, we all know that if a man manages to get hold of a tent pole, it's not because he's a collector of tent poles or because he wants gradually to assemble a whole tent: it's because he's preparing to escape . . ."

"And when his pal calls the guard he gets a hundred cigarettes for upholding the discipline of the camp. Go along, then! Run and tell them!"

I spat the words venomously into his face. He seemed to be wondering if he ought to feel hurt, and how to make a decent exit from an embarrassing situation.

Then he waved his hand wearily and said: "Anyone can escape now. Things aren't what they were. The war has been over for eighteen months. The British sentries don't worry about us much, but they still have permission to shoot, though they are no longer compelled by order to do so, and if you walk in front of a sentry's sights, he will certainly have a shot at you."

"Why do you tell me that?" I said, for I was still not sure if I could trust him. The shrewd grin on his face softened into a sympathetic smile.

"Yes," he said, "anyone can break out now and you look as though you weren't making your first attempt."

"You're right. Six months ago I tried to get away with a couple of friends."

"You don't seem to have got very far."

"No. Someone gave us away. In a short time we were hauled in. The usual routine. I was sent to Camp 307 at Fanara in the Canal Zone where they put me in Cage 6 with an attractive mob of corpse robbers, homosexuals, camp thieves and suchlike."

"Is that so? I thought no one ever left Cage 6 in Fanara. You must have got ill. You're a doctor, aren't you? And I suppose you managed to contract some plausible form of sickness and get yourself sent to the hospital at Fâyid. Afterward, you were transferred here for a few weeks to convalesce."

"Yes, that's about it."

"As far as I'm concerned," said he, "you've got no cause to worry. I won't give you away, but if I were you, I'd give up this nonsense. Life is more or less bearable here."

"Yes," I said, "here perhaps it is. But tomorrow there's another batch of prisoners going to Fanara and I'm dead sure to be on the list. Up to now, I've been making good use of a varicose vein in my left leg. When I was in Cage 6, I pretended it gave me cramp. After the medical orderly had tried unsuccessfully to cure my complaint, they had to send me willy-nilly to Fâyid for an operation—which was just what I had been working for. Here there was at first no need for faking. It hurts a lot to have a vein pulled out of the calf of your leg. After a while I had to start play acting again. I cultivated a limp, and made the most of my discomfort so as to gain time and recover enough strength to undertake a long march through the desert."

"March through the desert!" exclaimed my neighbor scornfully. "How far do you think you'll get? It isn't difficult to die of thirst in the desert, but there are other ways of dying before that one. You'll always find Egyptian gangs in the neighborhood of the British camps. Should you fall into their hands, you'll be spared the necessity of worrying about your future. If they take you for an Englishman, though you don't look much like one, they'll kill you, for they hate the English like the plague. If you tell them you're a German prisoner of war, and they believe you, they will first beat you up and then hand over what remains of you to the British in return for the customary reward of two pounds. That's all you're worth. The members of these gangs are mostly employed as casual labor in the British camps by day and while they work, or pretend to work, they find opportunities for scrounging weapons for their nocturnal campaigns."

"Yes," I said, "I noticed some of those fellows hanging about by the fence the whole afternoon. Dirty, ragged brutes with long beards; they looked as if they had never washed in their lives. One can expect anything of them. All the same, it's useless for you to try to dissuade me. I can't take it any longer."

"If I had to choose between Cage 6 in Fanara and the desert, I'd probably do the same as you. Go along, then, and start soon. The longer you travel in darkness, the better your chances. Good luck to you!"

My next action was to tear off a few squares of newspaper from the nail and to make for the latrines, which were about fifty yards distant from our huts. Meantime night had fallen, and the darkness was only lit by the electric lamps on the posts in the barbed-wire fencing. The English didn't credit the sick prisoners or those recovering from operations with any serious intention of escaping, and the fencing around the camp was not difficult to get through. Instead of the deep entanglements which were usual in other camps, there was a line of single strands, not too close together, running from post to post and serving rather as a symbol of confinement. They were meant to remind us that though we were in a hospital camp we were still prisoners.

I sauntered between the huts to the latrines and halted by the washbasins. I had to avoid looking suspicious, but it was difficult. The whole camp was enveloped in an atmosphere of lazy immobility. The sentinel posted in the middle of the camp, whom I could see very well from where I was, stood as if hypnotized by the darkness of the desert, at which he was staring through the dimly lit fence. He was a young fellow who had probably never fired a shot, except on the range. We were both afraid of the desert, he and I. On the other side of the fence was the dark unknown. Formerly the sentries had to patrol along the inner side of the fence, but the marauders outside had often fired on them, while they were on the move. In the ensuing confusion the natives had broken into the supply stores and stolen anything they could use—and there was nothing they couldn't find a use for.

The sentry seemed harmless enough. There was more to be feared from the German camp-watchers, mostly parachutists, who for thirty pfennigs a day kept an eye on their comrades, even as late as this. They did not hesitate to use their cudgels to knock the homesickness out of any escaper before they claimed their reward in cigarettes from the sergeant of the guard.

However, I reckoned that these fellows must, by now, be going off duty. I looked out and waited, hoping that none of my comrades would come to the latrine and engage me in conversation, and then insist on my going back to the huts with him.

At last I was sure that the German camp-watchers had gone. I took a quick glance at the sentry standing there in the middle of the camp, young and almost pitiable in his fear of the dark wilderness.

I murmured to myself the opening words of *Tipperary*. Now for it! I strolled out casually, though I wanted to run at full speed. I found my tent pole lying by my hut, picked it up and trailed it along the ground behind me.

From the spot where I picked up the pole to the kitchens was about fifty yards, and I had to cover that distance at an easy casual pace, being the whole time within the sentry's field of vision. It would take me perhaps two minutes to traverse those wretched fifty yards—if I didn't want to attract attention. I had to keep my head down but not to crouch; to reduce my height somehow without bending my body. If the sentry turned only a little to one side, it would be all up with me. Then I would either have

to drop my pole and go up and explain that I had lost my way
and next day be sent back to Fanara; or I could run for it. If I did
that, I should risk being shot at by the sentry and the whole camp
would certainly be alerted behind me before I had gone more than
a few yards.

I got over the first thirty paces, and what my intention was
became more obvious at every step. Now if the sentry challenged
me, no excuse would be believed.

Forty paces: from somewhere in the waste came a hollow,
howling cry. I started, in spite of my resolve to show no fear. Who
could have imagined that fifty yards was such an endless distance?
The two minutes seemed like a whole ghastly hour during which
I stepped slowly, slowly forward, while my need urged me to
hasten and all the time I felt as if the muzzle of a rifle was pointing
at my back.

At last it was over and I was out of sight behind the wall of the
kitchen hut. It was only a few steps from here to the fence and I
covered the distance at a run. My legs could no longer stand the
strain of pacing slowly forward step by step. There I was at the
fence at last. I had long been reconnoitering it to find a place where
I could slip through under the bottom strand, which was only a
foot from the ground. I found the place I had chosen, and when
I lay down there was just room for me to crawl through without
hurting myself, but I was so excited that I managed to tear a piece
off my jacket on the jagged line which separated freedom from
servitude.

Freedom!

As soon as I had the wire behind me I ran straight out into the
desert, not knowing where I was going. The intoxication of freedom possessed me. It was real intoxication with the promise of a
hang-over. I was free, free as a bird. But soon I realized what this
freedom meant to a solitary wanderer in the wilderness staggering
through the shifting sand, his strides robbed of half their length,
his feet clogged in the sand drifts as if in soft snow, as he trudged
painfully forward.

A hell of a freedom!

My first job was to find the highway and then to keep off it.

On what was called the desert road I was likely to run into a British truck at any moment. I needed to find a way aside from the beaten track which would lead somewhere and help me to real freedom. In the dome of heaven above me the stars were so clear that they looked like throbbing points of light. High above the horizon hung the Great Bear. One's simple, schoolboy knowledge comes back and reminds one that by prolonging the line between the two hindmost pointers to a point five times the distance between them one comes to the Pole Star, which gives one the North almost exactly. Ninety degrees to the left would be due west and that was my direction. My freedom depended on my getting as far to the west as possible. I looked for a bright star in the west and set my course by it. But, I thought, what shall I do if it wanders and leads me astray?

Before my flight I had been practicing walking as far as the limited space of the camp permitted and had thought myself very fit, though my estimate of my strength was more adapted to camp standards than to the stress of the open desert. I had hoped during my first few hours of freedom to cover a long distance on the way to my ultimate destination, and I had felt that much, if not everything, depended on how far I could travel during the first night. However, after wading for ten minutes through the soft sand and losing half the ground I gained at every step, I was so exhausted and the wound of my operation hurt so much that I had to stop and rest.

I sat down on a boulder, panting with exhaustion, and looked back on the camp which, looking threateningly near, lay like an illuminated square in the darkness of the desert. I was still so near the point where I had made my exit that I dared not light a cigarette, though I needed nothing so much as a few breaths of tobacco smoke to calm my overstrung and agitated nerves. The darkness lay so heavily on me that I felt I could grasp it in my hands. Only the lamplit square of the camp held some brightness, and that made the darkness elsewhere seem all the blacker. I grasped my tent pole tightly for comfort but I realized that it was not much of a defense against an uncertain future which threatened me with hunger, thirst, sickness and ghastly loneliness, or the prospect of meeting men who might well be much more brutal and cruel than those from whom I had escaped. I could still return to the oasis of light, order and security which I had left. The way back was not more difficult than the way out. In an hour I could be back in bed. My neighbor would be surprised but no one else would have noticed my absence. The war had ended so long ago, that they were bound to send me home in a few weeks or, at latest, a few months, for what was the point of feeding us any longer? Yes, but tomorrow they would send me back to Fanara and stick me in Cage 6 again. Maybe I should spend months there—possibly half a year.

No! That I couldn't stand . . . so onward to the west! My tortured body had to obey the orders of my will, and my will was governed by the fear of going back to Cage 6.

Only, I had to go slowly so as not to waste my strength—if one could call it strength—senselessly. I followed the classic route of German escapers—first three hours march due west, so as to get clear of the British Canal Zone and then turn northwest and make for the Sweet-Water Canal, which runs from Cairo to Ismailia.

How I managed to keep going all night, plodding mechanically on step by step, without relaxing every ten minutes and looking for some place to rest, was a mystery, and I still don't know how I did it. My whole body was in agony, but after the decision I had taken when I looked back at the camp, I knew I must not slacken even now. I stumbled on through the dawn feeling that every step brought me nearer to safety.

As day broke my guiding star vanished. I wondered if it had fooled me but couldn't know for certain. Now I had to look for landmarks in the desert, which were hard to find in the monotonous landscape. One picked out a few boulders or a strip of dark or light ground or, maybe, a miserable thornbush. The rays of the eastern sun shone hotly on the back of my head and seemed to burn into my skull as I set my course on these selected landmarks—and often failed to come up with them.

The sand kept getting into my shoes and chafed my feet like emery powder till they were almost raw. The pain of my varicose wound increased as I went on and my muscles ached with weariness, but though I was so dog-tired and broken that I was ready to collapse I still denied myself all rest. I knew that after a while I shouldn't be able to go on any longer.

Then, as I stumbled forward automatically, stunned with fatigue and ready to fall asleep at any moment, I heard sounds. I had just gone into some low ground from which I had no view, when I clearly heard the sound of tank tracks. Where the tanks were going I couldn't tell, but I had just time to creep into a thornbush when the first tank came over the top of the slope. It was followed by a second, then a third, and finally a dozen of the steel monsters lunged over the edge and made straight for my hiding place. My miserable little bush presented no obstacle to the caterpillar tracks of these rolling fortresses, which could have obliterated it with absurd ease, and there was no reason for them to deviate from their course in order to avoid it.

Lying as flat as I could, with my nose in the sand, I debated feverishly whether I should creep out and give my presence away or let myself be rolled over, with the outside chance that the tracks would just miss me. Knowing what the spoor of these apocalyptic beasts looked like, I was making up my mind to dash away when the tanks drew up—I don't know why—a short distance before they reached me. Soldiers clambered out of the openings and sat on the tracks or lay down in the shade of their vehicles and started to smoke.

Hearing the report of small arms and hand grenades some way off, I concluded that I had stumbled into the middle of a field exercise. This knowledge relieved me to some extent, but I felt, to say the least, extremely uncomfortable in the near vicinity of these camouflaged monsters with their khaki-clad crews, who soon began to walk about for lack of something to do. They had halted within a stone's throw of my bush and, if they spotted me, it would be easy for them to deliver an escaped prisoner at the camp by noon.

As I lay with my face pressed into the undergrowth, I peered anxiously at the armored fortresses and reckoned up my chances of avoiding detection. Hardly daring to breathe, I wished these fellows and their field day in hell. In spite of my extreme fatigue and my belief that my aching and exhausted body was incapable of speedy motion, I had to think of the possibility of making a dash for it or alternatively continuing to lie there as still as a corpse, if curiosity or boredom led one of the soldiers up to my thornbush.

Then something very extraordinary happened to me—something which never ought to have happened. I actually managed to fall asleep in full view of the soldiers.

I remember raising my head and feeling indescribably miserable and then noticing with wonder that I was looking westward into the declining sun. I looked around the depression in which I lay and found it as empty and deserted as when I first stumbled into it. No tanks, no khaki uniforms. My sleep had been so deep that I hadn't even heard the soldiers starting their engines or the grinding of the tanks rolling by my hiding place.

Strangely enough, I felt the delayed action of fear more than joy. I was no longer capable of laughter. Although it was winter, the sun's rays shone strongly on the stony, sandy desert and, as a result of sleeping in the sunshine, I had a violent headache which made thinking a torment. I reckoned from the present position of the sun that the soldiers had long ago finished their exercise and were now, with their bellies full of an excellent dinner, playing poker or crown-and-anchor. My own last meal had been eaten twenty-four hours ago. But it wasn't my hunger that put me in a rage. It was the thought of the cold shower they had enjoyed when they got home that made me hate and envy those soldiers. I imagined them luxuriating in cascades of cool water and then tumbling into clean shirts and tidy uniforms and putting on shoes without a single grain of sand in them. They had had beer to drink, as much as they wanted, or perhaps only water. Water . . . water . . . fresh water from the tap, as much as they liked . . . and I would have given anything to lick the rim of a water bottle.

Inside my tortured head my brain seemed to have come unstuck and to be wobbling about at every step I took, as I limped along, trailing my tent pole behind me and occasionally stopping to lean on it before I started again in whatever direction my faith or instinct led me.

Soon daylight departed and everything around me grew dark, as did the thoughts within me. Nothing—not even the right way, not even my safety—seemed to matter. When I saw that I couldn't go on any longer, I let myself fall into the sand and went straight to sleep, holding my tent pole slackly in my hand.

I awoke next day with a splitting headache to see nothing but the sunlit desert ending in the swimming haze of a mirage. I stumbled on aimlessly, no longer able to keep my eyes fixed on a landmark long enough to follow it. Tortured with headache and thirst, I hated the thought of anyone else being able to put even his toes in water. When I stopped, all was silence, but as soon as I started moving, I kept hearing taps being turned on and water rushing out of them. I thought of the taps in my Berlin apartment and counted them. There were nine altogether, five for cold water, and four for hot. One could drink warm or even hot water, if no cold was to be had. Cold water at a temperature of 47°! My mouth was so dry that my tongue lay in it like a stiff piece of leather, and it hurt me to move it. My lips were swollen and cracked.

Suddenly another thought came to me. I must have lost my direction. Probably I had been walking too long due west. Yes, that was it. If I had turned northwest as I had meant to do, I should long ago have reached water. At present my stumbling progress had a single goal—water—to reach the Sweet-Water Canal and follow it upstream. There must be enough water in the canal to quench thousands of thirsts like mine. But I felt that I could drink it up all alone, with its Bilharzia worms and its billions of microbes. Everything else subsided into my unconscious mind— the agony of marching with raw and blistered feet, my headache, my worn-out legs, my searching for the right direction and my anxiety to avoid danger. I didn't care what bandits might fall on me and beat me up, provided they first held a cup of water or a gourd to my lips and let me once more learn what it was to drink.

I had long been unable to see in what direction I was moving, and if I had been able to do so, I could not have coordinated my observations. I was unable to look in front of me, as my head hung down on my breast, and all I could see was the yellow sand which shifted and reformed under the pressure of my feet. After a while I could no longer make out the sand or my own shoes: all I could see was a swimming sheet of yellowish-brown.

Then suddenly I stumbled onto a human skeleton—another victim of the desert—complete with a solitary human thighbone beside it. Nearby was the wreck of a truck with which I nearly collided since, being unable to lift my head, I couldn't see anything till I walked into it. The truck had stopped in a depression and still carried the faded pennon of a British division.

I suddenly realized how the tragedy had occurred, and had a fellow-feeling for the victims. The truck must have been attacked by Bedouins who had killed the driver and his mate and then driven the vehicle far out into the desert, where they had unloaded and dismantled it and carried off on camels everything they could use. The corpses had been stripped naked. The Arabs had left them only their shoes and belts, because these objects might have betrayed the origin of the other stolen goods, just as they revealed to me who the victims had been and by whom they had been murdered.

The bodies had been eaten and their bones picked clean by hyenas, jackals and birds of prey. The second skeleton had been pulled to pieces, and only the remaining thighbone showed that its owner had been a young man.

These dry bones aroused my fears again. I had no longer any wish to be knocked on the head by bandits and have my body gnawed by jackals, even on condition that in the hereafter I could forever slake my thirst in fresh cold water!

No, indeed.

So I aimed to move away as far as possible from the scene of the desert tragedy, as far, that is, as my parched and feeble body would carry me. My strength was failing me and it was only the fear inspired by those ghastly skeletons that drove me away, step by step, from the gruesome hollow.

But even my fear was not strong enough to stiffen my knocking knees. I stumbled and fell down and had the greatest trouble in getting up again. My mouth was full of sand and I hadn't enough control over my tongue to be able to spit it out. If I fell again, it would be for the last time. I could just walk, leading off with the right foot and then planting my left foot laboriously in front of it.

At last I came to the end of my walking. I could go no farther. My mind was obsessed with the thought of water with which to moisten my parched and swollen lips. "Water" was my last word and thought. Then the yellow sand rose up to me and the ground struck me in the face.

Chapter II

I BECOME A BEDOUIN

I AWOKE from a deep swoon with a strange, uncomfortable feeling that someone was near me. It was a great effort for me to open my eyes, though I sensed danger at close quarters. Then I felt a strange pair of hands fumbling at my clothes and I smelled an unfamiliar smell. At last my eyes saw, as if it were happening to someone else, a pair of nimble hands feeling in my pockets and the face of a Bedouin boy of about thirteen years, who grinned confidentially at me when he saw that I was awake.

His face and hands were unbelievably dirty and he went on grinning with a sort of apologetic friendliness as his hands pursued, undeterred, their investigations in my pockets and the other recesses of my clothes. There he found matches and a packet of cigarettes which he fished out and stowed away under his filthy galabia.[1] But the thing which struck me most was the penetrating stink, which seemed to fill the whole desert. It was this stench, I fancy, that had restored me to consciousness. It was strong enough, it seems, to reanimate a man on the threshold of death and to restore him to the horrors of existence.

The most unwashed of Bedouin lads could hardly have disseminated so fierce a stench all by himself, and I soon perceived that it came from a herd of goats which were grazing round about in the dry and scanty herbage. From going around with goats this young Bedouin had acquired their aroma, which in combination with the perfume of his herd had brought me back to life.

After frisking me deftly, the boy came to the conclusion that I possessed nothing more worth stealing. He nodded with the satis-

[1] galabia—robe.

faction one feels at a routine job well done and then, with the same courtesy with which he had emptied my pockets, he handed me his waterskin, which he had put down beside him in the sand. Half-dead with thirst, I put my lips to the mouth of the bag as greedily as a calf runs to its mother's udders, and I tried to hold it to me until I had drunk the last drops of water it contained. Finally the lad tore it from my mouth. He somehow made me understand, though I hardly knew a word of his language, that if I wanted more water I had only to come with him. I gathered from the expressive language of his hands that we should soon reach the tents of his tribe, where I should be much better off than in this sandy hollow. I felt too weak to stand up and begged him for more water, which he curtly refused to give me. When I sank back in the sand, he turned on his heel, drove his goats away and left me to my fate without even turning around. He knew that I would follow, impelled by thirst and the hope of a resting place in the Bedouin camp. As a matter of fact, I had gained so much strength from the brackish water that my body and brain began to revive and I felt once more the urge to live. So I rose to my feet and hastened in the direction to which the boy had pointed before departing with his goats.

If I had known, before I collapsed, that human beings and water were so near, I might perhaps have found the strength to struggle on till I reached them.

After a short hour I caught sight of palm trees in the distance. Bushes and vegetation became more frequent as I drew near the desert's edge, and here I saw some bitter Dead Sea apples which need so much moisture to keep them alive that the Arabs always reckon to find water by digging where they grow. I had now recovered myself sufficiently to use my reason and began to wonder why I had been so slow in recognizing the signs of approaching vegetation.

I had just reached the edge of the flat depression through which I had been marching, when I came in sight of an Arab encampment consisting of a number of untidy tents made of goat's hair, with huts built of palm branches and maize straw leaning against them.

Here I was mobbed by a pack of barking dogs which had scented my arrival. As I had foreseen, I was able to use my tent pole to some effect against these half-starved mongrels, and a few shrewd blows taught them that the stranger was not altogether unused to the ways of the desert.

I heard children crying in the first tent I came to. I meant to go in and ask for water, but before I reached the entrance a toothless old crone rushed out and struck at me with a palm branch. Her language seemed anything but welcoming.

When I came to the second tent I was luckier. I asked for water, and a middle-aged Arab with a silver-streaked beard listened to my few words of broken Arabic in which I tried to explain that I was an escaped German prisoner and that I needed water. He nodded in friendly fashion and led me to a small guest tent which was pitched about fifty yards away under the shade of three date palms. Here they brought me water in an earthenware vessel—they call it a *zeer*—with an unglazed surface through which the liquid evaporated. The evaporation keeps the water cool inside the vessel. The Arabs know all about desert thirst which can only be quenched by a whole bottle of water drunk at one go. They also know that a thirsty man with a tongue swollen to twice its natural size can't talk, and they wanted to find out who and what I was before deciding how best to make use of me. It soon gets about that a stranger is in the camp. The neighbors came and sat around me, firing off questions. The Arabic vocabulary I had picked up in the POW camp by questioning other escapers did not even enable me to understand what they were asking. I knew only a few words, but two of them kept recurring in their questions. One of them was "*feloos.*" Even if I had not known its meaning I would have understood the sense, for a Bedouin, when he uses it, always rubs his thumb against his forefinger. The most sensitive spot in the *nervus rerum* is touched when the thumb makes contact with the forefinger.

"*Feloos?*" No, I hadn't any. I shook my head. The few pounds I possessed were hidden in my shoe.

"*Sa'ah?*" No: I hadn't a watch, either, and had not had one since I had been taken prisoner. I had to pull out my empty pockets and show my wrists, which I did without misgivings. My total lack of possessions was a useful passport. The Arabs became perceptibly friendlier when I had convinced them that I was as poor as they were. The sight of wealth always irritates the poor and makes it hard for them to treat the rich humanely. I had taken to heart the lessons I had learned in Camp 307 from escaped prisoners and knew that the questions "Have you money?" and "Have you a watch?" must always be answered in the negative.

It is true that the Egyptians hated the British and always harmed them, when they could, and also that they liked the Germans and were not inclined to hand over escaped prisoners merely for the reward of two pounds a head, but it was tempting to do so when you could collect money plus a watch from the German and two pounds extra from the British. My poverty was my protection.

Soon they brought coffee in small cups without handles and I began to feel the life flowing through my veins. I drank no less than four cups of the powerful brew. It was only later that I learned that it was impolite to drink more than two. No doubt, also, my table manners left much to be desired, as I wolfed down all the food they brought me—boiled eggs, onions and pieces of bread.

When my meal was over, I became conscious that the atmosphere had changed. The rules of hospitality had been observed. Now there was serious business to be done. At the entrance of my tent a fire of palm branches alimented by cakes of camels' dung—the briquettes of the desert—was lighted, and a flickering gleam illuminated the picturesque scene. Around the fire sat the tribesmen and discussed my fate. Should they get rid of me or let me live? It is true that I did not understand a word they said, but I listened intently to an elderly, stout, gray-haired man, who harangued the audience without pause like a professional prosecutor. His hate-filled eyes and the way in which he spat as he looked at me told me enough.

I picked out one word, which he kept repeating, and noticed that he punctuated his monologue with an expectoration, whenever he used it. *"Taliani"* was the word.

Good Lord, I thought. So I would have to find words to explain that I was no Italian, though with my black hair I didn't look like a typical German. I spoke, but I spoke in German which no one understood, and whenever the old man said "*Taliani*" I obstinately interjected "*Alemani.*" Not much of a speech for the defense in this desert court.

Near me sat a lean man of about thirty. He looked like a Semite, with his hooked nose, but he had thick lips which indicated a strain of Negro blood. The way he kept curling his thin black mustache was as provokingly curious as his silence. He had a scimitar tattooed on the back of each hand, and his long blue robe, embroidered at the neck and on the sleeves, showed that he was a man of some position. But he said nothing, while the old man went on speechifying and spitting, and every now and then straightening the Webley-Scott revolver in his silver-studded belt. I felt sure that this weapon had once belonged to an Englishman who had crossed the man's path. I was crossing it now, and I was not sure if my own path led any farther.

In spite of the coffee and the need to utter my sole word of defense when I heard myself accused of being an Italian, I eventually closed my eyes and fell asleep. Then, it seems, they left me, apparently satisfied that I was not an enemy.

Next morning I was awakened by the crackling of a thorn fire outside my tent. My host was there making tea, which he brought me in a glass together with some thin slices of toasted Arab bread. He looked at my uniform disapprovingly and shook his head, as if he were thinking: you can't go on like this. I looked down at myself, too, and came to the same conclusion. No, that really wouldn't do. So I was presented instead with a well-worn and correspondingly dirty galabia and a brown woolen cap.

In order to help me on in my new life, I was also given a lot of good advice. The only thing I really understood was that I was on no account to mix with the fellahs, the peasants of the Nile Valley, but to consort exclusively with Bedouins. The latter in their pride spoke slightingly of the fellahs who, for their part, judged me to be a Bedouin by my dress and never condescended to say a word to me, even when I walked through their fields.

When I continued my march in a northwesterly direction, I took nothing with me except the good advice of my Arab hosts. I was no better than a dispirited tramp, but I had no longer to fear the pangs of thirst, nor was there any risk of losing my way. I reached the Sweet-Water Canal before noon, and was struck by the abrupt contrast between the lifeless waste and the fertile fields and orange gardens irrigated by its waters. Wherever the ground was watered by the complicated Egyptian system of irrigation channels, all sorts of crops could be grown; but when the water could flow no farther, the cultivation stopped suddenly and gave way to the barren wilderness.

In the fields stood peasants, their long galabias looped up between their legs, loosening the soil with flat-headed mattocks. This instrument, which they call a *"fass,"* serves as a plough and a general utility tool for the Egyptian peasant. It loosens the bone-hard soil and breaches the dams of sand, when the time for watering comes. Before the water is allowed to run into the fields, the fellah must break up the soil with his *fass* to enable the water to soak in. I tried to understand what the peasants were doing, but avoided speech with them as I had been advised. Up to now, I had no inkling of the historical grounds of the feud between the fellahs, descendants of the ancient Egyptians, and the Bedouins, who stemmed from the later Arab conquerors.

I had been told to go on till I came to the next Arab encampment. It was not very far and, shortly after noon, I found myself approaching a good-sized Bedouin settlement. My body and mind were tired, and I saw without interest riding horses and camels—already saddled—standing or kneeling in front of well-built mud-brick houses. The horses were hobbled to prevent them from straying.

The Bedouins were more observant than I was. I heard a shout of *"Alemani, Alemani,"* and a boy in his teens sprang out of the shadow of some farm buildings and, with outstretched hand, pointed to me. In spite of my disguise, the lad had at once spotted that I was a runaway German. I felt that if my mere appearance created such a commotion, it would be wise, however sympathetic the Bedouins might be, to clear out while the going was good. I turned and ran, as well as I could—which didn't amount to much—but soon I heard the patter of bare feet behind me. The Bedouin boy, for it was he, caught up with me and held me fast—no, that's the wrong word—he hooked his arm in mine with a brotherly gesture.

"*Istanna, Alemani!*" ("Stay, German") he said.

His words sounded friendly and reassuring. Subduing my fears, I yielded to the boy's friendliness and let him lead me back to his dwelling. He lived in his own little reed hut, leaning against the wall of a house. When we got there, he rolled out a straw mat and invited me to sit down. Of course I couldn't understand the torrent of words which he poured out at me, but I accepted his invitation to sit down and rest. He offered me some dried dates, which served for my midday meal; but I noticed that the words "*feloos*" and "*sa'ah*" cropped up in his talk as many times as there were stones in my dates. I had neither money nor a watch, and I was too tired to be annoyed by the naive cupidity of the lad, who obviously saw nothing wrong in his behavior, and actually seemed to welcome the sight of my empty pockets and bare wrists. The perpetual refrain of "*sa'ah*" and "*feloos*" had a stupefying effect on me. The boy's voice came to sound like the distant twitter of birds and I gradually sank into sleep.

When I awoke, a lively conversation was going on around me. I could see some shadowy figures sitting near me in the hut. Then my young host came in carrying a handful of maize cakes which he laid on the mat before me with a hospitable gesture. While I was eating, everyone seemed constrained to keep silent. Then a slender, youngish Bedouin with a short beard walked in, gave me a penetrating glance and sat down by the other men, who made room for him with gestures of deference. I learned later that he was the chief of the tribe.

As soon as I had finished eating, the discussions began again. It was obvious that I was the sole subject of their talk. I again heard the menacing word "*Taliani.*" The only person who said nothing was the young Sheik, but he kept looking keenly at me and was obviously making up his mind how to deal with my case. Suddenly he threw back his gray overgarment and drew from his belt a German parabellum. He made a sign to the boy who brought a little mat and spread it out on the ground. Then he took the pistol to pieces and threw down the different parts at random on the mat. Pointing to the dozen steel parts, he made a sign to me which I interpreted as an order to reassemble them.

God bless the Prussian drill which teaches us how to pull apart and put together all manner of weapons! I knew my stuff so well that I passed the ordeal brilliantly and in a minute, or less, was able to hand the Sheik the pistol in perfect order. I heard murmurs of approval and knew that I had established my identity as a German soldier.

Nonetheless, I hadn't finished with the word *"Taliani,"* which continued to crop up in the otherwise friendly seeming talk. When I made signs that I wanted to go on my way toward Cairo, they pushed me back onto the mat, saying *"Istanna."* It seems they wanted to clear something up, and after asking me to stay, I heard them saying *"Taliani"* once more.

At last a lanky, dark-skinned Bedouin with a long red scar on his right cheek came into the hut. *"Buena sierra,"* he said. I was not impressed by his bad Italian, but realized that the others hoped that by talking to me in that language, this fellow would be able to learn something about me. The Sheik told him what questions to ask, and the newcomer demanded of me in his brand of Italian details of my past and my profession, my capture and my escape. The Sheik was greatly pleased with the information I gave, but I admit that I was much upset to hear the interpreter invite me to stay on as the Sheik's guest as long as I liked. I understood very well that the invitation was an order.

I felt discouraged as I looked around at the ring of sitting figures. Outside I could hear a buffalo lowing. The Bedouins here had buffaloes and horses, camels and cows, as well as sheep and goats, which are the poor man's cattle. They were a prosperous, settled tribe with well-constructed, mud-brick houses built near the waterside, in addition to the tents they had retained from the days of their wanderings. They had invited me to stay with them, though all they could offer a civilized man was a mat to sleep on, and dates, onions, sour milk and occasionally mutton to eat.

"Have you any papers?" asked Scarface. I shook my head. "Money? Connections with Egypt or knowledge of languages?"

I had to say no. "Then," he said, "they'll grab you as soon as you come into the city; and if they don't, how are you going to live? Stay here until times are better. Learn Arabic and let your beard grow. You'll have *una bella barba!*"

I stayed, let my beard grow and became a Bedouin.

Chapter III

THE TRIBE OF THE SADDLED CAMELS

MY young friend whose straw hut I shared was called Mosallem, and Suleiman Hamada was the name of Scarface, the only person with whom I could talk. Very soon we became friends, in a manner of speaking, and I used to wait impatiently for his return when he was absent on one of his long journeys, in Libya maybe, where he had long resided and where he had picked up his smattering of Italian.

One day he said to me, "We are going to call you Salameh Suleiman. No one can say Herbert Pritzke and, seeing that you are a runaway, it is better that you should forget your old name." There were other reasons for which they wanted to give me an Arab name.

What the Bedouins were doing here, and from whence they derived such a good livelihood, was not clear to me. Their prosperity certainly did not depend on their livestock. When, as often happened, a man on a swift riding camel trotted into the village, heralding his approach with piercing cries, it was clear to me that things were not so fair and aboveboard as they seemed. The frequent nocturnal excursions on horse or camel back aroused my suspicions, and finally I began to remember that in the adventure stories that beguiled my boyhood the robber bands used to keep their camels always saddled, so that they could flit away at once when danger threatened.

The winter went by in deadly monotony. With the early spring rains, a fantastic carpet of rough grass and wild flowers mantled the desert, but as the sun grew stronger the splendor of the short-lived season withered and the desert became desert again. There was nothing for me to do except to adapt myself to my new life as well as I could, so I began to learn Arabic. Young Mosallem

was very eager and patient as a teacher. Anything more complicated than the substantives, which I wrote down with a stump of
pencil in a little exercise book, I referred to Scarface. The paper
on which I noted down what I had learned meant more to me
than the valuable objects in which the village abounded—modern
small arms, compasses, field glasses for night use and other relics
of a civilized war.

One evening Scarface brought me a little German-Arabic man-
ual, with the title printed in old-fashioned Gothic characters on
the well-thumbed cardboard cover. He told me he had a friend
in Cairo who had found the book for him, and he was clearly
delighted to have been able to do me this service. Now I set to
work in earnest, and the harder I found my task the more fanati-
cally I wrestled with the difficulties.

I began to understand what Goethe meant when he said that
learning a new language opened a door into a new world. In my
period of apprenticeship and slow initiation into the mysteries of
this difficult language, I learned much more than the grammar
and the words that was new and interesting. I began to realize the
meaning of many things which had formerly been veiled in
obscurity.

Only the secret of the nocturnal rides into the desert remained
undisclosed until, one night, I found myself obliged to flee with
the others into the wilderness. . . .

"Salameh, wake up, Salameh!"

I awoke to find Mosallem kneeling by me and shaking my
shoulder. "Get up," he said. "We've all got to ride off. The police
are coming to search the village and in ten minutes they'll be here."

There was no time to ask questions. I slept in my only garment,
the famous galabia which was now regularly washed, so I had only
to slip on my shoes and put my woolen cap on. Mosallem pressed a
water bottle into my hand and rolled up a few dried dates in a
cloth, before hurrying me out to the camel lines.

The whole village was alerted. Men, women and children, loaded
with bundles and parcels, were hurrying out of the houses into the
desert.

And now I had for the first time in my life to get on a camel's back

Dr. Pritzke in Egypt, where he practised medicine among the Bedouins as Salameh Suleiman or "El Hakim el Alemani" — "the German Doctor"

A Bedouin family in Egypt in their tent home

Photos from Egon E. Sch

Eid Abou Sueylim, whose son's life Dr. Pritzke saved after the fight at the pumping station near Tel el Kebir

and actually to ride the beast. The tribesmen would have sooner taught me camel-riding than Arabic. For them riding, running away and shooting were all more important than reading and writing.

Mosallem put the guide rope into my hand and I got into the saddle. I clutched the saddle horns in my two hands, but as soon as the boy gave the word of command and the beast raised himself on his long hind legs, I was on the point of falling off. Hardly had I recovered my balance when the camel got up on his fore-legs, driving the saddle horn painfully into my groin. I hadn't time to curse for Mosallem cried, "Yallah!" and gave the camel a slap on the behind. The animal bounded forward and ran on through the desert, with me bumping on his back.

Cage 6 was pretty awful, but this was ghastly. The beast ran on unchecked. I saw groups of men in the pale morning light burying in the sand the things the women and children had brought out of the village. Somewhere near me I saw a rider on a dun camel galloping full split over the desert. That must be Suleiman, I thought.

They call the camel "the ship of the desert," and a very good name too. On this one's back I felt as if I were sailing in a heavy sea. I gripped the front saddle horn with both hands and held on. The absence of stirrups with nothing to hold one's feet, which one had to keep crossed over the curve of the animal's neck, gave me a feeling of hopeless insecurity. The fantastic jolting caused a tumult in my innards. My bowels had long since been shaken out of the place designed for them at the creation, and my stomach was practically in my throat. Moreover, I didn't know in what direction we were supposed to be going and, since the halter had long ago slipped out of my hand, I was powerless to control the camel's headlong course. Just when I had come to the end of my strength and could hold no longer, a yellow dromedary came up close alongside and a practiced hand seized the hanging rope. My camel drew up and stood with heaving flanks and blowing nostrils, while I, without waiting for him to kneel down, slipped over his neck and dropped into the sand.

"Come, you need a drink of water," said my deliverer, and handed me his waterskin. I looked helplessly up and saw that it was really Suleiman, and that he was riding the dun camel which

I had caught sight of as we rode out. Not in the least excited or winded by his sharp gallop, he looked down calmly at me. Not even his mount, a light-colored Sudanese female, one of the loveliest beasts I have ever seen, was out of breath.

"We must get on." he said. "The ground here is far too exposed."

The people of the desert have an uncanny power of finding a depression in ground which appears to me perfectly flat. In one of these hollows Scarface ordered the two camels to *"barak,"* [1] and then planted himself on the top of the slope and looked fixedly in the direction of the village. He carried a loaded carbine and a belt full of cartridges, as well as a German pistol and a dagger, and there was no doubt what he would do if an enemy approached.

[1] *barak*—kneel down.

Chapter IV

SCARFACE'S CONFESSION

WHO was this Suleiman, who used to vanish out of the village in the gray of dawn and never return before nightfall, who remained absent, sometimes for weeks together, without telling anyone when he was coming back? He always kept a weapon within reach. When he spent the night in the village he invariably sat or stood with his back against a wall, in a position from which he could see door and window and any other possible approaches. I had already seen him sleeping, fully dressed, with his carbine and pistol within easy reach and his cartridge belt around his waist. He slept as lightly as a wild animal; in fact he was never fully asleep.

As we sat together on the crest of the desert hollow he said, "My friend, you are wondering about me."

I was startled out of my thoughts by the question. "How do you know that?" I asked. "You were not even looking at me."

"One can know without looking. One can learn to do that. When a man like me overhears another man thinking, then, maybe, that man will not think any more. Your thoughts are different; they hold no danger for me, but when you ponder and ask yourself who I am, what I am doing, why I live with an alien tribe, tolerated but not welcome, why the villagers look down on me, then probably you are embarrassed by the thought that it is just I who am your friend. But, if you think of it, haven't we got much in common?"

His meaning escaped me but I did not wish to interrupt him. He went on. "Are we not both outcasts, hunted by the law, homeless and forced to molder in a foreign land? You know that I do not come from these parts, but Libya, when all is said and done, is not very different from this country. What do frontiers matter to us Bedouins, who are split up into clans and tribes with our own separate pasture grounds? Here among strangers I am tolerated because I can no longer live with my own tribe."

I was going to ask why, but he had perhaps divined my thought, for he looked out into the desert and then seemed to feel obliged to answer my unspoken question.

"When the war began," he said, as if talking to himself, "the Arabs fell into two camps. Some of them favored the Germans and Italians out of hatred for the English and French, who rule most of the Arab world. The others wanted first to drive the Italians out of Libya, in order to have a chance of winning easy booty. I was young at the time and joined enthusiastically in the struggle for freedom against the Italians. I collected a group of partisans and carried out raids against the Italian columns, robbing or burning a number of their supply depots. In the eyes of the English we were a resistance movement, and they provided us with everything we needed.

"But you understand that in war the wind may change from one moment to another. When the Italians surrendered and joined the English against the Germans, could we suddenly treat them not as our enemies but as our allies? We could not, and so we went on just as before. Once, when we attacked an Italian settlement the English shot us to bits and chased us in armored cars like mangy wolves through the desert. Only a few of my band survived. I was one of them, but I could no longer live in Libya."

I believe that it was years since Suleiman had talked about himself and his life to anyone else. I did not wish to interrupt him, even by a gesture expressing astonishment or admiration. He continued: "A Bedouin without a tribe is like a grain of sand in the wind. I went hither and thither, and lived like a savage beast in the wilderness, my hand against every man and my rifle my only friend. I never took a prisoner, for only dead men tell no tales. The English chased me through Egypt and Palestine, and one day I was be-trayed by a tribe with whom I had spent the night."

I now knew why Scarface always sat with his back to the wall and kept his eyes on doors and windows. He stopped for a moment, as though he were reading the story of his hunted life from a diary and had to turn a page. The next page was the most gruesome of all.

"So weary was I of being ceaselessly hunted and harried that I actually found rest and relief in prison life. I was condemned to fifteen years' hard labor in the quarries of Tura. In the long run, however, I found that I could not stand the life of a caged beast. Better to be a hunted one! While a sandstorm was raging, I sprang on the sentry and tore his rifle from him—here it is." As he spoke he stroked the stock of his weapon almost affectionately. "I managed to get away. Since then my rifle has been all the world to me—my destiny and my life. I earn my living by killing men for payment. Sometimes it is the heirs of a rich fellah who hire me to get rid of their kinsman, or it may be a father who pays me to kill a pregnant, unmarried daughter. . . ."

After such a confession, I didn't feel able to comment or ask any questions. The final answer was given later by the desert, where Scarface was found dead after meeting someone who was quicker on the draw than he was.

Suddenly he told me in quite a different tone that I could now safely return to the village. "The raid must certainly be over," he said. "I'll come with you part of the way, until you are in sight of the houses."

Then I couldn't help asking him a simple and, in the circum-stances, almost frivolous question as we led the camels out of the hollow. "How came you by that scar?" I said.

He laughed scornfully. "I wish I could tell you that a man made this notch in my face, but the truth is that that little whore, the daughter of Sheik Saleh Abed, opened up my cheek with a kitchen knife."

The raid was over. Suleiman disappeared on his beautiful beast in the trackless waste to reappear the next day, or the day after or at any later date, when resting between two professional engagements. The Tribe of the Saddled Camels did not welcome him, but they bore with him.

Did he know too much? Anyhow, he had fled while the others were burying in the sand the things which must not fall into the hands of the law. Maybe he did not know everything.

Chapter V

THE AFFAIR AT TEL EL KEBIR

"I HAVE to speak to you, Salameh."

The young Sheik had walked up unobserved to the campfire and touched me on the shoulder. He made a sign to my neighbor Sueylim and another Bedouin to accompany him. Twenty yards from the fire, we squatted on our heels in Arab fashion and waited for the Sheik to speak.

"Listen," he began. "One of our men has brought good news today. It seems that there are some German soldiers at a pumping station near Tel el Kebir who want to sell us rifles and ammunition. Our informant is not certain of the details, as he knows very little English and the Germans speak no Arabic. He accordingly has made an arrangement for a meeting tomorrow night at eight o'clock."

I did not feel comfortable as the Sheik calmly lit a cigarette and looked around till his eyes rested on me.

"You, Salameh," he said, "will go with these two men to meet the Germans"—a categorical order. "You will make all the necessary inquiries, in particular about the number of rifles and the quantity of cartridges. In addition, you will scrutinize these men carefully, so that we may know if we can trust them."

In order to gain time and, if possible, to think up some plausible excuse for evading the job, I asked a lot of questions about the position of the pumping station and how it was guarded. I asked for a fourth man and named young Mosallem, as I would need at least two men with me as a protection, in case it turned out to be a trap, and a third to look after the camels. The Sheik agreed to my proposals and there was nothing for it but to obey.

Being a German, my job was to put through this shady deal with the other Germans, but I couldn't be sure from the data I possessed that a trap had not been laid for us. If things went wrong, I should be sent to a punishment camp by the British—with the subsequent prospect of a prison sentence by an Egyptian court. However, my hosts were now asking for my co-operation for the first time, and they had some right to expect me to do something to repay their hospitality.

Since the police raid, I had practiced camel riding for some hours every day, but the long ride from dawn to midday, cool at first and sweltering later, made me realize how far I was from being an expert and tireless rider. One sits on the saddle as on a chair with nothing to hold onto, and without being able to influence one's mount by leg pressure or stirrups. I found it almost impossible to keep in the middle of the saddle.

The undertaking was carried out like a reconnaissance action in war and was at least as dangerous. We left the camels in the charge of young Mosallem, in a concealed wady a few miles from Tel el Kebir with a dry water course running down it, and then moved stealthily on foot toward the camp. I surveyed the ground long and carefully through a pair of Zeiss field glasses, which a German gunner, or his British guard, had sold to the Bedouins. German prisoners under British supervision were working in front of the huge, wire-enclosed camp, which contained munition dumps, arms stores and various repairing shops. The enemies of yesterday combined to trade camp property to Bedouins or Egyptian dealers. Often enough, stores were loaded on trucks in broad daylight and dispatched with false manifests to unlicensed traders.

And there I made out the pumping station—a well-built pump house between two wooden huts. I thought to myself, if we don't want an unpleasant surprise while we are bargaining, we must get into the station as early as possible and certainly before the appointed hour. It would be dark at seven and that would give us an hour's start as our rendezvous was at eight.

I sent out one of my companions with orders to work his way slowly up to the camp and to keep moving between the camp and the pumping station. If danger threatened, he was to signal to us with his flashlight. There was no doubt that we were out on a perilous adventure and we had been armed accordingly. Sueylim, who went ahead of me, carried a Belgian carbine and they had issued me a large-bore Italian revolver, which looked as if it had come out of a museum. It had a formidable appearance, but was inconveniently clumsy and heavy.

When we reached the pumping station, I whispered to Sueylim to stand at the entrance. It was seven o'clock. "Let no one in," I told him, "and mind you keep your eyes on the camp. You may get a signal from our friend. One never knows."

From the powerhouse we heard the regular throbbing of diesels. One of the huts was shut up, but there was a light in the other. I was sure that this was where the German POW's lived. When I pushed aside the curtain, which in warm weather replaced the door, Sueylim gave a swift glance into the hut and then took up his station at the entrance.

"Evening, men!" I cried in a jovial voice, as I tried to take in the situation. There were five Germans, in the uniform of prisoners of war, in the room. Two of them were lying on their beds and sprang up when they heard my voice. The general surprise was so great that the three others who were playing cards dropped their hands on the table. They all looked at me without enthusiasm.

"Evening to you!" said one of the card players at last. "Sit down," he said, pointing to a wooden bench. But before accepting the invitation, I took a good look around the room, paying particular attention to the man who seemed to be in charge. He was a stockily built fellow, fattish and already over thirty, with hair like match stubs and a short bristly mustache—a typical German sergeant-major.

I had to be careful. Besides this man's appearance, there were a good many things which did not please me—and every good sergeant-major would have been proud that I had recognized and disliked them. The double-tiered beds had been made in the tidiest, most shipshape fashion, with the pillows under the blankets symmetrically tucked in on each side—everything in apple-pie order. No, gentlemen, I thought. Where discipline has kept the barrack room as perfectly as this, even in a prison camp, a dead soldier will be laid in his desert grave with his hands neatly aligned to the seams of his trousers, but there will be no scrounging of army property.

All this spit and polish does not go with the enterprise necessary for illicit trading.

"Go and fetch the tea, Vogel."

So one of the card players was called Vogel. He went and fetched it.

We talked and smoked over our tea. I refused one of Vogel's cigarettes and rolled one for myself from my own tobacco. If the expressions which I noted on the five faces reflected dislike rather than admiration, I couldn't reproach them. I had fallen very low. I lived with Bedouins and served as their interpreter in their shady transactions.

"Well, what about the guns?" I said. As no one apparently wanted to open the subject, I felt I had to do so.

"We can let you have forty," said the sergeant-major.

"And the price?"

"Shall we say," he hesitated a little, "ten pounds apiece? They all date from before 1942."

This last sentence was not unimportant, as in Egypt, where they know something about rifles, the weapons manufactured hurriedly in the latter part of the war were not thought much of. "Ten pounds," I repeated. The black-market price at the moment was between fifteen pounds and seventeen pounds. It was clear that any one who knew so little about prices had never done a deal like this before.

The sergeant-major looked at me with his honest blue eyes and said, "Mm, yes. Ten pounds, but if that's too dear for you. . . ."

Were they going to reduce the price of their own accord?

Really the hour I passed with these simple fellows was quite cosy. We stopped talking about the rifles, and Vogel asked me suddenly if I wouldn't like to hear some music. I said I would, and when I heard the tune and words of *"In einem kühlen Grunde"* grinding out of an old-fashioned box phonograph I felt quite moved. Every man, however artistic he may be, has a corner in his soul for sentimental music. I was no exception and, moreover, I had not heard a word of German for months. The old melody made me feel soft.

"Look out, Salameh!" hissed Sueylim suddenly from the entrance.

In an instant I sprang up from my seat and saw one of the five men with arms extended, standing in front of the muzzle of Sueylim's carbine. He had tried to take advantage of the musical diversion to slip out of the hut.

"Where are you going to?" I snapped out, all my suspicions reawakened.

"To the quartermaster," he stammered, "so that we can fix this business up."

"Yes, that's right," said the sergeant-major to help him out. Then to me, "What's biting you? We've often got rid of our spare guns this way. You must have been told that by your gypsies. And the quartermaster is a decent bugger and will never squeal on us." That sounded all right, but the sergeant-major really shouldn't have stolen a glance at the old turnip his grandfather had left him, which he kept in his breast pocket. He wanted to know the time.

I had come an hour too soon, and now the hour was over and our advantage had been frittered away in trivialities. We should have gone long ago. They tried to spin out the conversation; but Sueylim, who didn't understand a word that was said, scented danger and moved forward into the hut, holding his carbine at the ready. All the same, his instinct had played him false. While he was expecting trouble in the hut, our signalman was vainly flashing warnings to him from outside.

Too late! We were caught in the trap. From quite near I could hear the clatter of armored cars. "You damned swine!" I shouted to the sergeant-major and hit him in the belly with my fist. He folded up and gasped for breath.

Now I was alone, facing the four remaining men. Sueylim had preferred discretion to death. He had bolted, and one could guess where he was now from the barking of British automatic weapons. Meanwhile I was in a fix. It is easy to get one's weapon tangled in the folds of a galabia and, of course, that is what happened to my blunderbuss. I pulled it out by the muzzle and had no time to aim it as the four men came at me. I struck heavily with the butt into a broad white face in front of me, and its owner collapsed with a groan. At that moment one of his colleagues grabbed me from behind, pressing my shooting arm into my side.

"Help me, you idiots!" he called to his comrades. But they saw that my pistol—which I was now holding by the right end—was likely to blow large holes in them. So they left him to struggle with me alone. I had now gotten my arms free and knocked my man out with a blow from the butt end. Then, with my finger on the trigger, I made them walk to the wall and stand there with their hands above their heads. I shouted my orders so fiercely that they all obeyed like sheep. Only the sergeant-major thought it beneath his dignity to carry out my order quite literally. He only raised his arms to the height of his ears.

"Anyone who turns around and looks at the door gets a bullet in his belly," I said as I pulled the curtain aside and walked backward out of the hut.

I had not gained much by this move. Searchlights were scanning the darkness, and fountains of sand splashing up as bullets from Tommy guns struck the ground. Luckily, none of the searchlights picked me up. I pulled up the skirts of my galabia and bolted like a hunted deer. After a few hundred yards, I had to throw myself down to recover my wind. I saw the light shining from the entrance of the hut and heard the automatics coughing out their last rounds, but still I did not dare to get up. Light armored cars were racing to and fro through the darkness, turning as nimbly as hounds and scouring the undulating ground in threes.

Damnation! Now they must have sighted Sueylim, as heavy firing began again. They couldn't have been aiming at me, as I was more or less under cover, and the shooting seemed to be in another direction. But I figured that Sueylim had probably come this way; and that perhaps the English were just firing blindly into the bushes. The cars were moving away from the spot where I lay, so I got up and ran, bending forward as I did so, and sometimes stopping to hide behind a bush. Meanwhile the full moon was rising and pouring a stream of pallid, ghostly light on the wilderness, and painting a landscape more fantastic than any I had ever seen.

But the moon helped me, for I picked up footprints in the sand—the tracks of a single barefooted man, clearly an Arab. I had learned something about tracking during my stay among the

Bedouins, and noticed that the toe-prints were separated and that the foot, which no shoe had ever pinched, was broader than that of a European.

The late Karl May could have learned something from me even in my early Arab days. I observed that this man's footprints had been far apart from one another, and that at each stride he had thrown up a little hillock of sand. Therefore he had been running, and I can imagine how Sueylim was running. What I could read from the tracks would of course be no mystery to an experienced Britisher, and there were many of them. What I had to fear was that our pursuers might chance on these same tracks, and that the infantrymen sitting in the cars would dismount and follow the spoor with their noses to the ground. The cars were still zigzagging around, but in a routine sort of way.

For a while a cloud darkened the face of the moon and prevented me from seeing the tracks, even when I went on my hands and knees. I had to wait for more light.

Then I came to a place where Sueylim had thrown himself down and sought for cover in a little hollow. When he had come out of this, he had turned off at right angles to his previous course. Now his footmarks were nearer together and his paces of unequal length. The man who had passed this way had been dragging his right leg. Ha! here there was a dark, wet spot on the sand. Sueylim was wounded in the right leg but was still able to walk, though his tracks looked unsteady and the length of his paces was growing shorter all the time.

On the edge of a small depression there was a thick growth of thornbushes, which the Arabs call " *arfag*." The tracks ran close by it.

I heard a hushed voice behind me say "Salameh."

"Yes, here I am, Sueylim," I answered. I reckoned that he couldn't be so badly wounded; if he had still been able to play the old trick of first bypassing the place in which he meant to hide and then approaching it circuitously from another direction. A pursuer would naturally follow the spoor, but long before he made the circuit the fugitive would be able to shoot him down at leisure from behind—that is, if he had a gun—but Sueylim did not have his any longer.

"What's the matter with you?" I asked.

"*Ma'alesh*," he said. "Nothing to matter. Only a scratch in the leg."

However the "scratch" turned out to be a bullet wound in the thigh, which was bleeding profusely. The ball had entered about a handbreadth above the hollow of the knee and had come out an inch or so above the kneecap, leaving an exit wound about as big as a quarter. Judging from the position of the wound, the bone was undamaged, but it was clear from the profuse bleeding that an artery had been severed. To stop the hemorrhage, I tore off a strip from my galabia and pressed the piece of cotton cloth firmly into the wound. As this proved ineffectual, I took Sueylim's belt and made a tourniquet above the wound with the help of a piece of branch which I plucked from the bush.

It was not yet safe to go on. I had to be pretty sure that the bleeding had stopped, but we were losing time. The English would be sure to send out a few Sudanese patrols who would have no trouble in picking up our tracks, and I remembered that the desert motto "Shoot first and then challenge" was common both to robbers and the British. With his sure Bedouin instinct, Sueylim led the way toward the wady where we had left the camels, but after a short distance he slumped. I took him on my back like a sack of corn and carried him, but I could not manage more than fifty paces at a time. He groaned and I panted. We couldn't go on like this. At last he told me to go, so that at least one of us should get away safely. I declined his generous offer with big words, but I knew in my heart that we should never reach the camels together. Sueylim had realized that long ago. He said, "Carry me as far as the bushes over there and then go on by yourself." Whether I acted shamefully or rightly I don't know, but I carried him a few yards farther and deposited him in some thick bushes, after which, when he had once more pointed the way, I left him and went on.

I found my own behavior abject and uncomradely, and when I had gone a few yards I remembered that Sueylim had no weapon. I turned back and gave him my powerful shooting iron.

"Take my pistol," I said, "you could use it, if need arose. Anyhow I can run and you can't."

The Bedouin smiled and said, "Keep it, *ya akhi*, it doesn't shoot."

"You son of a dog!" I growled. So these people had sent me on a dirty dangerous job, which turned out to be nothing but a trap, and had armed me with a stage pistol that wouldn't fire. That seemed to me the worst part of the whole business.

"Don't make such a noise, Salameh," he said, "you'll set the English on our trail."

But I went on, "A pistol that won't go off, an escort that runs away at the first shot." I spat all the curses I knew into the fellow's face, but he went on smiling a superior smile. "You don't understand, Salameh," he said. "You're a German. Why do you want a pistol as well?"

I thought to myself what a wonderful and somehow disarming recognition this was, coming from a Bedouin, of Rommel's heroic achievements against overwhelmingly superior British forces!

Sueylim went on, "And I didn't run away. When the cars came up I had to lure them away from the pumping station. If I hadn't done that, you would be a dead man by now."

Allah alone knows what is in the mind of a Bedouin. It may be that Sueylim had really run into the fire of the armored cars for the reason he gave, and that he had taken this enormous risk in order to save his unarmed comrade from the enemy. Now my job was to save him. I ran with all the strength I possessed to join up with the others and tell them where Sueylim was, and get them to bring the camels to fetch him away.

In the wady I found Abdurrahman, our signaler, with the camels waiting with Mosallem for us to return.

"Come quick," I said. "Get the camels moving. Sueylim is lying back there, badly wounded."

"No, we won't take the camels," said Abdurrahman thoughtfully. "We don't know if there are patrols around. The camels groan when they get up and they might scream on the way. Besides, they would make too good a target in the moonlight."

So Mosallem stayed behind with the camels, and we two went back on foot to find Sueylim and carry him to the wady. We found him where I had left him, and I bandaged him afresh in the shaded light of my flashlight. His first bandage was drenched with blood. . . . I knew that death was riding with us as we silently rode off the wady in single file—a mournful procession of shadows in the wilderness.

"That is Ain-Dar," said Abdurrahman, as the barking of dogs announced that we were approaching habitations. We were at once admitted into the big tent, and Sueylim was bedded down on straw mats. There was light enough from two oil lamps for me to see what I had to do, but my services were firmly but politely declined by the Bedouins who said, "You can do nothing: only Um-Fahed can save him."

Um-Fahed, the healer, kept us waiting for a long time. Finally she rode up on an unsaddled donkey. Till that moment every one had been staring curiously at Sueylim, who had meanwhile been losing blood fast. The healer had first to push her way through the gaping onlookers, and then she boldly pulled off her veil, hung with coins and pearls, and revealed a thin, brown face with tight lips and an aquiline nose. She examined the wounded man perfunctorily and then called for burning charcoal on which she threw some long sticks of incense. The ceremony, designed to exorcize the evil spirits, was as impressive as her medical treatment was barbaric. She made a thick paste from crushed coffee beans, sugar, samh and opium, then pressed it firmly into the two wounds. Sueylim was roused from unconsciousness by the pain and screamed and lashed around him, but the bystanders held him fast till Um-Fahed had bandaged his wound with some dirty rags.

The Bedouins waited in tense expectation for a miracle of healing to declare itself. They waited in vain. Meantime Um-Fahed sat rigid on the ground by the patient, her thin lips framing soundless invocations. The lamps cast huge, grim shadows on the walls of the tent. But Sueylim's face grew paler and smaller as we looked at him. His new bandage was soaked with blood.

At last I felt I must persuade the persons who seemed to me to have most influence that Sueylim had not long to live without surgical intervention. The native love of a sensational spectacle may have induced them to allow me to act, in spite of the protests of Um-Fahed, whose dignity was deeply wounded. The spectators watched with interest when, at my request, a long, curved needle, some thread, a pair of scissors and a sharp knife were procured for my use and sterilized in boiling water.

The strongest men held Sueylim still as I knelt on the ground to operate. He uttered a terrible, animal cry as I started to make a deep incision above the wound but soon he fainted again, and my work became easier.

The light was inadequate, and I was ringed by a crowd of spectators bending down to look at what I believe was the most primitive and difficult operation of my whole professional career.

When at last I got up slowly, sweat-drenched and with aching back, the artery had been tied up with black thread and the wound properly bandaged. So far, so good. I had the leg tied up and watched the bandage anxiously. Half an hour after the operation no blood was seeping through. The bleeding had stopped.

While I was asleep, messengers were sent to tell the news to Eid Abu Sueylim, the wounded man's father. Late next afternoon, just as I had finished examining my charge, Eid rode up to Ain-Dar with five armed companions. The strongly-built, gray-headed man, who had procreated his species generously with the help of his three wives, was as worried about Sueylim as if he had been his only child. He descended heavily from his camel and, coming up to me with outstretched arms, kissed me warmly on both cheeks. Then he asked me to take him to his son who, as I explained to him, was, in my opinion, still in grave danger. He listened to me and said he would do anything to save Sueylim's life. He knew a Greek pharmacist in Ismailia. Just what I wanted. I made a list of the things I needed for this particular case, and which were essential generally to a doctor undertaking this kind of rough-and-ready treatment.

By noon next day, a mounted messenger, sent by the old man, brought me a parcel containing a stethoscope, syringes, scalpel, needles, scissors, bandages and various medicines. I was able to obviate the risk of inflammation by injections of tetanus serum, but even Sueylim, who had the constitution of a horse, was not out of danger till four days had passed.

On our return to the tribe, we made a triumphant entry into the village.

Thirty men riding beribboned camels came out of the village to meet us. We rode in amid a storm of welcoming cheers, and when we arrived we were taken to the great guest tent to feast with Eid.

There I found in the place reserved for me a costly Arab outfit, complete from sandals to silken kaffiyeh,[1] and with it a German parabellum.

When I mistrustfully began to take out the magazine, Sueylim laughed and took it out of my hand.

"This one does shoot," said he and, to dispel my doubts, he shot a hole in the roof of the tent.

[1] kaffiyeh—headcloth.

Chapter VI

THE EX-CORPORAL

NOW, after being at first barely tolerated, I had become El Hakim el Alemani, the German doctor, a man reputed and esteemed. I was given a tent to myself, which I divided into a living room and a consulting room. People came to me for treatment and advice about medical and other matters. I was visited by Bedouins from other tribes, as well as my own, and even the fellahs from the surrounding countryside sought me out and waited patiently for my return, when I was away visiting my cases, often in remote villages.

I used to look around the curtain that hung across the entrance into my waiting room.

Five more patients. My consulting hours were crammed with them. Before disclosing their symptoms to me, my clients would unashamedly retail them to the other people in the "waiting room."

"Next, please. . . ." It was almost like my clinic in Berlin.

When I had listened to my patient's story I would look for a suitable remedy in my medicine chest, which had constantly to be replenished from the Greek pharmacy in Ismailia. I kept a regular supply of routine drugs by me for daily use. One day a patient needed something I didn't have, and I had to prescribe. At first I felt reluctant, but—as there was nothing else to do—I wrote out a prescription for him to have made up at the pharmacy, before he came back to me for instructions as to use. I attached thereto a mysterious signature, *"Le Docteur Inconnu."*

It gave me a strange and sometimes uncomfortable sensation to remember that, though I was an escaped prisoner, listed among the persons wanted by the police, I was living and practicing my profession half a day's ride on camelback from Ismailia. I had ceased worrying about the chances of being discovered and hauled back, but I felt it would be tempting Providence to sign my prescription with my own name. So now, for the first time, I took a chance and my prescription, signed "The Unknown Doctor" was duly honored.

After that I always signed myself "The Unknown Doctor" when I had to prescribe some drug which I did not possess.

My next client was one of those lingering types who waits till he is last in the line. We doctors know him very well. He is either afraid of being hurt, or if he is an Arab, he has come to chatter with the patients and learn from them the latest desert gossip.

"Your turn," I said to him.

This lingerer was not quite the last on the waiting list and he would obviously have preferred to let the few remaining patients go in first. But when I called him, he followed me into the tent.

"Well," I said, "what's the matter with you?"

"Nothing," he said. "I'm perfectly well."

The man was dressed like a fellah. He quietly drew from his pocket a folded piece of lined paper and handed it to me. On it was written: "Please visit me during the next few days. I have some important business for you. Urgent." The word "Urgent" was underlined three times and the message was signed "Helmut Schneider, *Obergefreiter A.D.*"

Helmut Schneider was already a legendary figure, and I was likely to become one too after I had been practicing a bit longer in the desert as the *"Docteur Inconnu."* But Schneider was known throughout the Canal Zone. He was, like me, an escaped POW. He was reported to be engaged in unsavory activities and, of course, any illicit business carried on in the desert is always dangerous.

The fellah didn't start by asking if I would come, or if I had a message for Schneider. He simply told me how to get to the farm in the *rif*[1] where Schneider was living.

"All right," I said. "I'll come," for Schneider interested me.

I had to take precautions, so I arranged for Sueylim and Mosallem, the two friends in whom I had complete confidence, to ride with me.

It was a completely different world from that of the Bedouins which we now entered. The village children shouted after us "Thieves! Tramps! Vagabonds!" when we asked the way to the isolated building outside the village in which Schneider was living. A man like him needed a remote hiding place.

It was unpleasant to have to listen to the insulting cries of the children and the contemptuous remarks of their elders; and it occurred to me that the peasants, with their different way of life, looked down on the Bedouins just as we in Germany looked down on the gypsies. The fellahs are the settled indigenous inhabitants, who for thousands of years have been living in the fertile lands of the Delta and the outlying regions of the Nile Valley, and who stay put where they belong. A move to the next village is regarded as emigration. That is why the fellah attaches so much importance to a good and durable house, though by our standards it provides him with little comfort. The point is that he lives in a *house,* made of mud or sun-dried clay bricks, with doors and windows, and a coat of whitewash.

Restlessness is the key to the Arab nomad's existence. He cannot help wandering and moving around, even when he finds a place which contains all the conditions for a stable tribal life. When nomads do settle down, exchanging their tents for houses, the dwellings they erect are so ramshackle and so casually constructed that one gets the impression that they only mean to stay in them for a short time. Their untidy, ill-kept houses increase the contempt the fellahs feel for the tramps of the desert—and this feeling is as old as the history of mankind in the Orient.

When we rode through the open gate in a whitewashed clay wall into the courtyard, the fellah who was waiting for us had to throw

---

[1] *rif*—cultivated area.

stones at his dogs to drive them away, before the camels would "*barak*" for us to get off. Mosallem remained in the yard to look after them.

"This is the German to whom I gave your letter," said the man, introducing me to my host as he led me into a small mud-brick dwelling which looked like an annex of the farmhouse. Then I met ex-corporal Helmut Schneider for the first time. When he saw more people coming into the house than he had expected, his hand went to his pistol butt instinctively. He was sitting on a sort of homemade couch, which he had covered with a rug, and the primitive comforts of his room accorded ill with the pistol that hung in an open holster from his belt.

"Sit down," he said.

He was a lean, wiry man with a healthy, sunburned face and almost invisible lips. He wore a white silk shirt and gray flannel trousers.

He looked at me with some astonishment and said, "So you are the man who was mistaken for me."

I didn't understand.

"Tel el Kebir," he said, to help me. "When the Germans from the pumping station reported that a German was coming to the camp to do a deal, the Tommies thought it must be me. And they are anxious to get me out of the way"—he spoke with a certain pride—"and now there's a danger mark against your name in the police lists."

Flattering, very flattering, but a compliment from this thin-lipped mouth seemed more like a knife thrust.

"Why have you got me to come here?" I asked. Schneider told the fellah to bring coffee. It seemed that the man acted as his servant and guard. The fellah was obviously unwilling to leave the room and looked suspiciously at Sueylim's carbine, as he went out to prepare the coffee. When it came, Schneider offered me a Gold Flake cigarette and got me to tell him how I had escaped and what I had been doing since.

"They are saying," he remarked, "that your practice is flourishing." The slit beneath his nose seemed to indicate that he was smiling.

"Yes," I said, "it's not going badly."

"I started my own practice some time before you did," said Schneider leaning back on the couch. His fingers played nervously with the pistol.

"Seeing that we have both belonged to the Afrika-Korps and both were taken prisoner, you must be as familiar as I am with the conditions in which we lived before and after capture. You will therefore appreciate the way in which one works oneself into a profession like mine. You begin with a blanket and some underclothes, or a few pieces of uniform. You can always find buyers, but the price you get for the goods doesn't provide you with much food or tobacco, because there's always someone else who skims the cream. To make good the losses in your personal kit you have to join the organization."

"Yes, I know. That's the usual way."

"You may have other views, but what is the point of hampering yourself with inhibitions, when the British supervising personnel is an active partner in the racket and takes the lion's share of the spoil? One day I was caught and sentenced to thirty days in the cells for stealing army property."

"I was in Cage 6," I said, "and have some idea what it means to be in the cells."

"Well, my principle is not to sit down and let people put upon you. In our camp there was no lockup, so two British soldiers were detailed to escort me by rail, handcuffed like a dangerous criminal, to the main camp. Raw, inexperienced boys, both of them. We traveled in an open corridor coach which was full of Egyptians. True love, somehow, doesn't seem to exist between the Gippos and the British, and I took advantage of the fact. Besides—but do you already talk passable Arabic?"

"I'm progressing. It wasn't easy, but you learn it, as you learn how to swim when you're thrown into deep water."

"You learn it still quicker, if you don't want to be done in the eye over every deal. Now I speak Arabic as fluently as German, and I succeeded in hotting up the Egyptians in the train to such a pitch of rage that my two greenhorns, without knowing why, suddenly found themselves facing an infuriated mob. You can always kindle the fires of nationalism. The fuel catches in a moment and then there's a blaze. One of my two guards received a blow in the eye. In a moment both were disarmed and pushed into a corner. I don't know or care what happened to them. I tumbled out of the train, as it was moving, and rolled down the embankment just as I was, handcuffs and all. For a day or two I wandered around by the Sweet-Water Canal, and then I found a good-natured fellah who filed off my bracelets and helped me on my way." He paused. "Now it seems high time for me to do something for my friends the English. Some of them will like it, some of them won't."

"The desert winds have already carried your fame far and wide," I said.

"Yes, but I'm still as poor as a rat."

"What? A man who does his job as well as you do?"

"Ah, you don't know the whole story. The scoundrel who owns this farm picked me up when I was on the run and offered me a lodging here. He knows all about me. Look, here's my identity card. You see, I haven't changed my description. When necessary, I am still a prisoner of war; I have my uniform and can get into the camps without interference and do my business there with the British just as well as with the Germans."

"You've got a nerve—with a warrant out against you!"

"Naturally, and I take much greater risks than that. The owner of this farm gives me two trustworthy fellahs to accompany me on my trips, and when I come back he takes everything off me, but at what a price! I'm sure he gets ten times as much as he gives me for the stuff, but I'm dependent on this damned bandy-legged, poxy-faced son of a bitch. I have neither the time nor the opportunity to hawk the stuff around. I need his house, his people and his protection. If I press him too hard, the bastard will give me away. But I can't stand it any longer. It's got to stop."

Schneider, who had talked himself into a regular rage, sprang to his feet and, after rummaging in a little box, brought out a glass tube for me to look at.

"See that," he said. On the label was "Morphium hydrochloric."

"Well, what do you say to that?"

"Leave it alone," I said.

"How do you mean?"

"If you once get into the habit, you'll never be able to free yourself of it."

"Do you think I'm such a damned fool as to take the stuff myself? I'm going to sell it, and this time that bandy-legged brute will not be in on it. What do you think? You're a doctor. Can't you find a market for the stuff? We'll split the proceeds fifty-fifty."

He walked grimly up and down the little room. Sueylim looked on, uncomprehending, but his eyes never left Schneider. He must have been thinking: you never know where you are with these Germans.

Schneider continued. "This is my one and only chance of getting out of the dung heap I'm bogged in. Do you think it's a pleasure for me to live here like a native and risk my skin every day so that this fat hog may grow richer and richer, shoveling dollars into his moneybags till one day he makes up his mind to betray me?" He proceeded with impressive deliberation to point out that I was in the same situation as he was. "You want to get away as much as I do. You can't pretend otherwise. You're as sick of vegetating between the desert and the stinking canal as I am, and you want to get home."

He was right, but it was hard to admit it to a man like him. He went on. "We can never get away legally. We'll need false passports, clothes and steamer tickets. All that costs a hell of a lot of money. Only now, and only if we carry out my plan, shall we get the money we need. If we don't, we shall rot away here. And if the atmosphere of this cursed land doesn't destroy us, the most loathsome specimen of beasts of prey—the two-legged killer—will see to it when he blows a dozen holes in our bellies with a machine pistol."

Schneider was right—alas! he was right. I would gladly have

refused to touch the whole business, as I didn't want to be drawn into the dangerous vortex which surrounded Schneider. But this hunted man, sick to death of life among the natives, had diverted my thoughts so cleverly to the outside world, that I wavered. Once more, and then for always, to hear and speak my own language; to live as people live at home; to revel in the lights of great cities; to enjoy art in all its forms, to hear an opera again . . . !

"Have a look at this," said Schneider as he produced out of his box a folded booklet of yellow cardboard. "Only to be touched with the tips of the fingers. A thing like that is sacred."

On the cover were the words *"Laissez-passer pour les étrangers"*—a travel document for foreigners. Inside were listed Schneider's physical characteristics, and over his photo there was an official stamp in thick type surrounded by a blue circle.

"Genuine?"

"Of course not, but so well done that it looks more lifelike than a genuine one. The stamp is first-class, and the only thing one could recognize as false is the name. I can't very well leave Egypt under the name of Helmut Schneider. And what would you like to be called?"

I stared at the yellow cardboard.

He went on: "The whole business costs a hundred pounds. I can have the *laissez passer* ready for you in a week and, if my calculations are right, we'll make enough money to cover not only the cost of the document but also to pay for suits and linen and our steamer fares."

"All right. I'm with you."

The stakes were high. I would have to jettison my self-respect, my character as an honest man and my previous views on decency and morality, if I wanted to gamble for my freedom and a return to civilization. Best not to think about the means to the end. I aimed to be too busy in the interval to let my conscience eat me up. But to go home—home—was all that mattered.

A few days later, I was again dressed up in POW's uniform and found myself sitting next to Helmut Schneider in a decrepit jeep. It wasn't a comfortable ride, as the springs were collapsed and the potholes in the road past counting. However, driving even in this ancient bus was pleasanter and speedier than camel riding. Schneider had managed to procure everything we needed—the jeep, uniforms for himself and me, and prisoners' identity cards for both of us. The latter were genuine or copied from originals; and he could have supplied a dozen other people with all they needed down to the papers.

During the drive we wore long galabias which we took off shortly before reaching Tel el Kebir. After that we handed over the jeep to one of Schneider's myrmidons, who was to drive it to a specified spot, where he would take our purchases on board. From that point onward our progress was marked by the most bare-faced bluff. Standing by the road, we thumbed the first truck going in the direction of Tel el Kebir. The native driver picked us up and we drove into the camp without any questions asked. Thus, driving at the regulation speed of fifteen miles an hour, I returned to the world from which I had fled in panting haste. It was the summer of 1947, and the Germans working in the camp were no longer prisoners of war, but were considered as members of labor battalions.

Beside the camp gate was the usual hut for the guard, near which black soldiers were sprawling in the shade. In front of the soldiers' quarters there was a group of colonial blacks drilling and banging their rifle butts on the ground, with the exaggerated discipline which appeals to the children of nature. There was the officers' mess with a few Germans working at the lawn, without which Englishmen apparently cannot live, even in the desert. Behind were the tennis courts and cricket grounds. To the right of the road was an encampment full of tents for soldiers and POW's. I noticed a line of red fire buckets full of water, with a greasy scum of oil to kill the mosquito larvae. Everything in the camp was as empty and comfortless as one might expect. Our driver put us down in front of a supply depot where his journey ended.

"We've got to be lucky," muttered Schneider. "The camp is so big that it takes ages to walk from depot to depot. But our native has dropped us off at the right place."

In the sanitary office we found an elderly sergeant waiting for us. He looked slack but nervous.

Schneider introduced me as the friend who wanted to see the stuff.

The sergeant greeted me curtly and told me to come in.

"Now listen to me," said Schneider crackling with nervous tension. "I must go at once to attend to the truck and the other goods. Put out everything you can use and see to it that all the stuff is loaded on the truck. After that it must go to the clothing depot to take some more cargo. At twelve noon, precisely, we meet in front of the British canteen."

I was annoyed by his greediness and haste. "Stay here," I said. "We'll put the dope on board and cover it with sacks or sand, and then let's get moving. What's the sense of bothering about the other goods and wasting precious time?"

"You poor baby," he said with a contemptuous smile. "My bandy-legged landlord knows that I'm here, and I must bring him something to make him happy. Understand?"

"Whatever you say. Then at noon in the canteen, and mind you're punctual."

There was nothing to prevent my being on time. The sergeant did his job splendidly and never batted an eyelid when he put aside for me a box with a German inscription on it which had once belonged to the German commissariat. This box contained 10,000 tubes full of morphine tablets—an absolute fortune. As we had some time to spare, we searched the place for anything else I could use. I selected a few bottles of cocaine and eudokal which we then loaded onto the truck a native driver, in Schneider's pay, had just driven up to the depot.

"You still have time," said the sergeant when I had finished what I had to do; so I went with him to his office, a little wooden shed, where we drank tea and Gordon gin. At first more tea than gin and then more gin than tea, and the sergeant judged that I had plenty of time for still more gin and tea. Of course I had time, and I was no longer in the mood to worry about this pretty little racket. I had lots of time—and my head was swimming strangely. By the time the two of us had rearranged the world's affairs, with the help of more tea and gin, it was already after twelve.

Suddenly I remembered that Schneider would be waiting for me, and I set out for the canteen as fast as I could go.

I had to follow the camp road and then turn to the right, keeping on until just before the supply depot, then. . . . After a quarter of an hour I had lost my way so thoroughly that I had no idea where I was. But I couldn't ask anyone, or stand still to take my bearings as that would betray the fact that I was a stranger in the camp.

The buildings and roads became less and less familiar. I had certainly never been here, but if I could not find Schneider's truck, which probably would not have waited for me, I should have to get out of the camp by one of the gates and meet Schneider some time later.

But where were the gates? With the noonday sun in the middle of the sky, it was a problem to find one's bearings. I stood still—a figure of indecision.

There was the sun. . . .

"Hey, come here!" rasped a German voice. On the other side of the road, I saw for the first time two German policemen with white steel helmets and white strapping over their POW uniforms. Of course they carried truncheons.

Like good Germans, they earned their pay of thirty-three millièmes a day for doing their duty honestly and incorruptibly; and in a minute it would be their duty to lead me off and have me examined.

"Where are you going to?"

"To the East Gate."

"What, now, during the midday break?"

I hadn't thought of that.

"Show us your pass."

The Negro guards at the gate had accepted my pass as genuine but these fellows, trained to be thorough, would at once see that it was false, as it was not written on the regulation paper. And even if it had been genuine, they might have guessed that it had come from some escaped prisoner of war with a worse record than mine. The gin and the heat, combined with my fear and despair, put me in a turmoil. I didn't care much what happened—no one could help me now. For lack of anything better to do, I shouted at them, "What do you mean by holding me up? Don't you know your own hospital doctor? Have I got to hang a label round my neck with my name on it? I am assistant medical officer Dr. Pritzke."

The name had slipped out unintentionally. I froze, though I pretended to be in a towering rage; it was not till after I had said it, that I reflected it would be wiser not to boast of a name so prominent in the police records. My indiscretion did not seem to matter, and my outburst had a startling effect. The two soldiers sprang to attention with a smartness reminiscent of the old Wehrmacht, and apologized for challenging me. "Allow me, *Herr Doktor*," one of them said, "to mention that you are going out of your way." Then he pointed out the shortest way to the East Gate, in a very obliging manner.

It no longer seemed to matter how or when or where I met Schneider. After my long delay, I should be lucky to meet him at all. For me the only thing that mattered was to get out of the camp. The direction given me by the German was so precise that I couldn't miss my way to the gate. It was, in any case, the gate through which Schneider must have driven long ago in his truck. He was not the man to stay longer in the pen than was necessary.

At the gate the African guards were still sitting lazily on their bench, and they had brought in the knockers so as not to be disturbed during their siesta. The quiet and slackness of a summer noon pervaded the camp. I hoped that the man on duty would be too listless to verify my pass pedantically. I had the scrap of paper in my pocket. I prepared to take it out and show it as casually as I could.

But what was up now! I heard the sirens. All my fears and misgivings were suddenly reawakened. It would be the last straw if the police, alerted by some stupidity of ours and aware of Schneider's and my presence in the camp, were to shut the gate in my face.

I looked around me—without hurrying, as it was necessary for me to show no trace of anxiety before the gaping Negroes. I wanted to find out what the sirens were screaming about.

Ha! I saw with relief that it was just one of those normal incidents. A covered truck was approaching a good deal faster than the speed limit of fifteen miles an hour and behind it buzzed a military policeman on a motorcycle, who overtook and stopped it, taking down the number of the vehicle and the name of the driver. The summons would come later on, as it does in Germany. The motorcyclist then turned round and rode back into the camp. I felt that I really should not have allowed myself to be alarmed by such a trifle, and hoped that I should be as lucky when I presented my exit pass.

Then a British sergeant came out of the guardhouse to check the manifest. He looked at it for a moment, handed it through the window to the driver, and then raised his hand as a signal to the soldiers at the barrier to let the truck go through.

At that moment I heard a voice cry, "Hey, Sarge!" It must have been an African, to judge by the noise he made. The driver stepped on the gas and fumes puffed out from the exhaust. A Negro on sentry duty ran up behind the truck. "He take away socks, coats, blankets," he cried in broken English, waving his rifle excitedly in the air.

The barrier went down again, and the sergeant walked surlily to the backboard and pulled it down.

"Come out of that," he called and turning to the black soldier said, "Go and get the driver out and hold him."

Then a man in POW's uniform jumped down out of the truck just by the sergeant. Their bodies were almost touching. In his hand he held a pistol which he pointed at the sergeant's stomach. He pulled the trigger, and I heard an absurdly faint report, then another. The sergeant crumpled up without a word. The blacks didn't even shout for help. With open mouths they clung to their rifles, as if they were afraid they might lose them, and stared at the drama that had taken a few seconds to enact.

Helmut Schneider!

I was on the point of calling to him—I would have been cooked if I had—but I was struck dumb like the Africans; my mouth remained open but no sound came out.

Meanwhile Schneider ran past the man in front, making for the barrier. Two black soldiers barred the way. He was hell-bent to get out, so he shot them down. The other blacks scuttled into cover.

The guard was stronger in numbers than I had supposed when we came in through the gate. A second British sergeant came running out of the guard-room. "Come on," he shouted, "get the bastard!" Then he fired a few shots at the flying man. The sergeant's angry cries brought the blacks to their senses. They began to shout and to run after Schneider, firing from their hips as they went.

I saw Schneider suddenly shorten his stride and slowly sink to his knees. He turned around, clearly still determined to defend himself, and wearily raised his pistol. I did not hear him fire it for, as he knelt, he was riddled by a storm of bullets from the blacks firing at fifteen yards' range. He fell forward on his face, with his pistol still in his hand. Long after he was dead the soldiers went on firing at him, and it was not until an officer came up and laid about them with his cane that they stopped shooting.

In the short interval between Schneider's first shot and the arrival of the British officer, a crowd of British, Africans, Germans and Arabs had rushed to the scene, hungry for sensation. They all pushed out through the barrier and I with them. The exit was no longer controlled, for the guard had other things to think about.

There I saw the body of the man who had been Helmut Schneider. His arms were outspread and his feet drawn up under his body, like a Moslem in the attitude of prayer. The blood from his wounds formed a dark pool beside him. If I had not seen him when he jumped from the truck, I could not have recognized him. His face was shot away, and there wasn't a handbreadth on his whole body which hadn't been torn by bullets.

While everyone was excitedly crowding round the body I slowly moved away, sauntering casually at first, and managed to get farther and farther from the camp without attracting notice; but it was not till nightfall that I reached the point at which we had arranged to meet the jeep on our way back. Neither Schneider's men nor the jeep were there.

By now, everyone within a radius of fifty miles must have heard the story. When I reached my village of the Saddled Camels no one mentioned the affair, though I am sure they all knew about it. After all, Sueylim and Mosallem had assisted at my first meeting with Schneider and must have guessed what we were planning.

A police spy, masquerading as a hawker, in a Bedouin village

Captured narcotics smugglers under heavy guard

Photos from Egon E. Schleinitz

German volunteers in the Arab forces
in Palestine

This Israeli armored car was
captured by Arab troops

Sheikh Hassan Salameh, commander of Arab forces on the Central Front, stands sixth from the left, with open collar. The fat Sheikh fell in Palestine, shot in the back. Second man to his right, wearing bandolier, is commander of the Yugoslav Volunteer Battalion with the Arab armies

Photos from Egon E. Schleinit

"Stay with us," said Mosallem, "You will find happiness with us."

And Sueylim said, "Forget everything else. Oh, I know you will forget."

It wasn't easy to get away from the desert, as even Helmut Schneider, a hero of legend, had found. The desert clings to its own.

"Stay, Salameh!" The words haunted me.

"And forget," I added to myself, "that you were once Dr. Pritzke and that you lived in the great city of Berlin, among men of like nature with yourself. Forget, Salameh!"

Chapter VII

HASHISH DREAMS

THE realities of a life which held every possibility of coming to an untimely and violent end were so cruel and brutal that I slowly came to appreciate the methods by which the Bedouins of my village sought forgetfulness in dreaming, and from time to time transmuted the leaden metal of their daily lives into the fairy gold of hallucination.

One day Sueylim invited me to a party in a round reed hut alongside the settlement. I accepted with some hesitation, for I wished to experience and record what happens to a man when he intoxicates himself with hashish.

This was how things looked before we started smoking. There were five of us present, all young men, sitting around the fire under a roof of maize straw. Sueylim's brown fingers were rolling some grayish substance into a little ball, which he then heated to smoldering point with a burning corncob before inserting it into the bowl of the pipe. This, the narghile, was a short water pipe with a copper bowl and a thin bamboo stem.

From the moment when we gathered in the hut, no word was spoken. Silence was an essential part of the ceremony of hashish smoking, no less than the dignified gesture with which each smoker handed the pipe after two or three deep inhalations to his neighbor. Even when I interrupted the proceedings by choking and coughing after my first deep breath, no one gave a knowing smile. A solemn silence reigned. My second attempt was more successful, and I managed to inhale the smoke without choking.

The fire died down. Nothing happened. I experienced no feeling of excitement and saw no visions. My mind was still perfectly clear, and I watched with complete comprehension one of our party making up the fire with straw and corncobs. After a long interval, the pipe came round to me again. Still I did not dream, but I began to meditate on the realities of Bedouin life, made up as it was of excitement, unrest and worry.

I thought of their distant and dangerous expeditions in quest of this gray-green substance. It had long been no secret to me that, when they raided the village, the police had been after hashish. As they never ventured into the settlement at night, the Bedouins, who had a good intelligence service, were always able to bury their supplies of the precious drug in the desert just before dawn. It was a mystery to me how they found their numerous caches of hashish afterwards, as they never left a mark or a trace on the sand to show where the stuff had been hidden. But find them they did. As I sat there, I thought how sober and prosaic it all was. I had no dreams and didn't believe in them any more.

I felt tired, that was all. My limbs felt heavy. I could not sit up any longer and was obliged to lie down on my side. Then the hut began to turn round. I had to register and remember the sensation. I thought it wiser to shut my eyes, so as not to get giddy like a youngster after smoking his first cigar.

Then suddenly the hut stopped revolving.

No dream!

Now I could open my eyes again. When I did so, it seemed very strange that the reed walls were no longer there. But how had my friends managed to bring me into this Mameluke palace? I found myself standing all alone in a courtyard, with mosaics on the walls on either hand, pierced here and there with the filigree of *mushra-biyeh* windows. A fountain splashed before me, and in the pool below goldfish were swimming. Around me was a large garden with green lawns and bright flowers, with so sweet a scent that I almost ceased to breathe. Two dancing girls tripped in laughing and frolicking, followed by three stout Negroes who made music with tambourine, flute and dulcimer for them to dance to. Other slender figures followed, swaying their supple bodies to the ripple of enchanting music. Now I was sitting on a carpet, happy and relaxed as never before, watching these lovely creatures performing an oriental belly dance. I noticed that the figures on the patterned carpet were coming alive and throbbing like a beating heart.

On the far side of the garden sat a merry old man with a turban on his head and a beard which was dyed red. Before him, on a table inlaid with mother-of-pearl and ivory, lay great piles of yellow, printed cards. The old man picked up one of these on which, in spite of the distance, I was able to read, *"Laissez-passer pour les étrangers."* A long line of men in the uniform of prisoners of war came and stood before the table, and each received a passport.

He called across to me, "Well, Salameh, don't you want one, too?"

As I tried to get up and go to him, I felt a hand on my arm and heard a gentle voice saying, "Herbert, stay a little longer." Before me stood a tall, blond girl wearing a flowered summer frock. She had on slippers with high heels. Her eyes were gray-blue, her nose tip-tilted, her lips were parted. Oh, yes, I remembered well enough the happy hours we had spent together in her cosy little house near the Botanical Gardens in Berlin.

"Lisa," I cried. "Darling, where have you been all this time?"

She leaned against me, as though she could stand up no longer, then whispered, "In Warsaw at headquarters, under the ruins." I clasped her hand. It was icy cold. She smiled once more and then seemed to melt away, and there was nothing to see but a wisp of smoke such as one sees rising from a blown-out candle.

"Lisa, Lisa," I cried, as I wandered through the garden until I found myself facing the merry old man. "What has become of Lisa?" I asked him.

He quickly picked up all the remaining passes from the table, tore off the turban from his head and the beard from his chin with rapid, jerky movements, and I saw gazing at me from under bushy eyebrows the dark eyes of the Intelligence Officer from Camp No. 307.

"I knew you would be coming back," he said mockingly. "They all come back, but I have been waiting specially for you to come and answer the charges of theft of British army property and wanton destruction of equipment, not to mention misleading the camp authorities and breaking out of camp. You are certain to get seven years in a punishment camp."

I leaped backward and ran away from him into the garden,

which was now dark and empty. In the middle, where the fountain had been playing, there was now a small fire burning from which thick, poison-green smoke was rising.

It seemed that it was my fate to be always on the run. I was out of breath with running, but I noticed that I had not moved from where I was, as though I were running on a band which was being pulled in the opposite direction to that in which I wished to go. I made desperate efforts, but in vain: I could not get on. The copper basin was still there and the flames from it rose higher and higher. They gave no light, and the smoke which accompanied them grew thicker and more poisonously green. Through the smoke which threatened to stifle me, I saw the Intelligence Officer's face, which had become greener and thicker like a giant frog's head, and heard him say, "We are going to get you. We *have* got you. Seven years, seven years!"

Then I awoke.

That is what my dream was like. It was a dream, and yet I saw, just as I have related, the thinly veiled dancing girls, and was spellbound by the sound of such music as I had never heard. But the horrors inspired by my own anxiety had been projected into my trance so that my awakening was terrible.

The hut was empty and the fire had gone out. I was lying on the ground covered by a blanket which someone had thrown over me, but I shivered with cold. I felt as broken and exhausted as if I had just completed some tremendous physical task, and now I must drag my weary body to my tent. No: what was the good? After a few steps I staggered back and collapsed at the entrance of the hut, with the clear, cold stars pricking down on me.

Now the realities of my life seemed more cruel and brutal than ever. Maybe they would soon bring it to a violent end.

Chapter VIII

THE EXPEDITION TO KHAN YUNIS

NOT long afterwards Sheik Selim Khidr came to look for me in my tent. He found me busy with a patient.

"Hurry up," he said. "I have something urgent to say to you."

His voice was low, and it aroused my suspicions. I did not want to keep the Sheik waiting, so I examined my patient summarily and pressed a packet of entero-vioform tablets into his hand, to cure him of his dysentery, and told him that if he didn't feel better, he must come and see me again. Then I pushed him out into the road.

I found Selim Khidr sitting with crossed legs in my waiting hut. I sat down beside him. "Listen, Salameh," he said, "we want your help today. I suppose you can drive an American jeep." There was hardly a question mark in his voice. The Arab takes it for granted that every Westerner, especially if he is a German, has imbibed a knowledge of technical matters with his mother's milk.

Now if I had said that I had never driven a jeep, it would have been no less than the truth, but, as befitted a loyal subject of the Sheik, I solemnly declared that I could. I certainly could drive an ordinary car, and the peculiarities of the jeep, in respect to its four-wheel drive and its ability to cross rough ground, would not be very unfamiliar to a man accustomed to driving German army vehicles.

Then I asked him about our destination. "We are going to Khan Yunis, far up in Sinai. There are some goods I want to fetch from there."

There was no use in trying to back out. I probably would have had to drive even if I had said I couldn't drive at all. No one would have believed me. Khan Yunis, a little town just on the Egyptian side of the Palestine frontier, was, for the Bedouins at least, a great entrepôt for hashish.

The material, merchandise, or whatever you care to call it, was brought thither by ship, airplane or caravan and then carried on into Egypt by Egyptian dope-smugglers. The police, who in jeeps and armored cars patrolled the whole of the desert east of the canal as far as the frontier, knew more about the traffic than I did; though as a matter of fact the Sudanese camel patrols were in some ways more formidable than the police cars.

"Why isn't Ismain going as usual?" I asked, for I wanted at all costs to get out of going.

The Sheik smiled thoughtfully. He knew very well what I was after.

He said, "Sorry, but Ismain was arrested yesterday in Ismailia."

"Something serious?"

"He will be out again in two or three days. We have a certain pull with the police, but today, just when we want him, he isn't here."

I said, "He's an experienced man and knows the way. Wouldn't it be worthwhile to put off the trip for a few days, so as to be able to take him with you?"

I thought up a lot more alibis, and the Sheik listened patiently and gave polite consideration to each one. At last he said, "In the first place, in order that our plan may succeed, we have to bribe some particular police officers who will be on duty tonight. Secondly, the whole Organization has long been prepared to carry out the program tonight. Thirdly, the moon is in its first quarter and gives just enough light for us to find the way and too little for us to be spotted at a distance. In a few days it will be too bright. Do you understand now?"

Of course I understood, but the prospect didn't please me. What he had said about bribing the police could only have been partly true. The risk was great, and greater for me than the Bedouins, but I was dependent on the goodwill of even the chief. The outcome of Helmut Schneider's plan to traffic in morphia had been fatal for him and disastrous for me. I had lost my chance of a *laissez-passer* and a steamer ticket. There was now no prospect of my getting away, unless. . . .

But, when I came to consider it, I saw that this expedition held certain possibilities for me. If we once crossed the Palestine frontier, I might get a chance of clearing out and making my way north through Palestine and Syria. It was not likely that I should be offered another opportunity of slipping through the frontier. Anyhow, it would be bad policy to show enthusiasm now for a plan I had discouraged, so I made a few more objections, which the Sheik patiently disposed of.

So I sighed and said, "Well, if it must be so . . ."

The program had to be carried out punctually, so the Sheik, Sueylim, another Bedouin and I left before noon on riding camels. The way was more or less familiar to me. We passed the scene of my escape from the camp and the place where I should have died of thirst, if I had not been picked up by a grubby little goatherd. It seemed, in a way, an impertinence on my part to be riding past the camp from which I had fled and where I was very much "wanted," but in fact there was no practical danger. I realized that my flight had not carried me very far, and now I wondered if I should ever get much farther.

At nightfall we reached an Arab encampment south of Kantara and very close to the Suez Canal. Here we handed over our camels for safekeeping. Our plans had been carefully laid, and it had been decided exactly where on the canal bank two casually strolling couples of Bedouins should go into cover.

In those days the whole length of the canal was patrolled by the police, and the distance from post to post was from one and a half to two miles. Our Sheik knew that the sentries patrolled their beats along the bank at a slow pace. The problem was to know exactly at any given moment where the nearest sentry was. The Sheik and I got into cover and waited, while the other two men reconnoitered on either side of us.

We had a long and trying wait. I was pretty well accustomed to the night sounds, but couldn't help starting when I heard the screeching laughter of a hyena.

Suddenly the Sheik got up. "The boat," he said. All was silent.

I listened for the splash of oars, but heard no sound. Then a shadow came sliding over the water within a few feet of the bank and drew up in silence before us. I felt that this scene must have been enacted many times before. A figure stepped out of the boat, gliding noiselessly over the gunwale, and I sensed, rather than saw, that nimble hands were tying the boat to a staple in the bank.

We still had to wait until our two companions came back to report that the coast was clear. At last they came and nodded silently, without a word said. The Sheik gave us a sign to embark. We climbed with the utmost care into the little skiff, which was dangerously overloaded. We did not dare to move lest our craft, already far too deep in the water, should capsize. The black boy in charge knew his business. He made no sound as he rowed, and we could hardly feel that we were moving, but after a few minutes we found ourselves at the east bank.

The Sheik had not been boasting when he spoke of the Organization. Our program was being carried out to the minute, with a precision worthy of the General Staff.

Once ashore, we walked in silence for a couple of miles till we reached an inconspicuous wady. Here we found a Bedouin with camels awaiting us.

But why baggage camels?

These brownish, fat-bellied, slow-moving beasts had been selected in order to put the desert police off the scent, for they could very easily distinguish the clumsy tracks of these splay-footed animals from those of the narrow-toed dromedaries. If we had been riding the latter, they would at once have followed our trail. It was much safer for us to proceed at a leisurely tempo. We did not wish to be taken for smugglers, who hardly ever used anything but fast-riding camels in the frontier districts.

We rode without stopping through the night. At first there was a crescent moon, and then darkness. We could see almost nothing of the landscape. The ground was mostly flat—a crinkled sea of sand. Here and there, we passed a thornbush or a patch of scanty desert grass.

About dawn the landscape began to change. The thornbushes became more frequent and thicker, and the ground more stony.

We reached Abu Tarjuman, our next port of call, at about ten o'clock. I felt sure that we had arrived at the appointed hour when we finally dismounted at a Bedouin camp, where a man took charge of our camels. He, too, was doubtless a link in the chain of our very efficient Organization, and my confidence in their efficiency was enhanced when the Arabs produced a jeep for me to drive.

From then onward, a heavy responsibility weighed on me, and the fact that I had never before driven over this sort of ground made it none the lighter. We bumped over almost impassable, stony country but didn't get into serious trouble till after midday, when we ran into a deep declivity covered with good-sized round stones which slipped away under the wheels and made driving a torment. We swayed and skidded over this untrustworthy surface for three hours until we suddenly, without transition, found ourselves rolling over firm sand.

We needed a rest after this ghastly drive, so we drove to a clump of thornbushes in which we could camouflage the jeep. There was nothing to do but drive straight into the thicket, and let the radiator breach a passage for us through the dry branches.

Didn't I hear a camel grumbling?

Yes, and there was something else we became aware of much quicker—the click of a safety catch and the threatening, dumb mouth of a rifle barrel pointed at us.

The man behind the weapon was the poorest, raggedest-looking creature I had ever seen. The butt of his rifle was pressed into a naked black shoulder, and the remains of a tattered galabia hardly covered his body. A single lock of hair, mark of a Sinai Bedouin, hung down on his forehead from under his kaffiyeh. Only his forehead and eyes were visible. The rest of his face was covered with a fold of his headcloth, which protected him against dust, wind and recognition.

The rifle was suddenly lowered, for it seemed that the scarecrow and my companions knew one another. All the people who traded in hashish seemed to know one another. Our sheik seemed to be glad of the meeting. The masked man in the ragged galabia was carrying "goods" back with him and was able to exchange some information with us. He had his own method of traveling, and never moved except by night. He had just slipped into the thicket intending to sleep for the rest of the day, when we came and scared him out of his hiding place.

When we came in sight of the houses of Khan Yunis, we had to remark a small defect in the Organization. The agent whose business it was to watch the road and see if there were controls or patrols on it was not in his place.

Sheik Khidr waited patiently. You could never read his thoughts or feelings on his face. The absence of the agent might be due to some unimportant cause, or it might denote a breakdown capable of endangering our whole enterprise.

At last the man came and unobtrusively gave the go-ahead signal. We could drive into the town without interference.

We drove up to a house looking rather like my dream palace. I was too exhausted to notice what was beautiful or remarkable in Hadji Mohammed Abdel-Ghaffar's dignified-looking dwelling. The entrance, with its spiral pillars and stone filigree work over the gateway, suggested an old family mansion. In the courtyard was a fountain with a marble basin to remind me of the fountain of my dream, and in the basin swam some gleaming goldfish. I stared at them, wondering if they would take on other shapes like my dream fishes. Now all that was lacking was a bevy of dancing girls in filmy garments.

Good Lord! That I should be thinking of dancing girls, however lightly clad, when I ought to be remembering that we had now reached the Mediterranean coast and that, if I could slip away from my companions here, my journey home would be substantially shortened. But when our host showed us into a large room with beds prepared for all, I lay down and fell into a deep sleep from which I did not awake for many hours. I was roused by a servant who summoned us to a sumptuous dinner with Hadji Mohammed. The good food and comfortable quarters provided for us in this merchant's house, in the older quarter of Khan Yunis, did not make the prospect of our return journey any more attractive.

During the endless meal, our host did not say a single word about the business which had brought us to Khan Yunis. There was an incessant exchange of compliments and inquiries after the individual health of the numerous members of the Sheik's and our host's families, and in the intervals between courtesies we all concentrated upon a generous repast of fowls, rice, lamb, fish and a choice selection of sweet things. It was only after the coffee that our host and the Sheik withdrew to talk business.

I had long learned from the Arabs the art of going to sleep at any time, in any place, whatever the circumstances, and had accustomed myself to seize every opportunity for sleep that presented itself.

After dinner, my two Arab companions went up to our room to sleep and I accompanied them, but though the temptation to sleep after so heavy a meal was very strong, I now had to resist it.

I was sure that the negotiations would last a long time, and in the interval I had to try to get out of the house. Had not a distant glimmer of freedom on the horizon provided me with an objective, I would have struggled harder than I did to avoid taking part in this dangerous venture. Under my galabia I carried a goodish sum of money which I had myself sewn into a leather pouch. The fees I had received for medical services had mounted up to something substantial, and I was determined never again to try to escape without the wherewithal to pay for the services I would need. Now, as ever, all depended on the first bold step.

My companions were sleeping so soundly that I felt sure they would not awake and interfere with me. The people of the house were all occupied, and no one was at leisure to snoop around. Beautiful and pleasant as this great house was, I had to leave it. It was not quite the house of my dream. "Bon voyage, dear friends," I whispered as I quietly sauntered down the stairs to the ground floor.

"Do you want to go out, Salameh?" asked a voice behind me. I had just reached the foot of the stairs and was looking about me to find the shortest way to the front door, when I heard the voice and became aware that our host's son was sitting cross-legged on a cushion in the hall, smoking a narghile.

It wasn't the moment to lose one's head, so I answered coolly. "No, I am looking for the lavatory." The young man pointed to a door and I went in. Unfortunately these rooms have only a single door, which in this case was in full view of the pipe-smoking youth.

I shall not dilate on the characteristics of the Oriental privy, interesting as they are, nor upon the differences of technique employed by Eastern and Western users of these places, which it would tax my delicacy to describe. . . .

When I came out the Hadji's son was still sitting on his cushion, only he had shifted his position somewhat in order to be able to see the door out of which I had to come. I noticed in the hall a servant zealously dusting a piece of furniture. His presence may have been accidental, but it looked to me as if he had been called in to strengthen the garrison. I was properly blockaded. Sheik Khidr had obviously been expecting all the time that I would have a shot at escaping, and had set a guard over me, for my presence would be even more urgently needed, when we drove back with our precious cargo, than on our outward journey.

I thought I would have one more try. I didn't expect to succeed, but wished to confirm my suspicions. So I walked smartly to the front door. As I reached the top of the steps leading down to the garden, the young man came running after me.

"Do you wish to go out now?" he asked.

"Yes. I would like to have a look at the town."

"I will come with you."

"You really need not take the trouble," I said, striding out at a fast pace, but he walked step for step with me.

"My dear brother," he said, "I should never forgive myself if you lost your way, or if anything untoward should befall you. You know, it is the host's most sacred duty to watch over and assure the safety and comfort of his guest. And finally, let me remind you that you are the first German I have ever known. It is an honor and a pleasure for me to keep you company."

He delivered himself of these polite falsehoods with such amiable persuasiveness that I knew I could get rid of him only by forcible methods, but I could not use force in the open. I would have to put up with his company and hope for a chance of slipping away through the crowd in one of the narrow lanes. Unfortunately, the streets of Khan Yunis were open to view and sparsely frequented just when I could have wished them crowded. I had to give up my plan and make up for my disappointment by endeavoring to enjoy the delightful views the town provided.

Here was a British police barracks to which my companion drew my attention with a certain emphasis. As a matter of fact, I did not need his explanations to recognize for what it was the yellowish, oblong building, with its watchtower and loopholes, withdrawn somewhat from the street behind a fence of barbed wire. On the well-kept, grassy sward some English soldiers were playing cricket. Better give the place a wide berth, I thought.

So we went down toward the seashore and, sitting on a rock, gazed out to sea.

The young man said, "This is the Mediterranean. Its waters do not wash your country's shores, I think. Germany must be very far away."

I had no difficulty in understanding the warning which his words conveyed. Indeed, I almost forgot that he was an encumbrance to me for the pleasure I took in the charming landscape. Behind us was an orange grove with the young, green fruit hanging from the branches, while below, running down to the sea, were ranks of olive trees with the shimmer of silver on their trunks and leaves. In the background I could see the fanlike foliage of a dark-green banana plantation fringed by a few slender date palms. In front of us we beheld the blue expanse of the Mediterranean dotted with the white or colored sails of little fishing boats, while overhead the sky was blue and cloudless.

I began to wonder what was the point of trying to escape, if my flight would only take me back to our gray northern skies, in which every fine day was an unlooked-for blessing and the sight of every bright-hued butterfly a blissful experience.

"It is time to go back," said my companion, breaking in on my thoughts.

Yes, to go back, not to go home.

When we returned, we found our host and the Sheik still sitting in the hall smoking hubble-bubbles. It looked as if their discussions had proved satisfactory, particularly to the Hadji. But the Sheik also smiled contentedly, as our host patted him on the shoulder.

Our cargo was compact and took up very little space in the car. It was unobtrusively packed in cardboard cases, each of which had once contained a dozen bottles of "Saunders." These were stowed away, carefully corded, under the seats of the jeep. The small flat cakes of hashish, each wrapped in linen, were worth a large sum of money. It needed a great organization served by men, camels, motors, boats and, perhaps, even airplanes to convey these insignificant-looking linen packages from the producers in the Lebanon to the consumers in Egypt. Every individual who served as a link in the long chain of communications staked his freedom, if not his life, in the venture; but the rewards of success were dazzling, and the huge profits, shared among all who handled the business, seemed to justify the great risks.

In this particular enterprise I myself was an important link, but no part of the profits would stick to my hands. I was merely earning my keep as a refugee.

There was no difficulty about crossing the frontier between Palestine and Egypt on the return journey. On the Palestine side, the customs and police precautions were so inadequate that one had to be phenomenally unlucky, or criminally clumsy, even to catch sight of a frontier guard. Since the outbreak of the internal strife between the Arabs and the Jews, who were seeking to create in their ancient home a new state and a place of refuge for their persecuted brethren, almost all the units of the British army of occupation and police had been withdrawn from the frontiers to the interior.

But if the task of the smugglers on the Palestine side was facilitated by these events, the Egyptian controls were correspondingly tightened as the policy of the government was to make it as difficult as possible for dangerous and disturbing elements to find their way into Egypt.

With dimmed headlights, the jeep ground its way through the sand. I peered with straining eyes over the draped radiator at the ground in front of us, so as to avoid crashing into a boulder or breaking an axle in a pothole. We couldn't afford to take risks. It is true that Sheik Khidr had bribed the police officers, but even he seemed uncertain about the positive value of such action. These gentlemen might take the money and then fail to honor their promise. Or again it might happen that, even if they did instruct the patrols to avoid a certain region on a particular night, an obstinate patrol leader might unexpectedly cross our route. The patrol routes crossed one another and, if two patrols happened to be working the same piece of country and one of them did not know what arrangements the other had made, the fact that we had bribed one of them might do us no good.

"Stop!" said the Sheik quietly.

"What's the matter?"

We stopped and the Sheik pulled out of the baggage a German machine rifle, model 34, and fixed it skillfully into the iron rim of the windshield, in which a hole had been bored. Khidr screwed it into place and the weapon sat fast. Elsewhere wipers are fitted onto the edges of windshields in like manner. *Autres pays, autres moeurs.*

"Have we got to have that?" I asked resentfully.

"It may be necessary. I don't know."

"Who is going to fire the gun?"

"You, of course."

A beastly job which I would gladly have avoided.

"And if I hadn't been here? If Ismain had been driving?"

"We are carrying this weapon for the first time today, just because you are here. I suppose you know how to use it."

So that was it. In a general way, the Bedouins were quite familiar with automatic weapons, but none of my companions had ever handled a German machine rifle. This was yet another of the duties they had thought up for me.

The Sheik pulled out a box of ammunition and set it on his knees.

"Drive on," he said.

So I drove on, peering into the sand and stones, and keeping as best I could to the line they told me to follow.

Suddenly the man behind me gave me a sharp push in the back. I nearly knocked my nose against the steering wheel. Everybody whispered, "Stop." I disengaged the clutch and trod on the brake. The Sheik quickly turned off the ignition.

We stood still.

What was that? No—yes, it was. I could quite clearly hear the throbbing of a motor.

They gave me no time to listen to the sound droning through the night. Anyhow, my heart was in my mouth, and its beating would have drowned the noise of the engine that was grinding around somewhere near us. Our conversation consisted of prods and pushes. Some one pushed me in the side, and I climbed onto my seat to get the machine gun ready for action. Leaning far forward, I stared into the darkness, from which the regular throb of an unseen motor drew nearer and nearer.

A dazzling white light suddenly pierced the darkness and focused on a sand dune. Then it swept around in a semicircle and went out as suddenly as it had come on. Then came another sweep from the searchlight; this time it passed quite close to us.

"Oh God! Drive on, Salameh," said a terrified voice from the back of the car.

"Hold your tongue, you dogs!" cursed the Sheik. "If we turn on the engine they are certain to hear us. Anyhow, a moving object is easier to pick up than a stationary one."

The sound of the motor grew clearer and clearer. Then I saw a huge dark shape appear on the crest of a sand dune. In the dim moonlight, I recognized the turtle-backed contours of an armored patrol car. If only the driver kept on in the same direction! Yes, good! He drove slowly on, parallel to our route. I began to feel relieved. But what was happening now? His engine stopped, and the heavy car stood motionless a hundred yards away.

"*Ya Mohammad! Ya Naby!*" whispered the panic-stricken men in the back seat. "They have seen us or heard us, and now they are coming to get us."

Of course they were. I was just as much afraid as the Bedouins behind me.

"Silence," hissed the Sheik, "bend down so as not to expose yourselves."

Then it happened. . . .

The searchlight shone out, feeling around with its dazzling finger until it got us into focus and remained fixed on us. I shut my eyes.

"Shoot, you sheep!" roared the Sheik. He no longer whispered, as all seemed to be lost. He shouted and struck me in the side with his fist.

"I can't see," I said and shielded my eyes with my arm. "Besides, there's no sense in shooting at an armored car."

In no circumstances did I wish to be the first to fire. Our shots would strike harmlessly against their armor, and then our enemies would fire a burst with their machine gun and let their 7.5 finish us off.

"Curses on you for a coward!" cried the Sheik and pushed me away from the gun. At the last moment, I succeeded in pulling out the magazine. The Sheik tried to wrest it from me. He grabbed me by the neck of my galabia, and I closed with him and threw him on one side. Now the men in the armored car were bound to do what we hadn't done, namely to open fire, though that would be hardly necessary. The mere weight of their car would be enough to roll us flat, if they charged. . . . We were in for it!

But what was happening now? The searchlight went out and our eyes, which had been blinded by the brilliant rays, were in black darkness. We stared unseeing at the spot where we knew the car was. Suddenly its motor started up and we clearly heard the powerful engine shaking the great body of the car. We heard the gears go into action, and in a moment the colossus was moving, not in our direction, but following its former line—on and on, rolling over the undulating sand farther and farther away from us, with its finger of light pointing in search of other victims.

"Why didn't they fire on us?" I asked, when it was safe to speak aloud, and we were getting ready to pursue our way.

"How can I tell?" said the Sheik, who had gotten over his ill-temper. He was clever enough to realize that I had done the right thing.

I shall never know what to make of our experience with the armored car. Possibly the policemen on board had taken us for part of their force, as jeep patrols were also employed along with the armored cars. Possibly, again, the officer who had received the baksheesh had told them to keep their eyes shut and to be satisfied with frightening us. But it seems hard to believe he would ever give himself away so completely to his own men.

I have thought, too, of a quite different explanation of our escape. The policemen in the armored car had, perhaps, made up their minds to take a spell of rest. They had been bumping around for hours in the desert and, as they were rottenly paid and brutally treated by their officers, they thought that they would knock off work for a while. If my guess is right, all the men in the car were asleep, including the driver who, before he took his nap, turned on the searchlight and during his waking moments turned it off and on again to impress a control officer, if one should appear, with the activity of his unit.

"Drive on, Salameh," said Sheik Selim Khidr in a tired voice, adding, as he slipped the amber beads of his rosary through his fingers, "Allah is great and merciful."

Chapter IX

THE PAYMASTER WITH THE MANDOLIN

OUR cargo of contraband reached its destination safely, there to create dreams and unhappiness—in any case unhappiness. There was not much further talk of our adventure, or the part I played in it. Those things seemed to be taken for granted. I was now left to divide my time between my medical practice, occasional conversations with acquaintances from the village, and the very serious study of Arabic.

"What are you working at?" asked Mosallem one day, when he saw me sitting in the shade of the hut practicing writing.

"I am learning to write Arabic," I said, "and your language is very difficult."

"What's the sense of learning to write?"

I had asked myself the same question, and the answer was that we have not got so many years to live that we can afford to waste year after year unprofitably.

It was very hard work learning to read and write, and it got harder as I went on. Arabic, like all Semitic languages, is written from right to left, and consequently one has to read a book backwards. And once I had got myself entangled in these curiously intertwined characters, which have nothing in common with our letters, I found myself caught in a thicket from which there seemed no way out. Arabic contains more letters than our alphabet and, moreover, many of the letters are written in three or four different ways according to their position in any given word. Then I had to accustom myself to the fact that the Arabic numerals, which we long ago borrowed from the Arabs, are now almost wholly unlike ours to look at.

The difficulty of my studies was aggravated, too, by the absence of characters to denote the vowels. This is a feature of all Semitic languages, in which the vowels are indicated by points placed under or over the consonants. Every divinity student who learns Hebrew makes use of this device. But the majority of persons who write Arabic do not take the trouble to put in what are called the diacritical points, which means, that unless one has a lot of experience in reading, one cannot at first sight be sure of the meaning of a word or the right way to pronounce it.

Perhaps the most confusing thing about Arabic is the fact that, when one learns to write, one must learn another language.

The numerous modern spoken dialects, which differ from one another almost as much as German, Swedish and Dutch, are never employed in writing. The Moslem Arab clings firmly to the language of the Koran and admits little modification. The difference between the spoken and written word is as great—and as absurd—as if we Germans continued to speak in an everyday form of High German, but employed for writing the Middle German of the *Nibelungenlied.*

At the start, I found this so exasperating that I sometimes used to throw my exercise books into the corner.

"That's right," Mosallem would say, "Throw them away. What's the use of them?"

"You don't understand, my dear Mosallem," I would answer and Mosallem would shrug his shoulders and keep silence.

One day Mosallem interrupted my studies to say, "There's a German to see you."

"Where?" said I, getting up.

"They are giving him water. He will soon be here."

There appeared a man who had been picked up by a tribesman of the Ateibeh, some hours back, near the Sweet-Water Canal. He looked very much as I must have looked when the grimy little goatherd found me and handed me his water bottle. His lips were cracked, his eyes sunken and his cheeks hollow. His hands groped greedily for the water jug, for, although they had already given

him a long drink, his dried-up body thirsted for more. I gave him
an injection of caffeine to bring him to life, and to enable him to
give an account of himself.

"You must come with me," he said.

"Come where?"

"I don't know. The canal. No, I really don't know."

"How many of you are there?"

"Five—five including me. The four others collapsed yesterday. I
left them lying in the desert and came on alone. I walked a long
way until I could walk no more. Then an Arab found me and
brought me here. We must go and look for the others."

The man who had found the German and brought him in, told
me roughly where he had picked him up.

I asked the German if he had ever been on a camel. He said he
hadn't. He was in no state to object when we strapped him into the
saddle and put the guide rope into his hands. We loaded up water
skins and medicines on my camel, and rode off to find the place
where the Bedouin had found my German comrade. From what the
latter said, it would be difficult to find the others, for, after leaving
them, he had wandered around at random, half mad with thirst,
and had several times lost his bearings.

"I left them lying under some bushes," he said. "I was to try to
find the Sweet-Water Canal and bring them water. I suppose they
must be somewhere in this direction if they are still alive."

"Can you stick it out a little longer?"

"Yes. I'm all right. But we must find my pals soon or we'll find
them dead. What fools we were! What frightful fools!"

"How do you mean? Did you take the wrong road?"

"You've said it. We went to Cairo."

"You got through to Cairo! My compliments. If I ever get as far
as Cairo, no one will ever see me here again."

"It was that crook Farouk. You know how things are. They
haven't really changed much, though former POW's are now supposed to be members of labor battalions. A lot of them got through
to Cairo. Then the Egyptians started informing the British counter-
espionage office about them and the trouble began all over again.

"We had read in the *Progrès Egyptien* that the King of Egypt had offered freedom to all Germans who had escaped from the British. So we suckers fell into the trap and were simple enough to go to a police station in Cairo and report ourselves. The word of a king, you know. We learned that he had engaged a former German prisoner of war as maintenance engineer for the pumping stations on the royal estates.

"Well, the police shut us up. It didn't look very dangerous at first, but then we were transferred to another lockup where we found ourselves being interrogated by a British officer and knew that we were in for it. On the journey back, the five of us jumped out of the train, not knowing where we were, and walked till we were half dead from fatigue and hunger and seemed likely to die of thirst."

Less than four miles away, we found the four men in a patch of scrub. The man the Arabs had found had taken a whole day to cover the distance, and he was the strongest of them. One of them could not drink. He was already in a deep coma when I arrived, and died soon afterward. As soon as I had brought the others around, and was satisfied that they would be all right for the next few hours, I rode back to bring camels and helpers in order to carry the sick men to safety.

But four sick Germans in the settlement! When I suggested it, the answer was a categorical no, and I could readily understand it. It was a serious offense, visited with heavy punishment, to harbor escaped prisoners of war; and in the case of a tribe already strongly suspected of other malpractices, it would be doubly dangerous to take any risks with these men. If we took them in, the whole desert would be talking about it in a day or two.

I had no difficulty about securing an awning, blankets, mattresses, food and water and other necessities. I loaded these things on a camel and set up in the place where the fugitives were lying a little hospital where they could recuperate while waiting for a chance to get back to Cairo. We buried the dead man nearby under a cairn of heavy stones, so that the winds should not expose the body to be torn to pieces by jackals, hyenas or pariah dogs.

From time to time I had been able to help in this way, since Helmut Schneider's death. Previously the Arabs had always sent the Germans they had picked up, or who had come into a settlement seeking help, to Schneider, who had invariably done something for them. The fact that he could always find a use for their uniforms and identity cards, which he received in exchange for the native dress with which he provided them, did not detract from the unselfishness of his efforts on their behalf. Now fugitives in need of help were brought to me, and I was able to assist many of them on their way.

It was an open secret that I was living with the Ateibeh and the news had filtered into all the camps. It says much for the loyalty of the German POW's that the English never learned where I was to be found.

In the desert we managed things somewhat differently from what senior paymaster Behrens had imagined.

One autumn day, amid the wild barking of dogs, a blond, red-cheeked man in a khaki tunic, airman's breeches and top boots strode through the village toward my dwelling, followed by a fellah boy who sweated and panted under the weight of two heavy wooden boxes and a mandolin.

"Is that he?" said the man in German, pointing to me. The boy nodded, and then the gentleman, standing stiffly to attention, introduced himself.

"Permit me, Behrens. Oberzahlmeister Behrens."

"Go inside and sit down," I said, but before following him in, I wanted to learn from the fellah where he had found him.

The lad said, "Hadji Eid smuggled him out of the camp and brought him to our village in a jeep."

That was all he knew.

I went in. "Do you mean to say you live here the whole time?" asked the Oberzahlmeister rather indignantly. "Where can one get a bath?"

"For that," I said, "You have to go down to the canal. But I don't recommend it as these slow-moving waters are full of Bilharzia and dysentery germs."

I don't remember ever having seen such a comic figure; but he was an escaped comrade, and I had to show him hospitality and overlook his oddity. I had a couple of fowls killed, and cooked them with rice for our supper.

"Have you no cutlery?" he asked with a superior air, as he sat by me on the straw matting and watched me tearing a fowl to pieces with my hands and eating the flesh off the bones without help from knife or fork. He was sure I could afford cutlery, he said. He himself took out of one of his two boxes a folding knife and fork, for field use, and made an elegant job of carving his chicken. Up to that point I had kept calm, but when he asked for a glass of water and I handed him the earthenware *zir*, he asked naively if the water had been boiled or disinfected.

That remark drew me. "It's easy to see you have never roughed it," I observed coldly.

"Oh yes, I have," said he modestly, "now and then." Upon which, after rummaging in his box, he brought out a glass tube full of tablets. Two of these he threw into the waterpot, saying with a superior smile, "For disinfecting purposes."

As we drank our coffee, I asked him what plans he had for the future.

He didn't know really what he ought to do next and spoke vaguely about a rich landowner in El Sanafin, with whom he had done business while in the camp. Then he took his mandolin, sat down in front of the tent and strummed German *Wandervogel* songs, to the great joy of a crowd of children who had gathered around him. The Sheik and some of the elders took a less favorable view of the newcomer.

When, on the following day, he repeated this performance serious representations were made to me. I was warned to get him away as soon as possible. It was enough to be a German to attract attention, but if the German wore fancy clothes and spent his whole day playing on the mandolin, it wouldn't be long before a police spy got wind of it.

I did not wish to push him rudely out, but polite hints made no impression on him, so I thought that a good way to discourage him from making a long stay would be to give him a vegetable soup with chunks of tough buffalo meat in it. On the day after, he only got flat slabs of Arab bread with raw onions. I expected Behrens to turn up his nose at my menu, but as a matter of fact he did nothing of the sort. He merely took a bottle of permanganate from his box and sprinkled it over the onions, which he then ate with evident satisfaction.

I counseled him in vain to sell his stuff, as I knew too well that other men's possessions always aroused the worst instincts of the Bedouins. Many a man had been made away with for the sake of belongings less attractive than those of Behrens. The man was impervious to argument, but my fellow tribesmen, whose resentment was growing daily, threatened to drive my guest away by force, if I could not get him to move on.

"Very good," I said, "lend me a camel and I promise to take him tomorrow to Bilbês." Why should I escort him, they asked . . . I must simply drive him out and lose no time about it. They would send a few men on camels behind him in order to make sure he had really gone. I didn't like the idea of leaving Behrens alone to face an unknown future, so I decided to accompany him for the next stage of his journey.

"Lend me your camel, Salaheddin," I said to one of the tribesmen.

No, Salaheddin wouldn't agree, even when I offered to deposit the value of the camel in cash as security.

"You don't know the country round Bilbês," he said. "The Arabs there are the biggest thieves and brigands in this part of the desert. I can assure you that if you go among them they will beat you up, and you will come back without your camel and without your clothes—if you come back at all."

So I didn't get a camel but only an ancient, worn-out donkey, a miserable creature with its belly hanging down to its fetlocks, all its ribs showing and a pair of dreary, flopping ears.

Its yellow teeth were worn down with old age, and its whole body was covered with festering sores from blows and goadings and tick ulcers. Still, it was a sort of beast of burden. For my own part, I was not intimidated by Salaheddin's stories of robbers. With my black hair, brown skin and tufted chin-beard, I could pass anywhere for a Bedouin, especially as I was master of their language and thoroughly conversant with the twists and tricks of the people of the desert.

We hoisted the Oberzahlmeister's two boxes onto the sore back of the pack-ass and went on our way, with me in front, pulling the limping animal along, and Behrens with his mandolin bringing up the rear.

At first the Oberzahlmeister marched in firm, soldierly style; but soon he began to lag behind until finally, about midday, he began to complain of thirst, headache and sore feet. We were about four miles distant from Bilbês when we came in sight of a Bedouin camp which Behrens at once made for.

"Come back," I called after him when he came hurrying past me toward it. "In another hour we shall be in Bilbês."

I knew that even if Salaheddin's picture had been overdrawn, it would be most unwise to get into contact with the Bedouins. But Behrens, exhausted and thirsty, refused to listen. He obviously imagined that a little digression to the Arab tents would be something like stopping at a village inn for refreshment.

"We don't need to stay long," he cried, "and if you haven't got the nerve to come, I'll go by myself."

I couldn't leave him to face the risks alone, so I followed him very unwillingly. Everything about the camp indicated the extreme poverty of the inhabitants. The sum total of their animals consisted of two or three baggage camels, sitting in the shade of the scattered huts and tents, and a few goats. To people as poor as these even a broken-down donkey was a temptation. The appearance of the women impressed me very unfavorably. They wore short skirts and were unveiled. They must be fellahs. And what were women from the cultivated region doing among the Bedouins? A Bedouin who married a fellah must have fallen so low in the world as to lose all self-respect. This was certainly the most miserable camp I had ever struck.

"Come back, you idiot!" I called. "Come back." But by this time the curs had caught sight of us. In a poor village the dogs are still more repulsive than in a rich one, as they get fewer scraps to eat. We had not enough hands to keep them off, but a man came to our aid, running out of a hut. With a few well-aimed stones he dispersed the yelping curs. "*Marhaba!*" he said. "Come inside, my friends. Rest yourselves and drink tea with me."

Behrens frustrated my last-minute attempt to refuse the invitation by walking, as though hypnotized, toward the hut, while the Arab grasped my donkey's halter and tied him to a post by the entrance. When I came in, I found Behrens drinking deep draughts of water from an earthenware jug.

The Bedouin was a long-legged, disheveled creature as dark as a mulatto. He wasn't even wearing a galabia, only a pair of loose, white drawers and a sort of waistcoat which they call a *sadriyeh*. Round his head was wound a cloth which once, like his drawers, had been white. He bowed deeply and introduced himself as the Sheik of this exalted tribe.

"Can you not give us coffee instead of tea?" I asked. I had a good reason for making this request.

"Unfortunately there is no coffee in the house," he said with a rueful expression.

"Then be so good as to fetch some from your neighbor," I insisted.

The man then had another look and, with a gesture of feigned surprise, found some coffee. When the brew was prepared, he poured some of it out of a beaked container into small, handleless cups, which he offered to Behrens and me with a deep, ceremonious bow, laying his left hand on his heart as custom prescribes.

"*Deyf min Allah*," I said quickly, as he handed me the cup.

It was for the sake of this little phrase that I had insisted on coffee and stubbornly refused the offer of tea. Coffee-drinking has been from time immemorial a semi-sacred ceremony; and anyone who uses this short formula, when offered coffee, places himself for three days under the protection of his host, who is bound to see that during that period no harm befalls him. The Arabs have a superstitious dread of infringing this taboo.

"Say the words after me," I whispered to Behrens, nudging him with my elbow.

"What words?"

"Say at once '*Deyf min Allah*.' "

"Why should I?"

"Don't ask silly questions: say it," I said angrily.

"I first want to know why," he said.

"It's a polite formula," I could not explain it at length.

"Pooh!" he said contemptuously. "What's the idea of using the polite formulas of these filthy natives?"

The Bedouin seemed to have some notion of what was happening. He smiled somewhat scornfully, and his expression caused me to fear an unpleasant surprise. Only Behrens was at his ease, stupidly ignoring the possibility of danger.

However, nothing happened. The Bedouin behaved as an Oriental host knows how to behave toward his guests. Our short visit was interrupted by no incident, and when we went out and untied the donkey before taking our leave, he smiled courteously and, bowing, wished us a good journey.

"You see, these people are quite harmless and well-mannered," said Behrens complacently when, to my relief, we had left the last of the Bedouin tents behind us.

It was not due to him that things had passed off so peacefully. Now, as the minutes passed, we were getting farther and farther away from this ill-omened village as we approached the fertile and closely populated delta with its promise of greater security. Far away, over the edge of a wady, we saw high palm trees on the horizon.

"That is Abu Zaabal," I said. "There we shall certainly find a cart or, perhaps, even a truck to take you to Bilbês."

Our road followed the line of a dry watercourse and, in order to avoid having to struggle up and down the sand dunes which fringed it on either hand and which our donkey could hardly have negotiated, we went down into the bed of the wady, which was full of stones and boulders.

"*Qif!*" shouted a high voice, calling on us to halt. We had seen and heard nothing, but a Bedouin had crept up noiselessly behind us, and when we turned around at his challenge we found him aiming a shotgun at us. Behrens instantly put up his hands, saying, "What are we to do now? What does the fellow want from us?"

There was not the slightest doubt about what he wanted. I had good reasons for hating shotguns and had no desire to remain within range of a spreading charge of small shot. A shot at close quarters was even more unattractive, for it was practically impossible for a doctor to save a casualty riddled with pellets at short range.

I walked slowly and casually up to the Arab and began to talk to him, in the hope that I might get a chance of closing with him or drawing a pistol and pushing back the safety catch.

But before I was near enough to do anything, a mob of armed Bedouins appeared on all sides, as if the sand had given birth to them, and ran down the banks of the wady waving bludgeons, knives and palm branches.

The position couldn't have been clearer, and Behrens trembled with fear as he asked again, "What do they want of us?"

He was a pitiful object as he stood there with his hands above his head, casting anguished glances from one Arab to another. I don't suppose I looked very heroic either, when the screaming horde of Bedouins crowded around us and pinioned our arms behind our backs.

Behrens started yelling as if he were being torn to pieces and, indeed, the treatment he was getting was not much better. The Arabs threw him on the ground and started beating him with their sticks and palm branches, while others trampled on his stomach with their bare feet until he ceased his cries as he lost consciousness. Then they stripped him down to his short underpants, which they left him, not out of any feeling of humanity, but because a Bedouin has no use for such a garment.

Only two Arabs stayed with me, holding me fast, while the others were handling Behrens. When he was down and out, these rascals began fighting over his things, and I saw one of them stretched unconscious on the sand.

Then it was to be my turn, at least that is what I expected, but just as the mob turned toward me a loud voice shouted, "Leave him alone! Leave him alone! By God! He is my guest."

My former host came stumbling down the slope gesticulating wildly. He was only just in time. The Arabs, who had set on me, withdrew sullenly after freeing my arms. One Bedouin who had come away empty-handed from the loot of Behrens' baggage wanted to make up for his bad luck by robbing me and tried to rifle my pockets. I had prudently brought nothing with me except my pistol, which I had no wish to lose. I succeeded in gripping his thievish fingers before he was able to get them around my pistol, and I ground his knuckles so hard against one another that he sank groaning on his knees. He did not dare to attack me now that I had been claimed as the Sheik's guest.

Meanwhile, Behrens had recovered consciousness and was at last behaving sensibly. That is to say, he lay quietly where he was, though it must have been a bitter experience to watch the Arabs rifling his two boxes.

They also wanted to take the ass, but the Sheik intervened, crying loudly, "Do not take the ass; it belongs to my dear guest."

The swarm of robbers disappeared all together, carrying off the boxes, as no one wanted to be late for the sharing of the spoil. The only thing they left was the mandolin.

The Sheik bade me farewell in fitting terms and as he wished me a safe journey, he laid his hand on his heart with a sincerity which I did not doubt.

His Grievousness Oberzahlmeister Behrens rose groaning to his feet. "What am I to do now?" he moaned expecting, it seemed, that my sympathy would find some way out for him. But, to speak the truth, my sympathy had evaporated and I gave him a curt and cold dismissal.

"I suggest," I said, "to the Oberzahlmeister that he should clear out of here as quickly as possible."

I took the donkey's halter and turned to go.

"Where can I go, dressed like this?" he groaned.

"You will get through just as you are. No one will suspect you of carrying treasures in your pants. Climb up to the top of the slope, and from there you will see the palm groves of Abu Zaabal. You have only got to make for them. You got us into this damnable mess and you can get yourself out of it."

What a picture he made crawling up the steep slope in his underpants and nothing else, with a mandolin slung around his neck! A happy journey to him!

Chapter X

CHOLERA IN THE DESERT

YA hakim! Ya hakim!

The desert was calling for the doctor.

The desert, like Pharaoh of old, would not let me go, however often I planned to get away and however energetically I tried to force a decision and find my way back to civilization.

I had long ago tired of the adventure of life in the wilderness and had done my part to deserve the hospitality I had received. It was true that I was not a prisoner, was not forcibly prevented from going; but I was subject to a constant, steady pressure, not heavy enough to produce revolt but sufficient to leave its mark on a man who belonged to a wholly different world.

I remained the desert doctor. And the desert I served was as sober and prosaic as the conditions of life it imposed, with no hint of Oriental glamour. Nevertheless, it held a magnetic attraction which held me back whenever, after searching my heart, I came to the conclusion that the time was now come for me to go.

By now I was hardly considered as a stranger, and when the muezzin chanted the call to prayer in his high, far-sounding voice, I felt that his words were meant for me as well.

The tribesmen of the Ateibeh treated me as one of themselves and, after the Friday prayers were over, they would come to me in my tent and talk over the latest news of the desert. I used to prepare a bowl of tamarind juice, from which they drank in turn, and they would share their anxieties and problems with me.

We would talk of dangers too, for danger was never far away, even if it was only the danger that people should know exactly what profits the Ateibeh made from their contraband.

Lately, for instance, Gandil, the servant of Salim Khidr, had reported that he had seen a man called Abu Khaled—whom everyone knew and no one trusted—leaving the police station at Ismailia. This man was of no importance in himself. He was a sort of tramp who wandered round the Bedouin settlements hawking cigarettes, tobacco, sweets and knickknacks. The fact that Gandil had run into him as he was coming out of the police station was proof enough for the Arabs that he was spying for the police. . . .

The Egyptian police did not need to be told by this old rascal that hashish was being smuggled. No one knew better than they what was happening, and if the officers had felt they should do something about it and pay a surprise visit to the village, they could have done so long ago. Raids were in fact staged from time to time as a matter of form, but these perquisitions were disagreeable only by reason of the fact that the police were apt to impound anything which took their fancy.

A serious, unannounced raid against our village of smugglers would have cost the police officers the monthly payoff they got for leaving us alone. This amounted to a sum many times greater than their wages. For that reason, both sides were content to live and let live.

Nevertheless, in order that their monthly takings should be kept at a proper level, the officers used to extract from creatures like Abu Khaled detailed information about the financial situation of each one of the tribesmen, on the strength of which the tribute paid for the privilege of being left alone was often increased. And if the contributions fell short of what was usual, the beneficiaries lost patience and stimulated defaulters with the kurbash.[1] Indeed, one might say that the information provided by Abu Khaled added to the burden of the unofficial taxpayer.

Yes, we had our worries.

My own were uncomplicated and consisted in daily bargaining about the price of meat and vegetables, bananas and fish and other things necessary for my diet. The business of procuring medicines and drugs also was not quite so simple as it had been at home and frequently provided me with serious problems. I had often to cover long distances on my visits to sick and injured patients.

---

[1] kurbash—whip made of hide.

And then there was the problem of contagious diseases or, God forfend, of an epidemic. . . .

"*Ya hakim! Ya hakim!*"

A Sudanese boy came running through the noonday sunshine shouting for me.

"What is it?" I asked.

"Come at once to Hadji Eid's house; a tinsmith is very ill."

A wandering tinker—probably a gipsy. I should have to charge the fee to God, as the pious Hadji would certainly not pay a piaster for a vagabond of that sort.

"All right," I said, "take my bag."

The boy took my bag, and I picked up my riding crop, without which one could hardly get out of the house on account of the dogs. To protect myself against the burning heat, I drew a linen hood over my head. Then I walked with measured steps, according to local custom, to the house of Hadji Eid.

I found the sick man lying under a straw shelter in a corner of the courtyard. His body was twisted with pain, and his two hands pressed against his belly. A crowd of curious sightseers stood around him. His cold hands, hardly perceptible pulse, sunken eyes, pinched nose and bluish skin, combined with continual vomiting and stools the color of rice water, left me in no doubt about his illness.

It was cholera!

Cholera—and in these insanitary conditions!

On his body and in his excrement had settled a swarm of those green, stinging flies one sees so often on the eyes of blind people or children in Egypt.

As soon as I had finished my examination, I rose hastily to my feet, holding out my hands, with which I had touched the sick man.

"Bring me a large can of water—at once," I said.

A servant poured water over my hands from a copper vessel, and I washed them thoroughly with phenol soap. Then I washed them again with pure alcohol. When I was satisfied that it was safe for me to come in contact with other people, I hurried into the house to inform the Hadji that there was cholera in the village and to discuss with him measures for disinfecting his courtyard.

I found Hadji Eid lying on a divan in his reception room, smoking a water pipe and dozing.

"*Marhaba!*" I said. "*Naharak saeed!*"

"*Naharak saeed wa mubarak,*" he answered.

"Sit down, my friend."

I was too excited to sit down and was beginning to break the dreadful news to him.

"Listen, Eid—"

"My brother, sit down here on my right." insisted the Hadji, and I had to comply with the etiquette.

"How is your health?" he asked quietly.

The compulsion of Arab courtesy was stronger than that of the cholera, so I said, "*Elhamdulillah!* And how are you?" As good manners required, I looked him full in the face as I spoke, as if I wanted to be sure he had no symptoms of illness.

"Praise to God!" he answered gently.

"What I wished to say to you . . ." I began, starting a new approach. There was not a minute to lose. It was cholera, and around the sick man everything was in a ghastly mess and clouds of flies were settling on his droppings—an absolutely impossible situation.

The Hadji interrupted me again, to clap his hands and order a servant to bring us coffee.

"We have a sick man in the courtyard," I said, coming straight to the point, regardless of the laws of politeness.

"Yes, I know, I know," said the Hadji, with a gesture of boredom, and looked at me critically as if resenting my bad manners.

"The patient has cholera and must go at once to a hospital." What did I care about manners now! "The disease has made such progress that he can only be saved by hospital treatment."

"You mean that he is dying?"

"Probably; his only chance is to go to a hospital."

"Allah is great and all life is in His hands," broke in the Hadji. "If he has to die, he can die here."

I could not hold myself in any longer. I sprang excitedly to my feet.

"Don't you understand?" I said. "It is not a matter of a single sick man. If we don't at once take all possible precautions, we shall have cholera in the village."

"Our lives are in God's hand," he repeated and put a fresh charcoal brand in the bowl of his pipe.

"The man must go at once to a hospital."

"Salameh!" he said.

All at once the sleepiness had gone out of his voice. Then he said to me in a normal tone, "Sit down." I had to obey him, I had to sit down beside him, condemned to listen patiently to what he said.

I remembered that some time ago Faraj, one of my neighbors, had come into my tent for a chat and had shown me a newspaper on the front page of which was printed the news that cholera had broken out at Port Said—was it four or five weeks ago? Faraj had commented on the news, which had been given such a prominent place, by saying that the English had brought the disease from Calcutta. Everything bad always came from the English, might God strike them blind and destroy them with cholera, plague and abortions—these infidels who sucked the blood of true believers like bugs! Yes, the English were getting what they deserved—and anyhow Port Said was far away.

That was four or five weeks ago. And now?

"Now, I want you to listen to me," said the Hadji. "If the man goes to the hospital, we shall immediately have the Public Health people on top of us. They will put the village in quarantine and surround us with a cordon of police and soldiers. No one will be able to come in or go out. Our business will be completely interrupted, and you know how difficult it is to arrange. We simply cannot risk losing it."

Even had I wished to, I could not fight against this argument. If I had attempted to go and inform the health authorities at Ismailia I would have had a poor chance of reaching them alive.

Finally I said, "Well, it is your responsibility."

"Allah's responsibility," he corrected, "for all life is in His hands. What is the use of a hospital, when we have a doctor in the village? You are responsible for the health of the inhabitants. You can have everything you need, but you must keep the cholera away from the village."

What else could I do but assent?

I then said, "I shall have to put up a tent outside the village to serve as a cholera hospital. I shall prepare a list of my needs at once. When shall I get the things?"

"*Bukra.*"

The routine of Arab procrastination, when it is desired to postpone any particular action indefinitely, prescribes that the adjournment should be qualified with the consoling word "*bukra*" meaning "*tomorrow.*" On this occasion everything I had asked for was ready for me on the following day. Everything, that is, but the cholera vaccine, which was not obtainable, though of course it was due to arrive "*bukra.*"

We learned only later that at the outbreak of the cholera epidemic, there were no more than eighty ampoules of cholera vaccine in the whole country. Eighty doses for a population of twenty-two million, at a time when cholera was threatening the country! The eighty ampoules were immediately appropriated by the Palace, and those who moved in Royal circles were the first to be inoculated.

The villagers feared the disease less than the disclosure of the single case that had hitherto occurred, which would involve them in all sorts of unpleasantness. Stimulated by anxiety, the village elders made a point of seeing that all the precautions on which I insisted were duly carried out. Eight days passed before another case occurred. Then a young girl belonging to Hadji Eid's household was brought into my hospital, and in a few days we had as many as eight cases. I was fortunate enough to get all of these through the critical period in a comparatively short time. Only a girl of twenty hovered for a long time between life and death. She was my last cholera patient from the village.

What made the treatment of this young woman particularly difficult was the fact that her whole family—father, mother, two uncles, several cousins and a grandmother, as well as the father's second wife—spent their whole time squatting on the floor around the patient's sickbed. It was impossible to get them to go away. At this time, I was not aware that this practice prevailed in all Arab countries; and that even the city hospitals often had to accommodate an entire family when one of its members was being nursed in a ward. But my violent protests were completely unavailing. When I wanted to examine my patient I had to force my way through the family, who all the time were exposing themselves to the danger of infection. And not content with inconveniencing me by their presence, they used to give my patient camel's milk, strictly against my orders, and contrived in numerous other ways to aggravate the difficulties of my task.

Into the midst of this confused mass of work, which left me hardly any time for meals or sleep, there burst one morning an unexpected element in the shape of a corpulent Arab, riding on a she-ass. He was accompanied by a gigantic black man, who respectfully took charge of his master's mount. I had just given my patient a salt-water injection when Mosallem introduced the unwelcome visitor.

I received him with the customary friendly greeting. Mosallem prepared coffee, which my guest drank with an air of boredom before putting me right as to the proper way to cure cholera.

I already knew this dark-skinned desert dandy, Sheik Hassan, and had no wish to know him better. He wore a low, dark-red tarboosh encircled by a neatly wound turban and a spotless caftan of dark color. His beard was carefully trimmed and he made an impression of well-groomed prosperity, confirmed by his smart-looking servant and his well-fed ass. As a matter of fact, he was of lowly origin—just a Bedouin like any other. But thanks to his knowledge of the Koran and his ability to write Arabic, two comparatively rare accomplishments in our community, he performed the functions of imam, as well as teaching in the little village school; and gave himself out to be an authority on many subjects. Too lazy to work, too clumsy to steal and too cowardly to smuggle, he earned his living by manufacturing charms—which were as easy to make as they were costly to buy—consisting usually of triangular pieces of paper with a text from the Koran written on them, before they were folded up and placed in a leather pouch to be carried around the neck.

He looked at my stethoscope and the other instruments of my

profession with a contemptuous air of superior knowledge, and expressed strong disapproval of my clinical methods.

"What foolish ideas you have about this sickness which you call cholera! We have known this sickness for many hundreds of years. It is nothing else but *hawa asfar*—the yellow wind. And what is the yellow wind? Merely miasmatic exhalations from canals and watered fields which, when the constellations are unfavorable, especially when the moon is waning, cause this disease to break out."

I had to be careful with this chatterbox. He was quite capable of accusing me of blasphemy, if I annoyed him.

He went on: "Against the yellow wind all your drugs are useless. The only thing to do is to drive the miasma out of the fields after morning prayer with palm fronds, sticks and switches. We shall arrange for that tomorrow morning. And I want to tell you that a hejab talisman is a sure protection against the disease. I shall make one for you. As you are my friend, it will cost you very little. For one pound you will have a charm against all dangers. Just give me the name of your father and your mother and the month of your birth."

With that he took out of his caftan a stump of pencil and a creased piece of paper, and looked at me expectantly.

In such a case silence was better than any reply, however well-considered. Silence brought down the price.

"You are like a younger brother to me," he said, "although you are an unbeliever."

The fat man panted with brotherly affection.

"I will let you have it for half a pound, though that is no price for a permanent protection against sickness and death."

Softened by my silence, he sighed and came down still further. "Very good," he said, "I will make you a present of it for five and twenty piasters."

With his cunning eyes narrowed, and his head cocked innocently on one side, he waited for my consent.

But I still kept silence.

"With a talisman like this around his neck, even an infidel may enjoy the delights of Paradise."

He proceeded to describe those delights which the payment of twenty-five piasters would one day entitle me to enjoy, but I was not to be tempted. At last my patience gave out, and I left my visitor abruptly in my waiting tent and began my daily round of the houses and tents in the village. Sitting by the bed of my sick girl, I found her multitudinous family. They were fanning her and giving her camel's milk to drink.

Meanwhile the Health Authorities of the U.N. had flown in large consignments of vaccine. The daily press, supported by leaflets and itinerant loudspeakers and not least the doctors, instructed the people in their duties. Sanitary brigades from the Ministry of Health and teams of foreign doctors scoured the land. The affected districts were isolated, and the further spread of the disease was checked. In a short time, the epidemic was unmistakably on the decline.

Chapter XI

ABDUCTION OF A DOCTOR

I HAD a presentiment of trouble when I looked up, as I was boiling my instruments, and saw a couple of camel riders coming over the village square, leading a third saddled camel.

The scene was significant. To judge by their appearance and demeanor, these men were complete strangers, and yet I noticed that they waved their hands cordially to the first villager they passed in the road. I judged that even though these men came from far away, their acquaintance with our people should be attributed to the fact that they belonged to the same profession which had spread its net not only over our desert, but over a much wider area.

I saw the man to whom they were talking point to my tent. One of the strangers nodded his thanks and came right away to me.

"*As-selam aleikum!*" was the greeting of a dark-skinned Sinai Arab. He did not look as if he had come on a peaceful mission, in spite of his words of greeting. He held his rifle between his arms, which were crossed on his breast, and stood before me in a ragged galabia, faded and discolored by sun, sand and dirt. His hair was plaited in a pigtail, hanging down from under his headcloth, which also hid the lower part of his face.

"Are you the German doctor?" he asked.

I said I was.

In that case, I should come at once with him to treat the head of his tribe, who was ill.

"What is the matter with him?"

"You are a doctor. You must find out."

He clearly thought my question out of place.

"But I must have some idea of what is wrong with him," I said.

It seemed a waste of time to try to explain to him that one needed a different set of instruments to deal with shot wounds, or a broken leg, from those one would need to treat a case of dysentery.

"He has a pain," said the Bedouin, and that was all I could get out of him.

What was I to pack in my case? On reflection, I equipped myself to deal with all the normal emergencies, and followed the Arab to the camel.

When I saw that my camel had no bridle and had been roped to one of the other beasts by a cord from the saddle, it became clear that I was to be their prisoner, with no chance of escape.

"We don't want you to have an accident," he said. "Your beast is rather wild." The smile that accompanied these words was the first I had seen on this man's face.

We rode southward. When I saw in what direction we were going, I began to understand why my camel had been roped to one of theirs. It was possibly an act of kindness in disguise for, if I had broken away from them, I should have found no water, no pasturage and no human habitations in this area—not even an Arab encampment. My two taciturn companions, riding on either hand, refrained from conversing with me. Anyway, they talked a dialect of which I understood only a word here and there. So we rode on past the Bitter Lakes, from which the Bedouin women still supply themselves with salt.

I really felt, when I thought about it, that I ought to be proud of the fact that my help was sought by people living so far away. It seemed that my fame had been noised afar.

South of the Bitter Lakes, my companions swerved away from the normal camel route, which led through the wadies, and rode off diagonally across the high dunes.

"*Ya Saater! Ya Rabb!*" they cried anxiously as the beasts painfully and stumblingly made their way down the steep slopes.

The first person who crossed our path as we were riding through a bush-grown region was a Bedouin woman, a ghostly apparition looking like a wandering bundle of brushwood, who was going home with the fuel she had collected. We saw no one else, and I began to ask myself where we were going.

It was clear that the Arabs were in a hurry, but the camels, which had obviously been ridden hard during the past few days, now fell into a slow, shuffling pace. The elder of the two Bedouins stretched out his arms in front of him and began to speak quietly—to his beast. Then he altered the pitch of his voice and pronounced in guttural tones the word "*Huirr!*" which he kept repeating. At once our camels pricked up their ears and broke into a fast trot which lasted, however, only as long as their riders continued to exhort them. When they no longer heard the magic word, they dropped back into their weary shuffle.

The country was quite strange to me. The great, blackish stones which formed the substance of a high hill away to our left became more and more abundant, till finally the tawny land gave place to a rough, stony surface. Eventually we had to get off and lead our beasts over a high, boulder-covered slope. The camels, which had up to now picked their way with great care, grumbled and groaned as we led them down the stony scree into the valley below.

Man and beast, we were near the end of our tether when the first sign appeared that we were reaching our destination.

"Look," said the younger of the two Bedouins, pointing to a pair of vultures circling in the sky. "They have killed a sheep in the camp."

Now we could remount and ride through the stony gully, scorched by the refraction of the sun's rays from the boulders and lava blocks. Soon the vultures were overhead, and a voice called "Halt!" My companions gave the countersign, and we rode on. Only then, the Arab on guard came out from his cover and looked at us as we pushed on toward a clump of brushwood, where a couple of dozen camels were ruminating in front of their fodder bags in the scanty shade of a few undernourished, yellow palms. There we found ten Bedouins sitting in two goat-hair tents.

The first thing I noticed, when we dismounted and walked stiffly to the larger of the two tents, was a pile of bales and boxes covered by a tent cloth, which the caravan had brought in from Palestine. A cargo of hashish. It was clear that the man to whose assistance I had been summoned had fallen sick on the way. There he was, lying on carelessly spread rugs—an Arab of some forty years, who in spite of his powerful, stocky frame was a picture of misery as he groaned and writhed with pain.

"Praise be to God!" he murmured in a husky voice. "I am saved!"

I knew all about that huskiness. A cursory examination convinced me that he had cholera.

"You must come to the village to my hospital tent," I said.

"Impossible," said the sick man.

"Impossible," echoed the Bedouins who, curious as ever, had crowded into the entrance of the tent.

"If we go into a village, the police will surely catch me," he moaned. "You don't know those blackmailers. If they see what we are carrying, they will suck my blood to the last drop. I shall have to sell my house and farm and my palm grove in Khan Yunis. My sons will beg their bread and my daughters will become dancers in coffeehouses."

These thoughts troubled him more than the pain of his sickness. That was why he had planned to abduct me. But now that I was in his power, he addressed me in gentle tones.

"The blessing of Allah be upon you, Salameh! Your heart is like honey and buttermilk. You will nurse me back to health, and I will give you a princely reward. Here, take this!"

With that he took two one-pound notes out of his belt and pressed them into my hand, in order to soften my heart and make it like honey and buttermilk.

The prospect of living for days in the desert with a cholera patient was not exactly exhilarating. But I was a prisoner and had not the slightest chance of escaping.

"Very well," I said. "But I must go back quickly to the village to fetch the instruments and drugs which I need."

"You cannot do that. I want you here. You must not leave me, but we shall send a rider on our swiftest camel to bring you what you require."

Here was a further difficulty, and one not easy to overcome. How could I explain to a Bedouin, for example, that he had to bring me a drip apparatus, intravenous needles and ampoules with saline infusions? And the problem of the drugs was even more difficult. The only person in the village who knew anything about the contents of my instrument case was Mosallem, who had often assisted me. And Mosallem could not read and would hardly recognize the description of the various objects. However, Mohammed Khidr had mastered the difficult art of reading, so I wrote him the following letter:

"To my friend Mohammed Khidr, whom may Allah protect!

"I kiss your hands in token of my deep respect and desire to inform you that I have arrived safely among our friends. Be so good as to read the enclosed lines to young Mosallem and tell him to select the things of which I am in need."

My letter ended with the usual long-winded politenesses, the composition of which must have added an hour to my patient's sufferings.

My instructions to Mosallem were as follows:

"I want, firstly, the large vessel with the tube with a clamp attached to it; secondly, the tin box with the needles which I stick into the arms of my patients; thirdly, the very big-stoppered glass containers in the white box."

As it would have been useless to try to explain to Mosallem what drugs I needed, I decided, after some reflection, to tell him to send all those that were stored in a big tin box which had formerly contained Black Magic chocolates. So my fourth point was "the large, black tin box which you once gave me as a present, and all that is inside it."

Late in the night, the messenger came back with everything I had ordered. Now I could begin the treatment. I tied the drip to the tent pole and inserted the needle into the brachial vein of the sick man. Then I stretched the arm out on a splint and put a cuff around the upper part, and then the infusion began. For the moment I could do no more.

Next morning the condition of the patient was as grave as when I arrived. The skin was dry and yellow. The vomiting and diarrhea were no better. After my examination I washed my hands in an old cooking pot.

"Come, please, and drink coffee with us," said a Bedouin to me, taking a soot-blackened copper bowl from the fire and pouring some of its contents into a cup which had clearly been often used and never washed.

I had long cured myself of fastidiousness, so I drank and handed back the empty cup. The Bedouin then refilled it and passed it to my patient, who drained it noisily.

Second round.

The Bedouin filled the cup, once more. I held it in my hand, remembering that the sick man had just drunk out of it. And now should I . . . ?

I couldn't think of anything better to do so, pointing to the sky, where the first flush of dawn was appearing, I cried, "Look, there are the vultures again."

All heads turned to where I had pointed, and I had just time to pour the coffee into my left sleeve. It was hot enough to burn my arm, but I preferred a burn on my arm to cholera germs in my belly.

"You are dreaming, Salameh," said someone who had noticed my action.

"Yes, of course. Just a little mistake," but I didn't mind their laughter.

I am not going to describe in detail the filthy and insanitary conditions which prevailed in the sick tent. There was no redeeming feature. Round the sick man, whose life was to remain for long in danger, arose a penetrating stink which was hard for European nostrils to endure.

The guards on duty around the man lying sick in the wilderness, beside his piles of costly merchandise, did their work efficiently. They gave the alarm when, late in the afternoon, a group of riders approached. The challenge was answered, and who should arrive but the sick man's uncle, with two women and two servants.

In spite of my violent protests, the uncle went straight to the sick man and kissed him. While he was invoking the grace of God on his sorely tried kinsman, the whole family planted themselves in a semicircle round the sickbed, and the women gave expression to their grief and sympathy by hysterical lamentations.

It is well known that the Oriental has the gift of working himself up into a passion of fear or anger or grief, or any other emotion, at

the shortest notice. The hysterical weeping of professional mourn-
ers at a burial is in a sense genuine, and the floods of tears they
shed for dead persons whom they never saw alive are not simulated.
It is true they earn their bread by weeping, but real tears deserve real bread.

The emotional grief of the relatives was quickly transformed into
lip-smacking enjoyment when the evening meal was prepared. The
visitors had brought with them a live sheep which the servants
slaughtered and quartered, and the flesh was now roasting in an immense cooking pot over the fire.

We all sat round a great copper platter heaped with rice on which
the chunks of mutton lay. Everyone, including my patient, rum-
maged in the mass to find a piece of meat to his taste, which was
eaten with a handful of rice. I was a privileged guest.

"Here is something you will like, Salameh," said the uncle, as he
passed me a sheep's eye in his dirty fingers.

I had faced death many times in the war, but I hardly remember
a moment when I was more intimidated than when I had to swal-
low down this awful tidbit. I sincerely hoped they would let it go
at that, but the uncle, who had taken me to his heart, pulled up his
sleeves and, leaning forward till his beard was nearly in the dish,
fished out pieces of meat one after another and tried them to see if
they were good enough for the honored guest and then threw them
back. At last he found a bit which he judged good enough for me
and handed it to me saying, "Here is another choice morsel,
brother."

It was a lump of fat from the sheep's tail, with a most unsavory
odor. The sight of my neighbor's unspeakably dirty hand gripping
this greasy offering, while the gravy ran over his hairy arm, was
too much for me. . . .

Nature came to my rescue and saved me from the obligation to
eat this delicacy, as well as restoring to the light the sheep's eye
which had spent a few minutes looking around my disturbed
stomach.

After supper, uncle and nephew started talking business. The
theme was, of course, hashish. Uncle wanted to buy the whole con-
signment and made an offer for it.

Then occurred a miracle. The sick man, who for most of the time had been dozing apathetically, suddenly came to life. His voice also recovered some of its tone. He sat up, leaned on his elbow and gesticulated. The uncle raised his voice but the nephew's husky growls drowned his words.

"By Allah and His Prophet!" swore the uncle. "I offer you 11,300 pounds for this lot and not a piaster more. Am I not a good uncle to you, my son? Have I not always treated you like my own boy? Did I not hasten to your side as soon as I had news of your illness?"

He certainly had hastened, but for other reasons.

Still his adjurations were impressive. He went on to say, "I am a poor man. My children are poor and ill-clad. My house is a resort of the faithful. By God! Eleven thousand, three hundred pounds is all I possess."

The sick man was badly handicapped by hoarseness. When he could not succeed in interrupting his uncle's resounding flood of words, he had to wait for a pause.

Then he said, "You know how much I honor and love you, dear brother of my father"—he waved his arm in the air to brush away the flies which were settling in the corners of his mouth and eyes—"but I swear to you by the tomb of the Prophet, by the life of my children and by all I hold sacred, that with the best will in the world I cannot let the merchandise go for less than 16,000 pounds, and even then I shall be losing money."

The old man smiled and stroked his sick nephew's arm affectionately. He realized that the sickness of the caravan leader offered him a wonderful chance of making a few thousand pounds. The cargo of hashish, stacked in front of the tents, was a serious responsibility. It was liable to be confiscated or to involve the owner in the payment of such large bribes to the police that the nephew would be well-advised to sacrifice some of the profits in his uncle's favor. The deal was finally concluded, amid cries and groans of protest, when the uncle agreed to raise his first offer by 500 pounds. Sheik Ahmed would have made 3,000 pounds more if Allah had not visited him with the cholera, but even so he had not done badly. Moaning, but not dissatisfied, he relapsed into apathy. Meanwhile, his uncle had the goods loaded on camels and removed under a guard of three armed Bedouins.

The condition of my patient remained grave. His small reserves of strength had been weakened by the effort of bargaining. Toward evening, I began to doubt if I should be able to save him, and next morning I was almost without hope.

The Bedouins now began to mutter and whisper among themselves in a manner that boded no good. I understood little of what they said, but enough to realize that they no longer trusted me. For them hashish meant everything, and they could not conceive that others should not be equally interested in it. They were beginning to believe that I had been bribed by a rival group to give their leader poison instead of medicine. It was difficult to follow their tortuous logic, and I had no idea in whose pay I was supposed to be. They muttered about the police and even the British Secret Service, and even went so far as to suggest that I was an agent of the Jewish Haganah organization. The final and, to them, most credible form their suspicion took, was to believe that Sheik Khidr had charged me to put his competitor out of the way.

As the Bedouins had no idea of medical practice or procedure, these suspicions might well involve me in danger, and it was not long before they made no secret of their mistrust. They now treated me as a regular prisoner and kept an eye on me at all times. A Bedouin was told off to watch my every action. When I got up from my sleeping mat to go out and relieve myself, a guard with a loaded carbine barred my way. I wanted to remonstrate, but the man pushed me back, saying, "If our leader dies, you die too."

There was no reason to doubt him. Men of that stamp mean such threats seriously. Meanwhile, my patient's condition caused me to believe that all my efforts had been and would be unavailing. Nevertheless, moved by hope and fear, I devoted as much care and effort to his treatment as if I were struggling to save the life of my only child. His life was ebbing, and mine with his. I became nervous and seemed to be losing my touch, however sure I was of the treatment I had to apply.

A fee of two pounds was not much to offer a man whose life was forfeit if he failed. And I was going to lose the game. That was clear to me one evening after attending to my patient. Next morning, there did not seem to be the slightest chance of saving him.

The final remnants of his strength would certainly give out before nightfall. I was quite calm, now that all hope was over for my wasted patient and myself. Besides, I had probably caught the infection. It would be a miracle if I had not. I had helped many in sickness; there would be no one to help me. Was it better that the Bedouins should make an end of me in their brutal fashion or that I should die as pitifully and painfully as the man before me, of the same disease and in the same horrible surroundings?

I revolted against my thoughts.

Was it certain that I had caught the disease?

No! No! I wanted to live and go home—to come at last to my country and my world, to breathe another air; to be free to do what I wished and not constrained in all my actions by another's will; to be where I could not be carried by force to a patient's bedside and where my fee would be something other than a pistol ball.

If I ever came alive out of this tent and got back to my village among the Ateibeh, I was resolved that it would be my village no longer. Many days had gone by; the year was nearing its end. Maybe an escaped prisoner would now have no great difficulty in getting through to Cairo, where he would find ways and means of leaving Egypt for good.

If only I could succeed in bringing the dying man to life again!

He was alive next morning, but no better. I had not slept the whole night, but had sat throughout by my patient's bedside in order to be able to detect any change in his condition.

Very early in the morning, one of the Bedouins rode off. I did not know the reason of his going, but felt that it certainly boded no good for me. Late in the afternoon the Arab returned, bringing with him an elderly man, who ignored me and began to busy himself with my patient. He raised Sheik Ahmed's drooping eyelids and spoke gently but urgently to him.

Now I was a spectator and was able to observe the traditional Arab treatment of sick people. A piece of iron which the old man produced out of his saddlebag was placed in the fire and left till the end was red-hot. Then he fished it out. Three Arabs held the sick man down. I heard a piercing cry and smelled the reek of burning flesh. The old man had pressed the hot iron against the soles of the sick man's feet to drive the sickness out!

Sheik Ahmed writhed in terrible torment and whimpered pitifully for half an hour. Then he fell into the sleep of exhaustion. But it was, in fact, sleep—no question of fainting or coma.

The vomiting stopped and, though he whimpered from time to time, the sick man had a comparatively quiet night. Next morning his condition so clearly improved that I felt the noose slackening round my neck. By the evening, the man was out of danger. I asked myself whether it was the intervention of the Arab *hakim* that had caused this wonderful improvement, or was it the patient's strong constitution together with the delayed effects of my scientific treatment? I prefer to express no final opinion. If it was really the Arab *hakim* who saved Sheik Ahmed's life, I am also beholden to him for my own. After what happened, it would be ungrateful to call him a charlatan.

A day or two later, it became possible to transport the convalescent on a canvas litter to his uncle's farmhouse. Nephew and uncle, with fulsome expressions of gratitude, both invited me to spend some weeks as their guest. But my memories of a coffee cup and a pair of filthy hands fumbling after tidbits in the dish, and above all of the terrible days when my patient and I were hovering between life and death, decided me not to take advantage of their hospitality.

When we parted, my patient with a generous gesture pressed another one pound note into my hand, which brought my honorarium for medical attendance to the handsome figure of three pounds. This almost pathological act of generosity had to be compensated by various economies. It was noticeable, for instance, that no one was sent to show me the way home, nor was a camel placed at my disposal. An aged donkey did just as well! Instead, fear was my companion—the fear that, though I had been recently innoculated, my close contact with the patient had infected me with his disease.

My apprehension left me only when a week had passed, and I

had shown no symptom of sickness. But the dark and gloomy impressions engendered by my experience still haunted me. I desired no longer to persist, from indolence and habit—due in part to the limitations of a life in captivity—in a lethargic routine to which death could be the only end.

I was now no longer alarmed by the hazards of the future and was definitely resolved to set out on my return journey to Germany, as soon as the rules of politeness permitted me to bid farewell to my friends of the Ateibeh. This time I would travel via Cairo by the shortest and easiest route available.

Chapter XII

A MAN CALLED IBRAHIM BEY

I KNEW that in Cairo several doors would be open to me, for I had the address of an influential personage named Ibrahim Bey.

Whenever, during my long sojourn in a desert prisoners' camp, I had the courage to dream, the name Cairo always held for me a vision of glamour and romance. Whenever we homesick prisoners, behind our barbed-wire entanglements and chevaux-de-frise, got talking of a civilized world in which there were still modern houses instead of army huts, women, bathtubs, motion pictures, radio music, opportunities to flirt and laugh, cabarets and beer—the name of Cairo was always mentioned. And it was with Cairo as his goal that many a daring man had broken out through the defenses and palisades—often to die of thirst in the desert.

In Cairo converged all the strings one had to pull in order to obtain false passports, currency and steamer tickets, and it was from Cairo that the secret roads by which men were smuggled into freedom, started. Cairo was the last station on the way to Germany; and there was much talk of the splendor of this station.

Besides, as I have said, there lived in Cairo an influential man called Ibrahim Bey for whom, so to say, I carried credentials.

I did not know him well; in fact, to tell the literal truth, I did not know him at all, though I had often seen him. Whenever he turned up in our village, I used to admire his flowing silk robes and, even more, the agal of gold thread which kept his white silk kaffiyeh in place. His dignified gait bore witness to his high position; the deference with which everyone in the village treated him showed that he was a man of great influence, while his comfortable rotundity led me to assume that kindliness of character which we associate with fat men.

At first I took Ibrahim Bey, whose name as yet was unknown to me, for a prominent politician; and since his appearance in the village coincided with the outbreak of troubles in Palestine, I inferred that he wanted to induce the Ateibeh to take part in the struggle. It was only later that I learned that he was one of the principal purchasers of hashish. Whenever I sought to approach this man, I was always prevented from doing so. Sheik Khidr and the other sheiks never left his side up to the moment of his departure, and it was clear that this close chaperonage was not accidental. I finally learned his name and, much later, his address from Sueylim's father.

I decided that this powerful man had to help me get away from Cairo. A man like him would be more useful to me than someone who had never fished in troubled waters. In the East, the bypaths are often more practicable than the highroads. When I announced my intention to depart, there was much lamentation among the villagers, who protested passionately against my decision to leave them and go home. The Bedouins appreciated me. I had shown a sympathetic understanding for them, I spoke their language and was necessary to them, both as a doctor and for other enterprises which needed nerve. I could not, of course, attribute my desire to go home to any dislike for their manner of life, so I explained to the chief men that I just wanted to go home; and they and my other friends gradually began to understand my point of view, though they used all their eloquence to break down my resolution up to the moment of my departure.

But when they found me unyielding, they gave me a friendly Godspeed. Sueylim came with me as far as Basatin Barakat, where I said good-by to him with genuine sorrow.

The young man had tears in his eyes as we waited for the bus and his parting words were, "If ever you are in trouble and need help, remember that I am your brother. You saved my life and it belongs to you."

I told him I was deeply grateful. Meantime the bus had come and was ready to move on. I kissed Sueylim on both cheeks in the Bedouin fashion. He turned away, overcome with emotion. Then I got in quickly, lest my resolve should weaken at the sight of so much friendship and loyalty. I looked lingeringly back from the moving bus and saw Sueylim riding listlessly away, while my camel followed, roped to his. Honest Sueylim had made the parting bitter, and now our desert village suddenly seemed to me like a lost home for which I should always hanker, wherever my destiny led me.

The bus was by no means full and the place next to me was vacant. All the other passengers were fellahs, and not one of these wanted to sit by a Bedouin as long as there was another empty seat. I had put on my oldest and dirtiest galabia, in order to look like what I pretended to be. I had my money in a pouch suspended around my neck and concealed by my garments. But I carried something else, a wonderful card of introduction, in the shape of a flat packet of hashish of the finest quality which I had procured from our abundant stocks.

Just as the bus started, a Bedouin jumped in and, of course, came and sat by me.

"*Elhamdulillah!*" he said. "Praise to God! What luck to be able to sit next to an Arab. One cannot talk to these fellah sons of dogs. Now I have company till we get to Cairo."

I grunted and drew the end of my headcloth over my face. I had no wish to be recognized as a foreigner and, though I knew the language well, I was not sure if my accent was good enough to pass muster with a Bedouin. As a matter of fact, I need not have been anxious because there is such a variety of dialects, with such marked differences, that Arabs often cannot understand one another. Even if my accent had been particularly rough and outlandish, I could have passed for a Kurd or an Armenian.

"Where do you come from?" he asked. "What is your tribe?" And as he spoke he showed his brown tea-stained teeth.

I did not want to have to join in a long conversation, so I pulled my headcloth still more tightly over my mouth and said, "I have the toothache. I am going to the dentist."

"Is it very painful?" he asked sympathetically. "Let me look!" and he grasped my head and tried to make me open my mouth and show him the aching tooth.

"Ow!" I exclaimed and shook myself free. "That's very bad," he said and looked at me pityingly. "Do you know my cousin's uncle once had a terrible toothache, just like you? That is to say, she was not really my cousin because my uncle's second wife, about whom I shall have something to tell you . . . " He droned on and on for hours, and when we reached Cairo he still had not finished tracing the many-branched genealogical tree of his tribe. He had been so much interested in what he was saying, that I never had occasion to interpose a remark.

When the bus reached the terminus, this philanthropic creature insisted on taking me to see a dentist—the best dentist in Cairo, he said. I managed to shake him off as we pushed our way through the crowds.

So this was the glamour city of a prisoner's dreams!

In order not to attract attention to myself by loitering aimlessly about, I got into a streetcar a few blocks farther on and let it take me wherever it was going. These streetcars repay inspection. They are open on both sides and are provided with seven wooden cross-benches, which in the rush hours are always full. There is also a good deal of standing room, but one often finds people standing on the footboards, and I have noticed porters placing their burdens on the roof in the dangerous neighborhood of the overhead cable.

I asked myself where I wanted to go. I had Ibrahim Bey's address in my pocket, but did not want to ask for the street. Here we were in the Station Square with the statue of Egypt, which I recognized from photos. From here we ran on to Ataba-el-Khadra, the central junction of almost all the streetcar lines. Somewhat later, when the car stopped at a roundabout, I forced my way through the clusters of boys on the footboard and stepped down onto the pavement.

I must have looked the picture of a simple, desert-bred Bedouin, with my few possessions wrapped in a bundle which I carried on a long stick over my shoulder, standing dumfounded by the bustle of the great city.

I stood by the wall of a house and stared. On the left were the brightly lit showcases of a textile house and on the right a shop in which white-smocked Egyptians were extracting the juice of oranges, grapes and carrots in a humming centrifugal press and selling it over a marble counter to the customers. I saw the steel arches of a bridge spanning the Nile. But it was the wall that interested me most. It was actually made of stone. I felt like a fool. How long was it since I had seen any but mud walls or the canvas walls of the tents in which I lived! I must, indeed, have looked a fool as I fingered this stony miracle. As I went on my way, I passed a policeman standing at a crossing and watching what was happening in the street. He raised his hand as though wishing to signal to me; then he lowered it again. I had put on my dirtiest clothes on purpose and I suppose that, on reflection, he found me genuine enough. I wondered if anything could go wrong.

As I strolled along, I came to a plaque at the corner of a street with "Rue Soliman Pasha" printed on it. That was just the street I was looking for.

The instructions I had received from Sueylim's father were to look out for a shoe shop on the corner of a street running into Soliman Pasha. A few steps farther on, I should come to a café through which I must go to reach the business premises of the dope trader with the gold agal. I followed the directions and found what I was looking for.

I stepped into a small, dark room with a few dusty electric light bulbs hanging from the ceiling. At rickety tables sat dark-skinned Nubians and Sudanis, noisily sipping coffee or tea, and others smoking narghiles or cigarettes. Among them moved an ambulant shoeblack and a vendor of lottery tickets, not to speak of beggars and street boys who came to pick up cigarette butts from under the tables. Everywhere one heard the tricktrack players calling the throws.

I ordered coffee, and when I paid I told the Sudanese waiter that I wanted to speak to Ibrahim Bey.

"What do you want with him?" he said. This Negro with a red cummerbund gazed at me disparagingly.

"Tell him that I bring news from the Ateibeh." The Negro disappeared and returned after a short while, saying, "You are to wait."

So I waited. I was an unimportant visitor, and Arabs always keep unimportant visitors waiting and waiting till they come to realize their own unimportance and the importance of the person they have come to see. I waited.

The short twilight waned and the street lamps were lit. I found this commonplace experience positively frightening. Since August, 1939, I had not experienced the normal lights of a city and had seldom seen well-dressed people in the streets. The sight of women in high-heeled shoes and nylon stockings, glossy automobiles of the latest make sliding by, neon lights and advertisements, the handsome faces of balanced human beings—all these I found absolutely overwhelming. I waited for my summons with my eyes on the street, in a condition of mental intoxication.

The black waiter appeared once more and beckoned to me to follow him. I walked past the little coffee bar at the back of the room, where coffee was being brewed in long-handled Turkish coffeepots on beds of red-hot charcoal. The waiter then took me through a low door leading into a sort of storeroom full of lemonade bottles, bags of coffee and other provisions, till we came to a steep flight of stairs which led to an office.

Surely that could not be the highly respected notable whom I had last seen wearing the golden agal!

Behind a table covered with books, documents and newspapers sat a fat, greasy Levantine wearing a tarboosh. He was writing in a notebook and smoking a water pipe as he wrote. The Levantine merely grunted as we came in, but didn't look up. The Negro went back into the underworld. I took in at a single glance as much as I needed to know: a dirty pair of trousers with several fly-buttons missing, greasy shirt cuffs, a frayed collar, threadbare sleeves and a day-old beard on his double chin. The Bey was busy picking his nose.

"What do you want?" said the fat man, without raising his head.

"I have brought something for you," I said, and laid my packet on the table before him.

The nobleman of my recollections, so common-looking without his make-up, sprang to his feet as if he had been stung by a tarantula, crying, "What's that got to do with me? Don't you know that it is forbidden to possess hashish? I shall call for the police and have you taken to jail where you belong. You are one of those vermin who undermine the health of the glorious Egyptian people."

Although I could see through his play acting, I did not feel happy. It might very well suit his book to play the moralist, when so little was at issue, so as to avert suspicion from his large-scale activities.

"I belong to the tribe of the Ateibeh," I said, determined to make an impressive entry. "We have often seen one another in the camp. You always wore a green silk robe and a golden agal."

"You damned swindler, you blackmailer, you rascal"—Ibrahim's face was as red as a turkey cock's comb, but as he looked at the packet he lost a little of his moral superiority.

"What is the name of the Sheik?" he asked looking at me keenly.

"Selim Khidr," I said, and added a detailed description of the man.

"And what is the name of the old man, his uncle, who has only one eye?"

Ibrahim's righteous indignation seemed to lose force in proportion to the number of people whose names I knew and to the detail with which I described things known only to the initiated.

"Oh, all right," he said at last. Then, after examining the packet from all sides, he went on: "I tell you again that I know nothing about this stuff and if I take it from you, it will be merely from good nature and to repay you for the trouble you have had to bring it all this way."

He took out a pocketknife and cut out a small triangular piece through the linen wrapping. Then he took the morsel of hashish he had extracted, pulled it in two pieces, rolled half of it into a ball, smelled it and, placing it on the glowing bowl of his pipe, tested the smoke. Next, he put the remainder of the hashish on his tongue and tasted it, smacking his lips the while to try the flavor. Then he added the portion he had tasted to what was already in his pipe and took a few deep inhalations.

This double test seemed to satisfy him, as he then put his pipe and the packet into a drawer and produced from his pocket a bundle of bank notes. Here is my money, I thought, enough for my passport, passage home and expenses.

He threw a few notes on the table saying, "Here's your money. Now be off with you!"

"But that isn't half what it's worth," I protested. If he didn't give me something like the market price, I was done for. I should not be able to get home.

"Well," he said indignantly, "that is my maximum. I am taking the stuff from you out of charity, so that you may have some pocket money, and you presume to dictate to me the amount I have to pay for it. Moreover the muck is of the lowest grade. I doubt if you could get the driver of a refuse cart to smoke it."

All my high hopes crumbled at his words. I had counted on an honest price and I needed it, as the savings I carried in my pouch would not suffice for my needs. This rascal, this distinguished personage on whose decency I had counted for the cost of my false papers and my passage money, this beast had swindled me.

I said, "You are lying and you know it very well. You are not taking the stuff from me out of charity and the stuff is good—first quality in fact."

The fellow boiled over. "You dare to doubt my word, you gypsy, you vagabond!" and he pulled the drawer open, picked out the packet of hashish and threw it into an overflowing wastepaper basket.

"That's where your filth belongs," he cried, "and that's where you ought to be."

"You rascal."

"What did you call me?" he yelled; then he shouted "Mohammed! Mohammed!" Before he could say any more I gripped my heavy stick and struck him. He tried to dodge and received a violent blow on the side of the head, which tore his ear open and sent the blood streaming over his cheek. He slumped without a word behind the table.

With all my hopes shattered and now ripe for the police, I stood before the table and realized in a confused sort of way that in a few minutes they would come and take me away. The door on the staircase was open, and I had no doubt that Mohammed had heard his master shout for him. There was no time to think things out.

I left the room at once and found the huge Negro coming up the stairs. My first thought was that if I wanted to get out of the house, I should have to strike the brute down. I was standing above him and his great strength would not have saved him from a downward blow. But he would probably have time to cry out before he fell and, even if he didn't, his fall would make so much noise that people in the café below would hear and I should run into the arms of the alerted mob. So I squeezed past him on the narrow stairway, jumped down the last few steps, ran through the storeroom and in a few seconds found myself in the street, uncertain in which direction to fly. Before I had gone many yards a black head appeared at an upper window and the faithful slave shouted "Thieves! Murder!"

I did not like the sound of this and liked it less when I saw Mohammed's outstretched, swarthy arm pointing at me and heard him say, "There he is—that Arab there!"

I now began to react. In a second I was across the street, but the people had spotted me and were beginning to come after me. I pulled up the skirts of my galabia, flung my bundle away, kicked off my slippers and ran at full speed in my bare feet, with the crowd running after me and shouting, *"Ya Muslimin!* Stop thief!"

In crossing the street, I had run just in front of a passing car, missing the radiator by inches. The car pulled up with screaming brakes. I heard the sound of a police whistle shrilling somewhere behind me. I had no idea where I was, nor in which direction to go, but I ran on. The shouts of the crowd alerted the people ahead of me, and a man came running out of a side street and tried to trip me up. I mechanically struck him a blow with my stick and was past him before he had time to cry out. The street in front of me was thronged with people, and it would be madness to keep to it. My pursuers were catching up with me, and I could hear them panting behind me. I shot right across the street, dodging the dense traffic. Better to be run over than grabbed by the howling mob and then arrested for murder. Somehow or other, I slipped through the streaming cars, which rolled on uninterruptedly behind me. Their drivers knew nothing of the man hunt that was going on. I had nearly got across the road when I saw a streetcar passing in front of me. I dropped my stick and, making for it, managed to catch hold of one of the stanchions, which nearly pulled my arm out of its socket. As I tried to get onto the car, I knocked my knee against the footboard. But hands were stretched out to help me, and the passengers pulled me on board.

It seemed that there were still some good-hearted people in the city of Ibrahim Bey.

"By Allah! You are crazy!" said a bearded old man as I sank panting and trembling on a bench beside him.

I still heard a few cries of "Stop thief," but they died away, drowned by the noise of the streetcar.

"Whither away in such haste, my son?" asked the old man.

"I am on my way to see a sick friend," I said for want of a better excuse.

The old man clicked his tongue to show sympathy and shook his head.

"What is he sick of?"

"He has fever."

"Does he live far from here?"

"On the other bank of the Nile," I said. The words suddenly came into my mouth as I saw that we were coming to a bridge. It wasn't the bridge I had seen that afternoon, but it was a bridge that obviously crossed the Nile. It would be some consolation to know that the river was between me and the scene of my crime.

"There is plenty of room on the west bank," the old man said. "Does your friend live in Zamalek or Giza?"

"I am a stranger and do not know the names of the districts, but I know how to get there."

"One can see that you are a stranger. I would not like to think that after you had risked your life jumping onto the car, you might waste your time getting out at the wrong stop."

The friendliness of the old man was almost alarming, but it was clear that he only wanted to be helpful.

"I think he lives in Zamalek," I said.

"Then he must be very rich. It is the best quarter of the town."

"He is a *boab*," I explained. Even a ragged Bedouin might have a doorkeeper for a friend.

"That is what I was thinking," said the old man with a nod. "To be a *boab* in one of those large new houses is a nice job."

"Yes," I said, "I know he has a good position." We rolled over the bridge, and after a while he said, "Here we are in Zamalek. Have a good look at the streets, so that you may get out at the right stop."

The nearest stop was the right one for me. The police might have taken it into their heads to follow the streetcar, and I thought it would be a good idea for me to be gone before they caught up with it.

"There is my street," I said, "there by the filling station."

I jumped down quickly at the next stop and walked toward the gasoline pumps. As I went, I heard the kind old man's voice saying, "I hope your friend will soon be better."

My knee hurt me and made me limp. I pulled up the skirt of my galabia and saw a streak of half-dried blood running from my knee to my ankle. I rubbed off the blood with a corner of my garment and limped on.

After passing the gasoline station, I turned into a side street where I found a public garden, almost abutting on the narrow western channel of the Nile.

Round about it stood the houses of the rich and fortunate who knew nothing of the anxious, harried lives the poor have to lead.

The lamps of the riverside road, reflected on the water, shone like jewels in the night. On both sides of the stream lay a line of houseboats moored to the bank. I could hear soft music from radios and phonographs wafted over the water, while on the terraced decks of the dahabeahs I could see carefree men and women sitting and talking. I think it was the cry of a night bird that first made me conscious of the excitement, the sensual attraction of the scene after the austerities of the desert.

I lay down under the drooping leaves of a dwarf palm and gazed up at the stars, feeling that they belonged to others, not to me. A man like me, an insignificant member of the refuse of humanity, who had been thrown up by the reverses of fortune like jetsam on a cheerless shore, had no longer anything to hold onto, not even a slender thread, which might lead him back to an ordered life. The stars could bring me no comfort.

I had sought by a devious route to assure my return to my country and my former way of life. My attempt had failed; and here I was, a mangy pariah, in a hostile society. It is true, I had money enought to hire a room in a hotel, but all the hotels were controlled by the police. I had not washed since the early morning, I was travel-stained, weary and hungry after my desperate flight through the streets. My galabia stank of sweat and camel dung. No *boab* whom I approached but would hand me over to the police. The sum total of my money might indeed suffice for my passage home but, without papers, I could no longer hope to get a steamer ticket nor a passport. I had staked all my hopes on the man with the golden agal and now my last hope was gone.

An automobile drove slowly along the riverbank. I rolled over as the headlights shone on me. I couldn't risk being seen. I was a fugitive. I was wanted by the police.

Chapter XIII

THE PASHA'S HOUSE

THE desire to be among my fellow creatures was stronger than my fears. I left my hiding place and stumbled, with uncertain footsteps, into the light, though the future held no possibility of a life for me. The circle of lights and the distant hum of the great city drew me to the haunts of men.

I was here in the garden city of Zamalek. Beside the asphalt road stood two- and three-storyed villas in the midst of beautiful flower gardens. Brightly lit windows hinted at comfort and luxury within. A woman was singing a French song, but the Venetian blinds prevented me from seeing her. There must be beds behind the windows, wide soft beds in which clean, well-cared-for men and women slept under soft eider downs when the laughter and singing was over.

Then I saw a house with no lights in the windows. It was not the only one which seemed to be uninhabited. I imagined that the owners would be coming back later, as the entrance gate was slightly open. This house attracted me. It stood in the middle of a large garden in which I guessed there might be a summer house or shed, good enough for a man like me to sleep in. The gravel crackled under my feet as I stole in under cover of some oleander bushes. No chink of light came from the house, no sign of life, and there was no dog to bark at uninvited visitors.

I crept round the house in search of a shelter in the back garden. Soon I came to a garage built into the side of the house. The door was of course locked. I could not open it, but thought I might have better luck with a small window in the back wall. I pushed the glass and the window opened very easily.Then I looked around, and as I saw no light and heard no sound, I climbed through the window like a thief.

There was just enough moonlight for me to see what was in the garage. I made out a barrel of gasoline, a jack and a number of shelves on which were tools and spare parts, but no car. The owner was away, and I guessed that he had gone away for some time as there seemed to be no servants about. He had careless servants, to judge by the open garden gate, the unfastened window in the garage and an unlocked door leading from the garage into the house.

From this door a carpeted staircase led up into the hall. I went up and stood listening there before feeling my way along with one hand on the wall.

I tried the handle of the first door I came to. It was locked—a prudent precaution against people like me. Then my hand came in contact with the banisters of a curving flight of stairs leading up to the next floor. I groped my way up and found myself in a broad corridor. The first door which I came to was unlocked and I found myself in a room. My knee pushed into a soft object—a bed. Moving on, I came on a door which turned out to belong to a cupboard set in the wall. In it were a lot of clothes, more than enough to fit a man like me, who would be wise not to run around in Bedouin dress on the morrow.

I struck a match, by the light of which I saw about twenty suits in a wide range of materials and colors. Before the match went out, I pulled out one of the suits. Hastily I tried on the trousers. The result was disappointing. Two men of my girth could have got into them easily. I threw the suit back into the cupboard and slammed the door in my annoyance. After this I went on groping around the walls, stumbled against a chair and finally found myself facing another door.

I opened it, struck another match and could hardly refrain from crying out aloud when I saw it was a bathroom. It had no window— only a ventilation shaft—which made it safe for me to switch on the light. When I did so, I was amazed by the startling black and white effects of the decoration. The whole room was lined with black marble tiles, but the bath, the washbasin and the bidet were of white alabaster. The taps and fittings were gilded and even the ridges on the glass door of the shower cabinet were overlaid with gold paint.

And what a curious refinement this door presented! The upper and lower surfaces were of clear glass, but the portion through which one might expect the bather's body to be visible from the knee to the navel was made of clouded glass, tastefully ornamented and perfectly opaque.

How long was it since I had bathed in such luxury! I asked myself the question only when my galabia and pants were already lying on the ground and I was standing in the shower cabin. The electric boiler was simmering gently, when I turned on the hot tap from which scalding water poured. I tempered the stream with cold water till my skin could bear it. There was soap too, lovely scented soap with which I lathered myself until my body was coated with foam.

I found a bath towel to dry myself with and then proceeded to wash my galabia and agal with lavender soap—starting a curious struggle between lavender soap and camel's dung, but when the garments were wrung out, I found that the lavender soap had got the upper hand.

As soon as I had finished dealing with my outer man and felt once more like a human being, an instinct which I had been obliged to fight down, rose to the surface. I was hungry. I had been hungry for a long time without knowing it, but now I had an appetite.

The house was so obviously deserted that I no longer needed to be chary about making a noise. With my freshly washed garments over my arm and wearing only my short woolen pants, I walked barefoot down the stairs in search of the kitchen. I had only to be careful about the light. It would be stupid to attract the curiosity of a passing policeman and get myself caught *en flagrant délit*.

I groped through the darkness till I found the kitchen door. In the corner of the kitchen there was a refrigerator. As I opened it, the interior lighting came on automatically. This gave me such a start that I instantly slammed the door again. I was in an awkward fix. In order to get some food to stay my hunger I had to open the refrigerator, and as soon as I did that the light would come on. Hunger won the day, I decided in favor of light and food. Anyhow, very little light filtered through the closed shutters.

I found a rich provision of the things people are accustomed to store in bottles, glasses and cans. I made a selection at random—a can of ham, some cocktail olives, a box of foie gras, half a Bologna sausage, a piece of cheese, bottled apricots and a bottle of champagne. There was no bread anywhere. I looked around for a can opener and knives, forks and spoons. For the first time in ages, I used a knife and fork to eat with, but here was nothing to remind me of Oberzahlmeister Behrens and the styleless field cutlery with which he ate his rough meals in my tent. I was going to use the refined tools of civilization to deal with the delicacies which fortune had bestowed on me. I would have scorned to use my fingers to fish out slices of ham or apricots from their containers.

I spread out a napkin on the table and laid myself a place, before I opened the cans and began my meal. I admit that I had to drink champagne out of a tumbler for lack of a suitable glass. I mixed up my courses somewhat and, after several hearty draughts of champagne, became more and more cheerful till I found I was talking aloud to myself.

"Won't you have some more of this delicious ham?" I said, offering myself the can.

"Many thanks, but no. I have already had four slices."

"Five," corrected my other self, "but who bothers to count here?" So, just because no one counted and no one had to pay, I helped myself to a sixth slice.

"What about some apricot compote?" I asked and held up the glass container for Dr. Pritzke to look at.

Then a door creaked faintly. My blood ran cold and I turned around in my chair.

The light from the refrigerator was sufficient to show that the man who had surprised me was tall and broad. He was also carrying a cudgel. Paralyzed with fear, I could not even get up. I just stared at him.

"How did you get in?" he asked in Arabic.

"Through the garage window."

"You speak good Arabic."

"I am of the Ateibeh."

"You are a German."

Then he turned on the light to see what I looked like. Up to then, the newcomer had been nothing but a great shadow. Now I saw that he was an elderly, muscular Sudani. I would have no chance at all in a rough-and-tumble with him.

The man looked at me earnestly from beneath his white turban and seemed to be reflecting.

"Why do you not tell me the truth?" he said in a tone of mild reproof. "Does a Bedouin drink wine? Does an Arab eat like a Frangi?" He pointed to the knife and fork. "Does he take off his kaffiyeh in a strange house? Does he ever wash his clothes except in his own camp?" That meant that he had already noticed my garments hanging up to dry. "And does a Bedouin talk to himself in a strange language which is neither English nor French?"

The old man was cleverer and quicker at putting two and two together than I was at answering him. I could not think of anything to say, so I just repeated that I was a Bedouin.

"Very well, then, if you insist on being a Bedouin, I shall treat you as such. You will first get a good thrashing, and then I shall hand you over to the police." He gripped his cudgel firmly and came toward me.

The *argumentum ad baculum* was too much for me, and I decided to tell the truth.

"Yes," I said, "I cannot deny it. I am a German." I got up and moved away quickly so as to get the table between me and him. "Now you can call the police. What is the market price of a German today?"

The old man lowered his cudgel and said in tones of genuine good nature, "Sit down again, my son. I only wanted to hear the truth from you, 'for woe unto them that speak with lying tongues,' in the words of the Prophet, on whom be peace!"

"Are you hungry?"

"No longer," I said pointing to the empty cans.

"That is good."

He looked disparagingly at the can which had contained the ham and said, "You are an unbeliever and so can eat the flesh of unclean beasts. You know no better. But my pasha was brought up in the true faith and nevertheless he pollutes himself by disobeying God's commandment. He also drinks wine and spirits, careless of the Prophet's word—'All is forbidden which causes drunkenness, even if it is only sour milk!"

"You are a pious man," I said humbly and in sore confusion of spirit, for the man's piety was an expression of true goodness. "I hope," I continued, "that you do not mind sitting with an infidel."

"God is great. He has His own reasons for granting the knowledge and light of the true faith to some and leaving others in the darkness of ignorance. But whatever you may do, however you name your god, all that happens redounds to the praise of Allah, the only true God."

The eloquence of this good-natured giant was not a mere excuse for quoting texts; it was the sign of a generous heart, which his treatment of me showed he possessed. As for me I had, in a sense, claimed the right of hospitality by entering the house and now desired to express my gratitude for the bounty I had received, before I took my leave.

But the old man insisted on my spending the night in the house. Of course his invitation might have been a trap, but I was sure it was sincere and so, without mistrust, I began to tell him all about my escape from captivity, my life among the Ateibeh and also the incidents which had led up to my damaging my knee. I wanted him to know that I was no thief and that it was only in desperation that I had entered his master's house, without knowing whither to turn for help when I should leave it.

"Tomorrow we will talk things over," he said quietly. "I think you will find a way out. If Allah places obstacles on our way, he also gives us means to overcome them." He stood up. "You must be right weary, my son. Come, I will take you to your bed."

I followed him into the hall, which was now discreetly illuminated by four corner lamps. From the ceiling hung a gigantic chandelier. The whole floor was covered with a thick-piled carpet from Tabriz and in the middle of the room stood a long, low table with a marble top. Ranged along the walls were a dozen high-backed, upholstered chairs with carved and gilded feet.

There was everywhere a prodigal display of gold lacquer, even on the stand which carried the marble table slab and on a shelf on which were numerous samples of tasteless junk gathered from the souvenir industry of the whole world. In contrast I noticed a Renoir hanging on the wall. Walking up the stairs, I observed further samples of an outstanding capacity to employ choice material to show off the most vulgar objects.

"Here is your bedroom," said the old man, as he opened the door of a room on the upper floor. "Good night, my friend."

If this friendly hospitality concealed a trap, then I was certainly in the most elegant and luxurious trap in which an aimless, wandering rat had ever found himself. My glamorously beautiful room was certainly a woman's bedroom. This was clear from the scent bottles and other apparatus for female embellishment that covered the dressing table, while the various French periodicals lying about suggested that a European lady had been the last occupant. I could not screw up courage to get into the great Louis XIV bed. It needed more nerve than I possessed to lie down between those carved bedposts under a red velvet canopy. Better to sleep on the floor as I had been accustomed to do among the Bedouins. After all I had spent the night before on the ground.

I heard a gentle knocking. The Sudani came in again and found me standing helplessly there. He said, "I have telephoned to the Brothers. They will certainly be able to help you on your way. To-morrow morning at nine you must be at the house of the Brotherhood. I wanted to bring you this good news at once, so that you should not lie awake and worry. Allah has already found you the means for overcoming the obstacles."

I wondered what brothers he was talking about and what might be in store for me on the morrow. After my lapse from misery into luxury, I still feared what the future might bring and my apprehension would prevent me from sleeping.

"I cannot stay here," I said. "I ought not to. If the lady of the house learns that I have slept in her bed, she will fire you."

"Lady of the house," snorted the faithful servant contemptuously. "My mistress has her room on the other side. This is the room of my master's concubine."

It looked as if there was method in his madness. The old man wanted to make me sleep in this bed, as a protest against his master's impious habits.

"All the same," I said, "I should prefer to sleep on a mattress on the floor—anywhere."

"Listen, my friend," he said sadly. "If you think you will be the first German to sleep in this bed, you are quite wrong. The Pasha changes his mistresses as often as his shirts. Most of them are girls from the Kit-Kat or women that he brings back from his journeys. And when he gets tired of women—well, you are dark-haired and a grown man—but I remember two young, fair-haired Germans, helpless and penniless, whom the war threw into his hands. . . . When he tired of them, he passed them on to some friends of his."

I was mildly shocked by these revelations and said something about law and order.

"Law!" cried the old man scornfully. "In this godless land money is the law. The lawgivers and judges are the traducers of the True Faith, the apostates from the way of Allah. And that is where we of the Brotherhood have our part to play. We shall put an end to the power of the rich and the Pashas, and set up once more the Kingdom of God. And we shall do it with fire and sword, if need be. Yes, with fire and sword." He repeated the words as if to himself. Then he said, "Good night, German. Sleep well. Tomorrow will be a fateful day for you."

In the subdued light of the bedside lamp, I took off the only garment I was wearing. The old man had kept my kaffiyeh and galabia in the kitchen; he would iron them, when they were dry. I could find nothing else to sleep in but a blue silk kimono; and as I closed my eyes in that heavenly bed, I sensed a soft perfume of women and long untasted bliss. But my body, inured to hard lying, refused to go to sleep in the springy softness of my couch. Tomorrow I should once more have a hard bed to lie on—harder, may be, than would please me.

The old man had spoken of the Brothers: the Kingdom of God: the True Faith: Fire and Sword, and once again of the Brothers. . . .

Chapter XIV

THE MOSLEM BROTHERHOOD

I MUST have gone to sleep then, for next morning I awoke refreshed and clear-headed. I perceived that my future was being arranged for me, independently of me, and began to understand gradually what the old man was talking about when he referred to the Brothers.

He came to my bedside, bringing me my headcloth and galabia and led me downstairs to a hearty breakfast.

"Now," he said, "you will come with me to the house of the Brothers."

"Just as I am?" I asked doubtfully.

"Yes," he said, "I shall take you there."

We drove together to the house, and my kind host only bade me farewell when he had deposited me in a waiting room hung with framed texts from the Koran.

An elderly man with a short white beard, wearing a long brown robe, came to tell me that I should have to wait for some time.

It was long since I had felt so shy and embarrassed. I was like a young candidate waiting for his entrance examination, or a barefooted peasant lad torn from the plough to work in a trade of which he knew nothing, for new masters in an unfamiliar world. I tried in vain, in spite of my good knowledge of written Arabic, to read the texts from the Koran written in florid cursive. Men came in and went out like brothers in a monastery. A silent Berber brought me coffee. The good-natured, slightly senile piety of the old Sudani and the appearance of the white-bearded ancient in the waiting room all contributed to my fear that I was going to work exclusively with elderly, religious men who had lost their manly vigor.

The old man broke in on my reflections and led me out of the ante-room into an office.

I was received with a handshake, across the table, which was anything but unmanly. It was the grasp of a man who knew his own mind, and the appraising look which accompanied it was calm and determined. The man appeared to be about forty. He was clean-shaven, but for a small mustache, and wore European clothes —and I felt that to Moslem eyes he looked as a man ought to look.

This was Hodeibi Effendi, then a leading member of the executive of the Moslem Brotherhood. In 1949, he became chief of the organization. He began to ask me in short, incisive sentences about my name, origin, profession, military education and war service. He wanted to know from what camp I had escaped and made me describe briefly my experiences since that time, taking notes as I spoke.

The interview, which was more like an interrogation, was being conducted with businesslike concentration, when we were suddenly interrupted by the entry of a short, thickset man. Hodeibi stood up politely, so I got up too. The newcomer, who wore nickel-rimmed pince-nez on an oversized nose, gazed at me over the top of his glasses with great, dreamy eyes. He exchanged a few words with Hodeibi and then left the room.

I learned afterwards that this man was Hassan el Banna, the founder of the mysterious Moslem Brotherhood. He had been a teacher in an elementary school in Upper Egypt, somewhere near the frontier of the Sudan. There he had collected around him a group of kindred spirits, whose deep sense of religion was expressed in resistance to the constantly declining standards of conduct and belief and a determination to build up a state in which men should conform to the Word of God and His Prophet.

The Moslem Brotherhood has passed into history. The circle of disciples and adherents gathered strength like an avalanche, and soon had spread all over Egypt and even founded branches in the neighboring Islamic countries.

In other circumstances, it is probable that the movement would have resulted in the emergence of a new branch of Orthodox Islam comparable to the Sunni, Shiite and Wahabi divisions of Mohammedanism, which consolidated themselves centuries ago. However, certain persons soon recognized that this mass movement could provide a powerful instrument for the realization of their political ambitions. This group, to which the Cairo lawyer, Hodeibi Effendi, belonged, created the Executive Committee to organize the association and provide leadership and, sensibly enough, appointed themselves as members of it. The dreamer, Hassan el Banna, was soon no more than a figurehead, and the real leadership was taken over by younger men into whose hands King Farouk played, when the unfortunate Hassan el Banna was shot by hired assassins. Hodeibi then succeeded as leader of the Brotherhood.

And Hodeibi was anything but a dreamer.

"Are you familiar with the use of dynamite?" he asked me, after Hassan el Banna had left the office with a friendly, absent-minded nod.

"No," I said.

"Are you a marksman?"

"No."

He proceeded to question me in greater detail in regard to any experience of secret service, or underground activities, I might possess.

I was obliged to tell him that I had none.

Hodeibi seemed to be considering whether a man with such limited experience of modern political life could be usefully employed at all.

"But," he said, "as a doctor you must have a good knowledge of chemistry. If we were to put you in charge of a well-equipped chemical laboratory, somewhere in the country, could you produce explosives or poisons?"

Up to now I had only helped to smuggle hashish or buy weapons for the Ateibeh. Was I now, perforce, to change the gentle drizzle of lawlessness for the thunderstorms of bomb making and poison mixing? So that was the good luck the old Sudani foretold for me!

"I am familiar," I said, "with the effects of certain medically tested chemicals on the human organism, but I am not a chemist in the proper sense of the word. And I know nothing about explosives."

I was conscious that my reiterated negatives were acquiring a tone of irritation, but Hodeibi ignored my mood, knowing that I would have to agree to something soon. He said that there was still a possibility of employing me as a medical officer for Arab units fighting in Palestine.

"There is something I should much prefer to do, Mr. Hodeibi," I said, "and that is to go home to my own country. It is four years since I left Germany and I want to get back as soon as I can."

"Unfortunately we cannot help you to do that," said Hodeibi so regretfully that I almost thought he meant it. "But service with the Arab armies will give you a good chance of eventually realizing your wishes. It will mean for you a passport, money and a road to a new future. Anyhow, the war in Palestine is bound to be over soon."

This man had the demagogue's gift—of making the impossible seem probable—so highly developed that one really couldn't resist him. He went on to say that I might not even be employed on active service and, if I were, I should be back in Cairo in a few months and free to go wherever I wished. He added that my services would be generously rewarded. When he saw an expression of doubt on my face he said, "You do not yet know the greatness and the gratitude of the Arab peoples."

I seem to remember hearing the phrase "*der Dank des Vaterlandes,*" "the thanks of the Fatherland"—here it was again.

Gratitude alone would not mean much to me. Here I was—barefooted, too tidy for a beggar, too well-off for a pauper, smelling of lavender soap instead of camels' dung, without confidence in my luck or in a sequence of lucky breaks sufficient to enable me to escape the clutches of the police. Emotionally drained by a succession of panic-stricken flights, I recognized in the open street my most deadly foe. If Hodeibi, after my successive refusals, decided to put me on the street, I would doubtless be in the hands of the police in a few hours.

When at last I had consented, ungraciously, to his final proposal, I was able to put my footslogging and streetcar-hopping behind me. I was sent in a taxi—with an escort, it is true—to Helmiyeh, to the headquarters of Hadji Amin, the former Grand Mufti of Jerusalem. He had been rightly reproached by the British for his sympathy with Hitler, and after a dramatic flight through Syria, had found his way to Berlin, where he had remained till the end of the war. In the Mufti's headquarters all the formalities were carried out according to normal routine. As soon as my personal file had been filled up and signed, I was relieved of my escort. The guide, who had been detailed by the Brotherhood to look after me, bade me farewell, and when I drove back to Cairo, the chauffeur knew exactly where to take me.

The recruiting commission for war volunteers had opened an office in the Victoria Hotel, and many guests before me must have come in through the stylish entrance hall and been carried up by elevator to the third floor.

"*Tafaddal!*" called someone when I knocked at a certain door. "Come in!"

I entered an ordinary-looking hotel bedroom, from which the bed had been removed and replaced by a writing table and a filing cabinet.

Sitting at the table, I saw a man of about forty with light-brown hair, very squarely built and wearing a check suit. Near him on the window sill was leaning a slender, blond man.

Odd-looking Egyptians, I thought.

"Good morning," I said, speaking in English.

"*Guten Morgen*," replied the man at the table with a good German accent. "I am Hadji Khaled. Sit down, please," and he pointed to a chair facing him at the table. "You are Salameh Suleiman, aren't you? Your arrival has been reported from the office of the Grand Mufti. Here is a countryman of yours, Herr Said."

The blond Hun gave me his hand with a grin, saying "Very pleased."

"You must buy yourself some slippers," said Hadji Khaled, pointing to my bare feet. "You seem to have been in a hurry lately."

I nodded. He wasn't wrong.

"A real Bedouin always carries a stick."

"I had one, but as you guessed, I was in a hurry and had to use it. Afterwards I thought it better to get rid of it."

Hadji Khaled had a charming way of starting a friendly conversation. "You are probably surprised," he said, "at my good German. I must tell you that some years before the war I was a student in Germany, and while I was there I learned to appreciate your country and your countrymen. When I returned to Palestine, where I come from, the war broke out. The British took me for a German spy and arrested me. I remained in prison till just before the end of the war, when I escaped. Since then I have been living in Cairo."

"I wonder the intelligence didn't pick you up. Under the British military administration, Cairo must have been a dangerous spot."

"It's not so easy to spot a local inhabitant. There is no general obligation to report to the police and the controls are not very tight. Even you, since you are not a typical German to look at, would have had a good chance of getting through unnoticed. But your galabia is far too clean and it really ought not to reek of lavender soap. Why, one could smell it from the other side of the street."

"Up to yesterday," I said, "it was dirty enough to have satisfied you, but last night an opportunity presented itself and I had it washed to get rid of the stink."

Hadji Khaled chuckled. "You Germans have a great failing. You are too clean. There are two ways of throwing dust in the eyes of the police—either to be conventionally dirty, with an unshaven face and a ragged galabia, in which case you are taken for a Bedouin, or else to wear a first-class suit made to measure and walk around as if you had bought the street. Then the police imagine that you belong to one of the numerous Allied legations and are afraid to speak to you. But what do most of the Germans do? They spend their scanty savings on cheap shoes, shirts and trousers and a jacket off the peg—all very simple and tidy and typically German. No wonder every policeman can spot them at sight."

They brought us coffee, and Hadji Khaled continued his lecture on psychology. He really seemed to know us Germans better, generally speaking, than we knew ourselves.

"Here is another typical mistake you Germans make. When you escape it is always in parties of two or three, and what makes it worse is that you go on sticking together. Quite intelligible from a human point of view, because company takes away the feeling of insecurity and forlornness in a strange city and among people whose language one does not understand, and whom one assumes *a priori* to be enemies. Good Lord, what mistakes you Germans make! One can tell a German from far off by his unsure manner and his horror of dirt, especially a Prussian. Your countrymen walk too fast and hold themselves too straight. Bedouins shuffle along unhurrying, while if several Germans are walking together, they march stiffly forward and actually keep step. Imagine Bedouins keeping step!" He laughed aloud.

"I haven't made any of those mistakes," said I, wishing to check his generalizations, "but I haven't got very far all this time."

"One always makes mistakes," said he with a rather complacent smile. Perhaps he meant me to understand that I was now on the point of making my gravest and most fateful error.

Then we got to talking business, and I had to tell once more the story of my life. My dossier was completed and I signed a declaration to the effect that I had volunteered for service as medical officer with the Arab army in the Palestine campaign.

Hadji Khaled wished me good luck and pressed the sum of twenty-five pounds in notes into my hand, saying, "Now go and buy yourself a decent suit of clothes. Said will go with you and take you to your new home."

"Come along then, new boy," said the fair-haired man. He took me to the elevator, brought me down and led me straight to a men's shop just around the corner.

I felt as embarrassed as a candidate for confirmation. The feeling was quite new to me, but it was so long since I had worn a suit of clothes that my judgment regarding color, material and cut was completely at sea. In my indecision, I left everything to Said. When, after examining a garment or a pattern, he said "This is all right, take it," I took it.

While I was slipping into a light-brown, single-breasted suit, hardly knowing where the buttons came, Said chose for me three sets of underclothes, several shirts and a tie.

The outfit of the newly created gentleman was incomplete in one respect. He still had bare feet.

The salesmen grinned impertinently, but Said put them in their places. Turning to me he asked, "What size shoes do you wear?"

"Forty-two, about."

"Tell one of your boys to bring us some brown shoes, size 8 to 8½," said Said to the manager.

A salesman broke away and came back with four cardboard boxes.

Now I need have no more fear or anxiety. In full view of the public, I had completed the change-over from a Bedouin to a European. No policeman now had the right to lay a hand on my shoulder for, by a wave of the hand, I had been transformed into a Fighter for Freedom, dedicated to the Arab cause in Palestine.

Still, I had lost my individual freedom, and there was nothing I could do about it. I had sold it, precarious as it was, for the sum of twenty-five pounds—quite a high price considering my circumstances.

When I was fully dressed in my new clothes, Said looked at me with misgiving. "You still look like a dangerous character," he said. "Off with you at once to the barber's."

He took me to a barbershop and gave instructions as to the sort of haircut I ought to have, as he turned my head this way and that and stroked my hair with an expert hand. Finally he decided on a crew cut.

"I'll leave you now, as I'm hungry," he said. "Join me at L'Americaine, across the way, when you're through."

Twenty minutes later, I found Said at the rendezvous. He had already lunched and was eating a slice of watermelon. In my new, ready-made suit and a neat little mustache, which was all that remained of my wild crop of face-foliage, I fitted very well into this cross between a bar and a restaurant on the watershed between East and West.

I asked him, over a cup of coffee, what his job was in our outfit.

"I'm a volunteer, like you. But I was the first of all the foreign volunteers and, as I speak English, French and Arabic fluently, I am acting as the Hadji's personal assistant until I go to the front."

"I don't suppose you are so eager as all that about returning to active service, or are you?"

"Hard to say. Life is very pleasant here, when one is accustomed to it. But war service, and my life in Libya and the Delta, got me so used to thrills and excitement that a normal existence bores me stiff. However, I believe we are going to stage something new shortly."

That sounded confidential, so I said, "What is your name?"

I could have dispensed with this question. Said looked at me with a serious and almost reproachful expression. "Didn't the Hadji mention my name? I am called Said. Your name is Salameh. We have no other names. And the other people you will meet have only their Arab names. They have forgotten their former ones. You ought to have learned by this time that one does better to forget one's German name, which one never uses."

To sell one's personal liberty! To forget one's name! To give up thinking of home and homecoming! A sacrifice, maybe, but better to be rid of all superfluous baggage.

"Here is your home," said my fair-haired companion, as he let me into a spacious apartment in a block in the old city. The owner had placed the apartment at the disposal of the Brotherhood to accommodate volunteers waiting to go to the Palestine front.

My companions in this home for the homeless were six Germans who, like me, had escaped from British POW camps and had been fished out of their hiding places; and a dozen Moslem Yugoslavs, who had fought for the Germans in Italy and had unexpectedly finished up in Egypt.

The food was good and plentiful, and a constant supply of cigarettes and sweets was maintained. A Sudanese servant looked after us.

But anyone trying to leave our roomy dwelling ran into a police guard outside the street door, and the man on duty barred the exit with his carbine, crying "*Erga*," "Go back."

So, in fact, we were prisoners.

Chapter XV

HEADQUARTERS IN JAFFA

"BOYS, the balloon has gone up!" cried Said one day as he hurried excitedly into the house, nearly beside himself with joy. He went on to tell us that he had persuaded the Hadji to let him go with the other volunteers. "Now get ready," he said. "Our car will be here in an hour."

As we had practically nothing to pack but soap and toothbrushes, there was plenty of room in our pockets for cigarettes and sweets to relieve the discomforts of war.

With our stuffed and bulging pockets, we did not look particularly soldierly, but not less so than the Egyptian army truck which drove us to the Palestine frontier.

A short way over the border we transshipped to a ramshackle bus which, after a long and tiring journey, finally deposited us at Ramle, a little town four miles from Jaffa.

The month was December, 1947.

The war as it was waged in these parts had already left its visiting card on the town.

The little market place, where we halted, showed fresh traces of serious damage which could only have been caused by high explosives. On one side of the square the fronts of the houses had been blown in. Poorly furnished rooms, looking like the rooms in a doll's house, had lost their front walls and were exposed to view from the street. The square was littered with debris from the booths and stands—fruit, vegetables, fish and ornamental trifles. Here and there people were dully collecting the scattered wares and carrying them into a house, and others were hauling damaged but still usable pieces of furniture out of the ruined houses. From

somewhere came the shrill wailing cry of a woman—a cry that de-
noted the presence of death. No one seemed ready to talk or to tell
us the story of the outrage. Something fearful had clearly
happened.

Finally, we managed to reconstruct the incident, bit by bit. A
truck had driven through the market place and had dropped a small
barrel in the road. Of course the barrel was the cause of all the
damage. Where else could the terrible explosion have come from?
And, of course, the truck must have belonged to the Haganah, who
had rolled out the barrel full of dynamite. Certainly the Haganah—
no room for doubt.

This incident was the sequel to a previous one, of which we
learned the details piecemeal from different sources. The two
stories were very similar. An Arab had driven a loaded ass into a
populous quarter of Tel Aviv. Who would bother about a donkey
which had to be tied up somewhere, while his master was attending
to his business in the town? Five minutes later the donkey's load—
some kilos of T.N.T.—exploded. The owner, after lighting the fuse,
had had plenty of time to slip away quietly. The ass and numerous
human beings were killed.

What had happened in Ramle was the reprisal. The reprisal
would be avenged by another outrage, just as crafty and foul.

These things were typical of the war in Palestine.

After this first experience of local warfare, we were driven to
the house of a rich Palestine Arab, who had invited the first German
volunteers on this front to have supper with him. This prosperous
citizen, whose name was Farouki, spoke fluent German. He offered
us a sumptuous meal, and was clearly delighted to have Germans
around him. There was a sort of irony in the manner in which he—
sitting in his fine house and secure in the possession of a solid
fortune—questioned us, not only about our war experiences, but
about our people at home, of whom none of us had had a scrap of
news for more than four years.

Everything had a nasty aftertaste in this reverberating dining
room, in which our host and his friends talked of the war as if it
were something remote and irrelevant, when only a few blocks
away the town looked like a regular battlefield. They spoke of un-

rest—or, at the worst, collisions between bands, at any rate in the Jaffa region, with a few bombs and mines exploding here and there. Neither the Jews nor the Arabs were organized for war, and the neighboring Arab states had not yet gone into action.

The principal strength of the Jewish army was constituted by the Haganah, the organization of the Resistance Movement in Palestine, with a good many members who had seen service with the British forces. At this time they were reckoned to number about 50,000. There were also some smaller and more extreme groups, among which was the Stern Gang, responsible later for the murder of Count Folke Bernadotte, the United Nations' mediator.

On the Arab side, the so-called Army of Freedom was composed of volunteers recruited from almost all the Arab countries, together with a few European officers; we were detailed to serve with this army. Sympathizers who preferred something slacker than the strict discipline of regular service were able to join the Haris al Watani, the National Guard. Most of these were Palestinians. They reported for duty wherever and whenever it suited them, sometimes went on sentry duty, shot and plundered a little, occasionally laid a mine and returned home when they had made enough money. From the self-satisfied viewpoint of Farouki Eff, a heroic campaign was in progress, but the undertones of his conversation hinted that he would find it advantageous to his moral equilibrium if the Arab army were formed exclusively of German veterans. Anyhow one could not expect much to happen as long as the Mandate lasted, and it would not expire till May 15, 1948.

Said whispered to me with a grin, "As long as the British are in the country the war will only be waged by night."

Farouki Eff, obviously interested, wanted to know what my comrade had said to me.

"We were wondering," lied Said calmly, "who our direct chief would be."

"Oh!" An expression of proud satisfaction came over Farouki's face as he said, "Sheik Hassan Salameh is going to honor us with his presence tonight, and I shall have the pleasure of presenting you gentlemen to him."

Our commander looked very different from the conventional

picture of a military leader. The man who came in shortly afterward, escorted by two bodyguards carrying carbines, pistols, daggers and hand grenades, was a tall bull-like man with fair hair and blue eyes. His coloring was surprising and his dress even more so. He wore gray trousers, brown shoes of untanned leather with crepe rubber soles, and a bush jacket. A broad leather belt with two pistols in an open holster completed his toilet.

Our host and all his guests treated Sheik Hassan Salameh with great deference. The respect they paid to him was doubtless partly due to his position, but I sensed that he was also personally popular. My feeling was confirmed when I observed that his intimates called him Abu Aly.

I had plenty of time to observe and study Sheik Hassan Salameh as he walked slowly around the company, greeting each guest with a powerful handshake. It was not easy to understand the peasant's dialect in which he made a speech of welcome to us. He said he was delighted to have us here in the country as comrades-in-arms of the Arab Fighters for Freedom. The fight would end in victory for us and them. His massive, sunburned forehead was that of a peasant, and peasant-like too was a crafty expression which seeped through his natural brutality. But he made a point of disguising these disadvantages behind a mask of good-fellowship. His forehead sloped sharply back and he had the underhung chin of a ruthless man, prepared to wade through slaughter to a throne. His eyes, almost lashless, were concealed between thick cushions of fat, but they observed everything with cunning precision, while wearing the good-natured smile which is the price a man must pay for his popularity.

That was our commanding officer.

The war he had to wage was as individual as his own character. Our conversation, which lasted until late in the night, was continually interrupted by the arrival of Arabs with rifles to sell. One batch brought a box of Italian hand grenades. All sorts of weapons were acceptable, as neither of the two contending parties possessed heavy arms. Pistols, rifles and submachine guns were the weapons in current use, and both sides possessed a few German and Italian mortars. As neither side was armed with cannon with which to fire explosive shells at the enemy or aircraft to drop bombs on him, each had to introduce bombs and homemade mines into the enemy camps or houses by stealth.

"You will drive to Jaffa early tomorrow morning and report to our H.Q., where you will supply yourselves with uniforms, kit and weapons," said our C.O. before leaving the party at a late hour. "I am now going on a visit of inspection to prepare our attack on a Jewish settlement. I shall probably be away for a week. In the meantime, I wish you to inspect the front and to write me your impressions confidentially. When I return, I shall have you posted to commands on the front."

Next morning we found three taxis in front of the house, waiting to take us to Jaffa. The Yugoslavs had already been sent on ahead in a truck. The respective treatment of Germans and Yugoslavs showed marked discrimination. Particular consideration was shown for the Germans, whereas the Arabs looked down their noses at the Yugoslavs, whom they planted out at random among the rank and file of their army. In contrast, every German volunteer was commissioned as an officer, regardless of his previous rank in the German army.

We sat six in our taxi, Said and I and two other Germans, while an armed Palestinian sat beside the driver. This man pointed out the interesting features of the countryside and drew our special attention to anything that indicated that a nasty form of warfare was in progress.

The landscape was charming. On both sides of the broad, as-phalted road, villas were standing among orange groves and palm clusters, and the slopes and valleys of the low hills were teeming into greenery. British armored cars reminded us that the atmos-phere was not as peaceful as the landscape. We passed a truck on the side of the road that had run over a land mine. No one seemed interested in removing the wreckage.

Suddenly the Palestinian in the front seat ducked his head and looked as though he were trying to get under the seat.

"Keep your heads down," he warned us. At a crossing in the road there stood a villa with a fence of barbed wire shielding the front garden from the road. Loopholed concrete bunkers commanded the highway, and this two-storyed sandbagged house with concrete shutters looked like a private fortress.

"That is the Villa Hasboun," said our escort. "The Jewish owners have made a stronghold of it." He spoke quickly and nervously, and got down into cover behind the door. "Cross your fingers and pray they don't fire on us."

"Don't listen to that trouser-messer," laughed Said and stood up to have a look. There was no one in the garden, but on the balcony we saw a girl behind a machine gun viewing us through a pair of field glasses.

It was not until we had left the villa behind us that the Palestinian resumed his normal dimensions. Turning round in his seat, he said, "Every time I pass by here I give myself up for lost. That house is a thorn in our flesh and must be removed. From here the Jews control the only road between Ramle and Jaffa. The house can't be captured without artillery, but now that we have a few Germans with us, we must see what they can do."

"I suppose you'd like the police to be patrolling here all the time," said Said scornfully.

"By day it isn't so dangerous," admitted the brave national guardsman. "British police are continually on the move in cars and on motorcycles, and they interfere at once if any shooting starts. And all around Jews and Arabs live at peace together and go quietly to their work. Of course, it sometimes happens that one of us or one of them gets laid out by a sniper. But by night! By night!"

Said pointed to some people who carried arms as they worked in the fields. He said, "I have heard they do it everywhere. It is the only sign that there is a war on—a war of bands under the eye of the police, a war without a front, which comes alive only during the night, when the British reduce their car patrols to the minimum. I don't blame them. Why should they get their soldiers shot in a war which doesn't concern them? Better to look on at these two Semitic peoples fighting one another. Well, we shall see. I rather think I shall find this sort of war to my taste. Oh—oh! This isn't quite what we wanted."

He had just caught sight of the British military cordon searching all cars as they came into Jaffa. We had to pull up and our taxi was thoroughly ransacked. It was typical Arab carelessness that had allowed us to run unsuspecting into this danger. After all, we were Germans and escaped POW's at that. Was it absolutely necessary to send us into a British occupied district when in the north, where the British evacuation had already begun, there were large areas without garrisons?

However, after thoroughly searching us, they let us go through. Another instance of Arab carelessness was the choice of a site for the Arab H.Q. Instead of establishing it in the middle of the Arab town, where it would be protected by the surrounding buildings, they had placed it in Jebeliyeh, a southern suburb easily commanded by the Jewish positions and particularly by the fortified watchtower.

The Arabs treated us more as if we were spectators and guests than participants in their war. They gave us food, tobacco and coffee and rooms to sleep in. But we had nothing to do but to hang about, and our enforced leisure was not made more agreeable by the fact that we were not allowed to leave our quarters. There was some justification for this because, it transpired, the Arab guards took all strangers not wearing uniforms for Jews and fired at them on sight.

All the same, we did not get our uniforms, though we did our utmost to persuade Major Adel Bey, the town mayor, a little middle-aged Iraqi, to give us them. What they finally did give us were some American uniforms, which we wore with headcloth and agal. They gave us no weapons.

However, from the time we were issued our uniforms, we had to circulate at night and had a chance of seeing the war at close quarters. It was unlike any war we had ever seen. The front line positions were in shallow trenches and behind the walls of houses and blocks of stone. They were badly and ignorantly laid out, and did not represent a real front line at all. At that time the Arab brigade in Jaffa consisted of 7 Germans, 150 Yugoslavs, 30 Egyptians and 200 Lebanese and Syrians. There were very few Palestinians among them, as these preferred irregular warfare with the National Guard, in which they could either be active or shirk at will.

There was no discipline, no military police, no muster rolls, no lists of personnel. No one ever knew who belonged to which unit or where the different units were.

This incurable disorder was shamelessly exploited. A man enlisted as a volunteer, received a weapon, went off to join his unit and was never seen again. He sold his rifle and uniform to a dealer who was prepared to pay from $60 to $75 for a rifle or a submachine gun. Later on, the same man reported as a volunteer to another unit and played the same game over again—as long as the supply of arms held out.

But now the supply was running short. At that time, there were only eight machine guns of British make in the whole of Jaffa. Still it was always possible to buy every sort of small arms from well-dressed Palestine Arabs, whom one could find sitting in cafés in the old city, carrying pistols in their belts with a martial air and spending the whole day playing dominoes or tricktrack.

There were other things to be bought—and from other people. One morning a British armored reconnaissance car drew up in front of our house.

"Dammit, Tommies!" cried Hussein, a Hamburger who was sitting reading at a window.

We all rushed to look and saw a young lieutenant and a sergeant get out of the car and walk into the house.

"They won't get us as easily as that," said Said, pulling out a hand grenade from under a mattress. "Run downstairs, you three, and see what they want." He included me in the detail. "The rest of you go and fetch anything there is to throw, then post yourselves on the stairs. If there's trouble on the ground floor, we'll send down our blessing from above."

While everything was being organized upstairs, we went down to reconnoiter. We could clearly hear the voice of the lieutenant coming from the major's office.

It seemed that after all he had not come to demand the surrender of a handful of Germans. He wanted to get rid of the armored car which was parked before the door. He was saying, "My unit leaves tomorrow. I have written off this car as unserviceable, but it would be a pity to blow it up. You can have it for 500 pounds." The sergeant translated the lieutenant's offer into broken Arabic. We signaled upstairs that there was nothing to fear, but in order to assist at such an interesting conversation we walked into the major's office.

Adel Bey was working himself up into a temper.

"What do you expect me to do with an old hulk like that?" he asked. "Its time long ago expired; besides, it hasn't got a cannon." He pointed through the window at the blunt turret out of which stuck the muzzle of a Bren gun. "Come again in a week. I'll think it over in the meantime."

"In a week, God be praised, I shall have left this country for good," said the young man smiling with, I thought, a touch of pity. "If you don't want the car I'll sell it in Tel Aviv to the Haganah. They will take it for sure." He beckoned to the sergeant. The engine came to life, and in a moment they were on their way to Tel Aviv. I thought it a good idea to memorize the number of the car in case we met it again. The number was 466.

The rented house in the old town of Jaffa, as well as the neighboring houses full of Arab families, remained unprotected, thanks to the slackness of the Arab command. In this very quarter stood the powder magazine, lodged in an ancient Turkish building with a domed roof. Said and I went to inspect it. A single sentry was on duty to guard the magazine against raids by the Haganah. This man let us in through a heavy wooden door.

A few unshaded bulbs hung in the dome. Below lay about in the utmost confusion all sorts of materials and instruments of destruction—explosives, aluminum powder, fuses, detonators, cartridges, and a large stock of unserviceable bombs, grenades and mines from widely differing sources, the separate parts of which, especially the fuses and the detonators, were to be extracted and employed for the manufacture of fresh bombs. When we came in, a couple of men were engaged in scraping the explosive out of some ancient Turkish grenades with knives. Above their heads a lamp swung on a much frayed, unprotected wire.

"Come out, my friend," said my blond companion in tones of horror, and drew me away from this fearful deathtrap. Said was not easily frightened. "I think," he said, "after what we have seen, we should be in the right mood to go over and pin the Sheik down to something definite."

"Is he back?" I asked.

"His tour of inspection lasted a fortnight and now he is ripe for some sleep. We have to be careful, or he'll slip away from us. It never worries an old thief to tell a lie, when it comes to the pinch."

"Was he a robber too? Someone told me he had been a peddler wandering up and down the Holy Land with an ass loaded with junk."

"Yes, to start with. But that didn't bring him in enough. He was also muscular, so he became a robber and a brigand, which brought him into contact with religion and patriotism. At the beginning of the Second World War, he attached himself to the Mufti of Jerusalem, with whom he was finally obliged to flee to Germany. And when Hadji Amin returned, Hassan came back with him and was rewarded for his loyalty with the title of Sheik."

"It seems that Hassan acquired the knowledge and experience which qualify him to be C.O., Central Front, during his career as a brigand, and that is all he will ever know. What the devil is the object of these isolated operations against Jewish settlements?"

"Booty," said Said.

We decided that we must somehow get hold of Sheik Hassan, who, we guessed, would want to disappear again after having his sleep out. Our idea was to stop him on the road, a proceeding which an ex-brigand ought to appreciate, and come to a clear understanding with him about the employment of our services. No doubt Hassan would want to evade his responsibilities, but all he had to do was to direct the Iraqi major to arm us and send us to the ports in which we were to serve.

The arms chamber in our house was, in a modest way, to be compared with the powder magazine. It was in the cellar directly below the rooms in which we lived. In this little room were strewn, in splendid disorder, boxes full of ammunition of all kinds and calibers, belts of machine-gun ammunition for German machine guns which did not exist, boxes containing dynamite and T.N.T., rolls of fuse tow, detonating wires, sidearms, a crate full of pistols of all sorts and eleven Canadian carbines.

I fished out from the stock of pistols a handy Spanish Star, but Said chose a heavy American .45.

"It makes bigger holes," was his grim comment.

The major let out a cry of protest when we began to pick up the carbines.

"Those are only reserve weapons," he said crossly. "We lend them out from time to time when rifles are needed and then we take them back into the store."

We did not want to deplete the arsenal to an extent that might prejudice the issue of the war, so we left him the carbines. The Sheik found the behavior of us Germans so disrespectful that he did not want us to stick together any longer. Accordingly, he dissolved our group by distributing us over his whole sector, so that we might have the fewest possible contacts with one another. Thus he transferred my six comrades, of whom only two had been officers in the German army, as lieutenants and troop leaders to six different units.

I was appointed staff physician and director of the polyclinic at the Christian Mission Hospital, which served as a military hospital. At the same time I was medical officer for the whole Jaffa front.

The old fox had judged quite rightly. It was the nature of the Germans to apply themselves with zeal and thoroughness to their new task of improvising an organization, which had not previously existed. It was not our fault that the success of our efforts was limited. It took us a few months to learn that the corps of Arab officers did not want to learn, and sabotaged our work out of ignorance, mistrust and jealousy, or "because they knew better."

It took us long to understand this and longer still before we gave up trying. Finally we made up our minds to regard ourselves as simple mercenaries, doing our duty as well as we could but regarding the war as a personal adventure. When things went well, we reckoned it a good day. But we knew too well that the small successes of the moment would have to be paid for. We could not foresee what the reckoning would be, but we were by no means willing to pay with our heads for the narrow-mindedness and incompetence of others.

Chapter XVI

GUERRILLA WARFARE

AS I WAS not only the oldest member of our party and the senior in rank, but I also possessed in my hospital a kind of sanctuary, my quarters became the meeting place of the seven Germans belonging to the Jaffa front. The material for our convivial gatherings was provided by an inexhaustible array of bottles which I kept on the top shelf of my wardrobe. But in case an unpleasant emergency should arise, I also kept in the self-same wardrobe, hidden behind a medical smock and my suits, two German machine guns, model 34, ready for action, together with a few belts of ammunition and a box of egg grenades.

With a side glance at our weapons and a mask of assumed jollity, we shouted down the fear we felt creeping over us as we said good-by to the Old Year.

"Let us drink to the Year of Disgrace, 1948," shouted Said. He drained his glass at a single draught and shattered it against the wall. As the fragments fell to the ground there came on us a dull feeling of disillusion.

We did not have to welcome the New Year with a salute of guns. Others would do that, as they always did. The war of bands was gradually turning into a regular war, as the British forces withdrew. What did we mercenaries know of the game that was being played out on the political chessboard? We heard rumors. King Farouk, it was said, wanted to incorporate the Sinai Peninsula into his kingdom. Transjordania had ambitions in Palestine, and Syria was also claiming a slice of that country.

The Arab states made hurried preparations to intervene in the Holy Land, but no attack could be made before the expiry of the Mandate, as that would involve an act of war against Great Britain.

The Jews knew all about the ambitions of their neighbors, and did what was to be done better and more thoroughly than their enemies. They bought weapons from all available sources, they formed their corps of francs-tireurs, and in addition turned all their men and women able to bear arms into efficient soldiers, who were to enable a nation of a million souls to stand up to the united forces of all the Arabs.

But the local war was still being waged according to the old rules. It was still irregular warfare, but it had now been developed into a very unpleasant science.

In Jerusalem the Jewish Agency was partly destroyed by explosives.

An Arab employed as a chauffeur at the American Consulate used his service car to unload two large cases at the Jewish Agency. Other Arab employees at the Consulate had falsified the delivery notes and a German, pretending to be an American, took over the receipt for the cases. Ten minutes after they had driven away, the cases blew up.

On March third it was the turn of the Villa Hasboun. Numerous attempts had been made to eliminate this Jewish strong point on the Ramle-Jaffa road. A night attack had been repulsed with bloodshed. A raiding party of three men carrying explosives, who had worked themselves up alongside the house, were discovered and shot down.

I had heard of this affair while I was on the way to start a sanitary personnel service in all the units and to put in sanitary installations, which I should subsequently have to inspect. The news of our final success reached me as I was walking through the winding streets of Jaffa on my way to do a job.

I suddenly saw the blond head of the Hun, Said, towering above a crowd of Arabs. He held himself as erect, and looked as self-conscious, as if he were marching at the head of the regiment of Guards. He was striding down the middle of the street and the Arabs gave way to him on either hand.

The old *Landsknecht*[1] caught sight of me and called, "Hasboun

---

[1] *Landsknecht*—mercenary soldier.

is eliminated," smiling all over his face. "We flattened it out yesterday."

"Tell me about it."

"Oh, it wasn't so difficult after all," he said and twirled the end of his mustache upward. "I had been thinking it over and had come to the conclusion that we would have to perform the operation by day, as those fellows always shoot at sight after dark. I had to think out a new trick. They knew the old ones too well.

"It was simple enough. I loaded a few boxes of dynamite on an ancient truck and laid the fuse through a hole in the cab. So I drove the old bus with my parcels from Ramle toward Jaffa, wearing my robbers' mufti, naturally, and Abdurrahman rattled on ahead of me in a jeep.

"When we came to the crossroads, I started hooting like mad as though I wanted to overhaul the jeep in my old crock, but Abdurrahman kept on right in the middle of the road and would not let me pass. Just in front of the house I drove straight into his tail.

"We both stopped, got out and began to insult one another. He called me a son of a dog and I told him he was as stupid as a donkey plus fifteen sheep. The Jews came out of the house to see what was doing and held their sides for laughter. A few ragged children ran up to us and clung to our arms crying, 'Baksheesh! Baksheesh!' I pulled out some millièmes from my pocket and threw them in a high arc over their heads for them to scramble for. This caused a lot of shouting and confusion.

"Then we both climbed into our cars. Abdurrahman switched his engine on while I lit the fuse. Then I jumped out again and ran toward the jeep with clenched fists, cursing at Abdurrahman. The Jews thought the play was starting all over again and began to enjoy themselves.

"But, instead, I climbed quietly into the jeep and Abdurrahman stepped on the gas. It wasn't till then that they smelled a rat and got busy with their machine gun. By that time, we were out of sight behind the cactus hedge and two minutes later the truck went up."

"Did the whole house go with it?"

"No—later on we had a look at the damage from close quarters. The whole front of the house was peeled off, including the balcony with that damned machine gun."

"Who was on duty?" I asked after a pause. I couldn't help thinking of the girl I had seen there when we first came into Ramle.

"Yes, she was," said Said, as though he had divined my thought.

"Pity!"

"Yes," he said, and suddenly seemed less proud of his exploit than he had been a moment ago. But the hard-bitten soldier of fortune was not inclined to indulge the softer emotions for long. Soon his flexible, inventive mind was playing with new ideas and thinking of new devices for inflicting as much harm as possible on the enemies of the Arabs.

One evening a few days later, he rang me up asking me to pick him up at H.Q. He wanted to tell me about something he had thought of.

We drove together to one of the narrow streets leading southwest out of Ramle, which the enemy from Tel Aviv were accustomed to keep patrolled. There Said brought me into an old stable, where asses had formerly been kept, and where now a dozen Arabs were sitting on the ground playing dominoes under the flickering light of candles. Hussein, the man from Hamburg, was smoking by the door.

"Has the lookout man gone to his post?" asked Said.

"Yes," reported Hussein, "I put him just on the bend of the road where he has an uninterrupted view for a mile and a quarter."

We had already smoked half a dozen cigarettes when the lookout man came running in.

"Three cars," he said.

Said sprang up in such a hurry that he knocked over his machine pistol, which he had stood against a tree.

"Lights out!" he growled into the stable.

The candles went out, and the men took up their positions on the other side of the road in selected cover. Said and Hussein tied grenades onto their belts and picked up their machine pistols. Hussein ran to the bend of the road to identify approaching cars.

It was a moonless night, with stars showing above the trees. Said

Wearing his usual Arab dress, Dr. Pritzke, in the photo above, looks
across the Saudi Arabian desert outside the massive city walls of Hofuf.
Below, he talks with friends in the city

Photos: Presse-Seeger

The Emir Saud Ibn Abdallah Ibn Jelawi, governor of the Saudi Arabian province of El Hasa, under whose orders Dr. Pritzke worked at Hofuf

Photos: Presse-Seeger

The imposing palace of the Emir. In foreground, Dr. Pritzke talks with Arab dignitaries and an engineer from an American oil company.

squatted by the wall of the stable, fiddling about with a little box with two steel pegs from which electric wires led outward. We could now hear the faint sound of approaching motors.

"Here they come," Said said. "Cross your fingers and pray the bloody gadget works. And you, keep your damned heads down, you rubbernecks," he cried to the Arabs across the road, whose faces showed palely through the dim light over the low wall that lined the road.

Hussein hurried back from his reconnaisance and told us that the convoy, consisting of three cars, would be here in a minute or two.

The noise of the motors increased.

I must admit that my knees were trembling and the palms of my hands were streaming with sweat.

Everything went like a slow-motion picture. Hussein took the two hand grenades from his belt and held them in his hands. Then he seemed to have thought of something else, for he took the machine pistol from his shoulder, loaded it and hung it on a strap which he looped over his shoulder again with the muzzle pointing forward. Afterward he picked up the two grenades.

From the other side of the road we heard the excited whispering of the Arabs, and Said bit off a curse between his teeth. Apart from this, he showed not the slightest sign of agitation. I watched him crouching behind a thick tree trunk, with machine pistol and grenades within easy reach, and his right hand holding the T-shaped handle protruding from the top of the black box.

"Go easy with the grenades, Hussein," he whispered to his comrade. "We've only got four of them and there are three cars. One for each and one in reserve. You take the last car; I'll take the first. When we've accounted for number one and number three, we'll attend to the one in the middle."

"That's right," said Hussein quietly.

"If only those bloody fools would keep their heads down, though it doesn't really matter much if some of them get their blocks blown off when the fun starts."

The headlights of the leader, like a couple of brilliant fingers, felt their way along the trees as the cars rounded the bend. Behind the glowing lights of the front car I guessed, rather than saw, its outline. Behind it two great shadows rolled, showing only their parking lights.

We ducked our heads and Said whispered, "An armored car," as the leader lumbered by—a six-wheeled monster with a small revolving turret from which a machine gun pointed. On the dark steel wall there stood in figures so white that I could read them in the dark, the number 466. . . . "We must get that chap," hissed Said, and took a tighter grip of his handle.

The second car was already several yards past us when Said jerked the handle downwards. We lay flat on the ground as, with a deafening roar, two huge mushrooms of fire shot up out of the roadway. There was a second of silence and then the rubble came raining down.

"At them!" roared Said, as he sprang up and pulled the safety peg out of a grenade with his teeth. Then he rushed toward the armored car, which at that moment began to spew fire from its turret. From the slits in the steel-coated sides of the two trucks, red and green tracer bullets came coughing out. One of the Arabs across the road let out a yell, which died away in a long-drawn whimper.

Then Hussein dashed toward the third car, which was firing as it retreated.

By now, Said had reached a point where he was out of the machine gun's field of fire and threw his grenade into the aperture. There was a dull, dry report as the bomb exploded inside of the steel colossus. The car reeled like a drunken man, and the engine stopped. The firing ceased, and the machine sank down like a pump handle.

The Arabs from the wall opposite stormed in to the car with howls of exultation and fired several dozen rounds through the aperture in the turret into the steel coffin, before they ventured to climb in and pull out the cargo—provisions of all sorts, cigarettes, ammunitions and arms.

At this point, Said got busy on the car in the middle, which was trying to squeeze past the wreck of the armored car, but had got itself jammed between the wreck and the trees. There was another well-aimed grenade, another dry report, and the firing ceased.

The Arabs, who had been plundering the armored car, were just beginning to turn their attention to this truck when a rifle barrel came through a slit, slowly and wearily, as though obeying the final order of a dying soldier's will. The man behind the gun fired straight into the middle of the charging Arabs. Said pulled his machine pistol from his shoulder and fired several bursts into the armor. His 9 mm. bullets rattled like peas against the steel, but there was a chance that one of them might find the opening and silence the shooter or at least divert his aim.

Meanwhile the third car, still firing, was working toward the point where the mine had destroyed the roadway, and Hussein was seeking an opportunity to throw his grenade. The driver drove desperately into the crater. The front wheels turned around in the air and the truck, top-heavy with the weight of its armor, staggered dangerously and looked for a moment as though it would overturn, but at last the wheels started gripping and the well-ribbed tires carried the vehicle up the other side and soon she disappeared, still firing, into the night.

Hussein broke away and turned his attention to the second car, which was still shooting. Holding himself erect, he ran forward grasping a grenade in his right hand. I watched him draw his arm back and bowl the oval projectile in a high curve toward the truck. Its outline was faintly visible as it lobbed through the air. At that moment, a projecting rifle barrel changed direction and a sheaf of tracer bullets passed through Hussein's body.

Hussein never heard the report of his grenade, nor saw his enemy's rifle flop forward. An enormous firework exploded into the sky as the truck's cargo of ammunition caught fire.

Next day the Hamburger called Hussein was buried with military honors in the Moslem cemetery at Jaffa. Just as his wife and child had been overwhelmed in an anonymous death under the ruins of Hamburg, so now he fell nameless, and with him the last remnant of his family was blotted out.

Chapter XVII

BOMBS AND ORANGE GROVES

THE rest of us Germans, whether we called ourselves Aly, Hassan, Said or Salameh, were obviously exposed to the same risk of extinction as Hussein, the Hamburger and, as time drew on, we became more and more convinced that our elimination was only a matter of time.

And yet I have never known a lovelier spring than that of 1948, nor a more heavenly landscape.

We lived surrounded by miles of orange groves which perfumed the whole region with their blossoms.

My memory takes me back to April twelfth. I had been sent for to treat a sick officer at the headquarters of the Central Front at Sarafand, where the orange trees were in their headiest bloom. Sarafand was a little place between Jaffa and Ramle, to one side of the main road. The British used to have a school for officers here, a long, two-storyed building, which now contained the staff offices, accommodation for the officers and, on the ground floor, two large rooms with barred windows which served as a prison for political detainees. The practice was that when an officer of sufficient seniority or political importance fell sick, the staff surgeon was sent for to treat him in his private quarters.

On this occasion I had an easy job. The officer was my only patient and, for once, I did not find him surrounded by a swarm of close or distant relatives, also in need of medical advice—for which a fee would not be charged.

When I had done what was necessary it was already after ten o'clock. As I did not care to return to Jaffa in the dark, I decided to pass the night at headquarters.

They brought me a mattress and bedclothes onto the roof, where I lay down to sleep under the starry sky. It was such a lovely spring night that it seemed a pity to waste it all in sleeping.

Below me was a vast orange plantation, in a small rectangular clearing on which stood the headquarters building, with the orange trees coming nearly up to the walls. The scent of the orange blossoms was wafted up to me from all sides.

I heard in the surrounding country the reports of single rifle shots, but very seldom the crackle of automatic weapons or the distant explosion of a grenade. I could see the searchlights in Jewish settlements lighting up the foreground, sweeping around in a semicircle before they went out. It was the usual orchestra of war, and I found it soothing rather than exciting.

"Are you asleep already?" said a voice. It was the machine-gunner, who had turned around in his seat and was looking at me searchingly.

"No," I said, "I'm still awake."

"What a lovely night!" he said dreamily. "Really too beautiful to be on sentry duty. One ought . . ." he stopped, apparently looking for the right word to express his thought.

"Yes," I said, "that's what we ought to be doing." Whatever he might have been thinking of, it was clear that anything was better than spending such a heavenly night in the senseless preoccupations of a repulsive war.

"Do you come from a large town in Germany, or from a village?"

"From the largest town, from Berlin."

"Is Berlin as big as Cairo?"

"Bigger, much bigger."

"That can't be right. There is no bigger town than Cairo anywhere."

"Do you know Cairo?" I asked.

I should like to have been able to see the expression of respectful wonder on his face, which must have reflected the tone of his voice. But I could see no more than a shadow—one of many faceless shadows which surrounded me.

"No," he said in answer to my question. "But I have seen pictures of it and heard people talk about it. There is no greater town than Cairo."

I said to myself that it is natural for anyone to think what he loves is more beautiful or greater than anything else. The massive trees of the Tiergarten are something quite different from the rustling orange orchards of Palestine, and the chirping of our cheeky sparrows makes a pleasanter melody than the thin sawing song of the cicadas. As I looked, a veil seemed to interpose itself between the brilliant stars and my eyes—the much reviled haze that floats over our great industrial cities, that mild and mitigating curtain of smoke so different from the cruel clarity of Palestinian skies. I lay awake dreaming, but soon I was asleep and still dreaming of Berlin.

My dreams were shattered by the sound of the alarm. But it was not the alarm clock on my bed table in Berlin. It was the cracking of a machine gun, quite close to me. The gunner was firing out into the darkness between the points of the battlemented roof—a new man, probably, who had replaced the fellow who was on duty when I fell asleep. All I could see was a dark, faceless shadow lying be-behind his gun.

Shrill cries of alarm came up from below. Then I heard confused shouts and steps running quickly up the stairs. Two Germans, Hassan and Aly, with half a dozen Arabs, all half-dressed, came rushing up onto the roof loading their weapons as they ran. They flung themselves down behind the pointed battlements and immediately began to fire into the darkness below them.

Some one called, "Turn on the searchlights." Time was lost in nervous fumbling before the light blazed out and the dazzling finger of light began to probe the foreground.

"There they are," cried a voice.

The searchlight had picked up three figures, who were gliding through the darkness with weapons raised aloft, and clung fast to them. Each of the men was shielding his eyes against the light with his arm, as he made for the cover of the orange trees. From every weapon on the roof a stream of bullets poured on them, and each of the fugitives crumpled as he ran. One of them pulled himself up and rolled into dead ground in a hollow. Suddenly, from the edge of the clearing, a machine pistol began to shoot. There was a sound of splintering glass above our heads. The light went out, and a spectral stillness supervened.

I heard a German voice cursing in the darkness. "Now we're in a bloody mess," it said. "It's a miracle that they have been so long in sending a storming party to attack the house, which they might long ago have taken. We've been telling the Sheik for God knows how long to have the orange trees cut down over five hundred square yards around the house and to secure the approaches with barbed wire, trenches and mines. But he always knew better."

I had heard the same sort of complaints from Said. But our commander had maintained that a sentry in each of the four corners of the clearing and a machine gun on the roof was protection enough, though whenever he slept in Sarafand there was a bodyguard posted in front of the door of his room to insure that he had a good night and to guarantee the safety of his irreplaceable person.

Hassan called out, "Come on. We must go down or these fellows will be attacking the house again." We all ran down with the exception of two men, who remained on the roof to serve the machine gun.

"Who is the fool who has left his junk in the middle of the passage?" stormed Aly, as he stopped dead. "There's a great damned steamer trunk in the way. Probably belongs to one of the gentlemen on the staff. Take care and come this way around."

We came out carefully onto the space in front of the house. Not a shot was fired, and no one was in sight. The enemy must have carried away their wounded. Only the bodies of the two dead men lay where they had fallen. But later, we found two of our sentries on the edge of the clearing with their throats cut.

"They've got clean away by now," growled Hassan. "There's no object in wasting time looking around for them." Then he came back with me onto the roof.

"Now let's get some fresh air," he said. "No use trying to sleep now, and anyhow it will soon be light."

We sat down on the mattress and lit cigarettes.

"Let us hope that the fat man will at last learn something by experience. If the lookout man hadn't had such sharp eyes, we would have been properly buggered up." No sooner had Hassan finished speaking, when the mattress began to shift and roll and the house below us shook as though the earth was quaking. A bursting crash assailed my eardrums, and I felt as if an iron hand were squeezing my lungs and I was tossed like a puppet into a deep, black hole, deeper and ever deeper. . . .

I felt lukewarm water being poured on my face, and a hand roughly shaking my shoulder.

"What are you doing with the water jug, Hassan?" I asked. I opened my eyes and saw Hassan and his water jug, and over his shoulder the light of the rising sun shining through the crenelations of the roof.

"At last," he snorted, "I thought you intended to sleep till evening."

My head ached fit to burst. As I put up my hand to touch it, I felt a bandage.

"We've tied it up with the sleeve of your shirt," said Hassan, pointing to my naked shoulder. "Too much in a hurry to find anything else. You knocked your head against the parapet. Now you've got a little hole in it to give your brains some fresh air."

"Don't be so stupid," I said—my splitting headache did not help me to enjoy his humor.

"You ought to be devilish pleased that the parapet was there. But for that, you'd have been carried overboard when the bomb went up."

"What bomb?" I racked my brains trying to remember about the earthquake. So is wasn't an earthquake after all. "Why man, it was the box in the corridor."

"Probably it was," nodded Hassan, "but we can't establish that now. Anyhow it's not important."

I sat up and looked around. Ten yards behind the mattress on which I sat, the roof with its crenelated parapet came to an abrupt end. Below I could see a few bare walls rising from a mountain of rubble. The whole clearing was strewn with stones and pieces of mortar. Down below men were working, and shouting as they worked.

"They're digging out the fellows who were buried," said Hassan.

"And the prisoners?"

"Yes, them too."

"Do you suppose any of them are still alive?"

Hassan shrugged his shoulders.

After that we had to look after ourselves, and then I had to return to Jaffa. We finally managed to get a damaged jeep into running order, in which we limped off on our way to Jaffa, Hassan sitting beside me.

The countryside was perfectly peaceful, as usual, and work was going on peacefully, though there were indications, which one could not mistake, that things were not exactly as they looked. Cultivators were hard at work in the Jewish orange groves on the left of the road. Weeds were being hoed up and irrigation dams made watertight. A few of the workers carried guns on their shoulders, and near every group of cultivators stood a sentry with his rifle at the ready. I imagined that similar working conditions prevailed 150 years ago in the western regions of America, where the farmers on the frontier worked under the continual menace of Indian attacks.

We passed the Villa Hasboun, which was in ruins. I was looking back at it, when the engine of our car began to stutter and after missing fire a few times came to a halt just beside a group of Jews working among the orange trees.

The sentry gave a warning signal. The workers immediately threw down their spades and hoes and grasped their weapons. In a few seconds they were all under cover.

"Get down," cried Hassan as he jumped out of the jeep. I followed him.

Then a few shots came in our direction; most of the bullets sang over our heads, but one struck a front wheel and ricocheted off it. Hassan was lying behind the front wheel, with the Arab driver cowering beside him. I lay protected to some extent by the back wheels.

Hassan was pushing his pistol over the edge of the wheel and looking for a target. I shouted to him not to shoot. "If you do, they'll wipe us out," I said. Hassan was sensible enough to put down his pistol.

The people in the orange grove also stopped shooting, after the first few shots which they had fired in the excitement of the moment. Now they were waiting to see if we would show our hand, and they seemed to be discussing what to do. They were lying under cover far apart from one another, so they had to raise their voices in order to be heard.

"No, in no circumstances," I heard someone say clearly in German. "I bet this is another of their swinish tricks like the Hasboun affair. They've got dynamite in their car and are out to blow us all up."

"Nonsense. The fellows are lying behind the wheels. They can hardly mean to blow themselves up, can they?"

"They are fanatics. They would gladly blow themselves up, if they could take us along with them."

I couldn't help smiling, in spite of the awkwardness of our situation. They seemed to have queer notions about our fanaticism.

"Keep down, for God's sake," said the voice of the cautious man. "The car may go up at any moment."

The accent was the unmistakable singsong of a Hamburger. If this man was really a Hamburger and I a Berliner; if the people over there were cultivating their orchard peaceably, and if we had had a breakdown—all of which was true—it seemed to me that neither group ought to be interested in blowing holes in the other.

I reached out carefully for the driver's rifle, which was lying on the back seat of the jeep, felt for the ramrod with my finger, and slowly unscrewed it and pulled it out. Then I tied my white handkerchief—we were civilized fighters—onto the point of the ramrod and waved my flag, to show we wanted to parley. The answer was a shot which came through the tin side of the car and passed close by my hand. I lowered my flag of truce as quickly as possible.

"What are you shooting for, you idiot?" said someone. "Don't you see they want to parley?"

"That's a damned ruse, I tell you."

I had to take a chance so I shouted, "Look here, we are

both Germans," as I stuck up the white flag once more.

I heard several voices say in tones of surprise: "A German!"

They consulted again together and finally one of them called out, "What do you want of us?"

"Nothing—we've had a breakdown—honest to God."

There was another pause, and then a voice challenged us to lay down our arms and come forward with our hands above our heads. Hassan's face showed mistrust, and the driver, to whom I translated the message, made a gesture of emphatic disapproval and said, "That is not good."

I called out, "I suggest that each of the two parties should send an unarmed man forward to parley."

"Agreed," said the spokesman, after a short consultation. "We meet at the fence."

I put down my pistol behind the wheel and got to my feet cautiously, with my flag in my hand. Not a shot was fired. I slowly walked around behind the car and went forward with half-raised hands up to the mesh-wire fence which enclosed the orchard. There I met a fair-haired man of about forty, who came up to me from between the trees.

"Good day," I said politely.

The other returned the salutation with equal courtesy.

"We really have had a breakdown," said I to explain our position.

"Yes," drawled he, "I should be glad to believe it, but you know . . ."

"Yes, I know."

He reflected for a while and then said, "Now listen. We will let your driver repair the car, while you and I both remain standing with our backs to our people and facing one another, so that neither you nor I can be shot down by the opposing side without the other being hit. I am quite sure that my people don't want any shooting. If you are equally sure about your people, you can accept my offer."

"I give you my word of honor," I said and shook hands with him through the meshes of the fence. When both sides had received their instructions, our driver got busy with his refractory engine, while Hassan and the Jews inside the fence lay mistrustful and tense behind their weapons. We two, living pledges of peaceful intentions, smiled at one another with a certain embarrassment.

"Where did you get that?" asked my opposite number, pointing to my bandage.

"During an attack on Sarafand last night." He smiled sympathetically and rather helplessly said, "I'm sorry."

"War is war," I said, taking refuge in the most banal of phrases.

"Where do you come from?" he asked me.

"Berlin. Niederschönhausen."

"Grand town, Berlin—at least it was before the war."

"I've nothing against Hamburg," I replied, returning the compliment. "Alster Pavilion, Rieperbahn—things we can only dream about today."

"Do you mind if I put my hand in my pocket?" he said. "I want to get out a cigarette."

I looked suspiciously at the pocket. It was too flat to hold a pistol.

"I'll use my left hand," he said, having noticed my glance.

I nodded assent.

He reached laboriously with his left hand into his right trouser pocket and slowly drew out a crumpled packet of cigarettes, one of which he passed to me through the fence. Getting a lighter out of his watch pocket was a less troublesome proceeding.

"Are you a volunteer?" he said as he lighted his cigarette.

"Yes, so to speak."

"Mm—escaped from prison, no passport, no money—bombed out at home."

"I have some money, but otherwise you're quite right."

We smoked a while in silence. Then he said, "Don't you think you're on the wrong side?"

"I'm a doctor. It's all one to me, whom I serve."

"All the same, you're on the wrong side," he insisted obstinately.

"Maybe, but that's where I am."

"You could serve with our troops as a doctor. In our organization there are certainly as many Germans as in the Arab forces. Christians too, former soldiers," he added to prevent my misunderstanding him.

By this time our driver had finished tinkering with the engine and Hassan called, "O.K. We can drive on now."

"Good-bye, compatriot," I said, stretching out my hand through the fence, "and many thanks."

He held my hand and said, "Won't you come over to us? The way is always open."

"Thanks for the invitation, but you know I don't believe that I've got any talent for changing my shirt from day to day."

"I can quite understand that," said he reflectively. "But it's a pity. Well, good luck to you."

Chapter XVIII

SHEIK HASSAN BECOMES SUSPICIOUS

WHEN I got to the hospital I found six new patients waiting for me. Said, whom I had patched up on various occasions for minor injuries, bullet grazes and slight wounds from bomb splinters, was now ready for a minor operation. A bit of a hand grenade was embedded in the upper part of his thigh and had to be extracted. He made light of it as usual.

I had, first of all, to attend to the five surviving prisoners from Sarafand. I was glad to find that none of them was seriously injured. And when I came to look into the faces of these brigands and gallows birds, as they had been described to me, I found nothing but intelligence, frank honesty and quiet confidence.

When it became known that I could be trusted, people talked openly in my presence about the reasons for which these men had been imprisoned. While I was dressing their wounds, they told me a lot of things and did not seem to fear that I would report them to the Sheik.

I found it hard to believe the reasons they gave me for their arrest. One of them, Abdunahman Abu Jarad, a young man of twenty-eight who belonged to a well-known family, had been put in prison by the Sheik because his family were active supporters of King Abdallah.

I asked myself whether that was a reason to arrest a comrade fighting on your side against a common enemy?

This young Arab in conversation with me developed a very intelligent, if confusing, picture of the territorial ambitions of the different Arab combatants. I had already heard a good deal about the claims of Egypt, Syria and Transjordania. Egypt wanted the largest slice she could get, Syria wanted to extend her territory by incorporating in it the northern part of Palestine, while Trans-jordania, originally an integral part of Palestine, sought to absorb the districts from which they expected shortly to expel the Jews and thus to create a greater Jordan.

The ambitions of these three states ran counter to the claims of the Mufti, who intended to found a kingdom of his own in Palestine as soon as the Mandate expired. In the last analysis, one could not overlook the Moslem Brotherhood, which by now had a firm footing in all the Arab states and aimed to set up an United Arab Empire, under the aegis of Islam.

Hassan Salameh, who commanded the Central Front, was a close adherent of the Mufti, on whose good will he was so dependent that whenever possible, he put out of business anyone likely to report to Hadji Amin on his incapacity. Thus, he was the enemy of all the Mufti's enemies and simultaneously the enemy of his confidants and partisans.

Fawzi el Kawukji, who commanded in the north, was a partisan of the Hashemite dynasty and had been made a pasha by King Abdallah. In return for this distinction, he lent his support to the King's Palestine policy.

In the Jerusalem sector, Abdul Qader Husseini commanded the Arab irregular volunteers in the interest of the Mufti, his kinsman.

In the central sector, the partisans of the King of Transjordania were already suspect, but anyone who did not truckle to the Sheik was ripe for prison. Moreover, the Sheik Hassan, who was nothing if not an autocrat, used to arrest members of distinguished families as hostages or for purposes of blackmail.

For example, Nimur Tuken, one of my wounded patients, was the nephew of the Mayor of Nablus. He belonged to a respected and powerful family and was a member of the Moslem Brotherhood. As he was driving to Lydda, he was hauled out of a bus by armed volunteers and brought to the Sheik's headquarters at Sarafand, where he was injured by the explosion of the "steamer trunk" bomb.

This bomb outrage had far-reaching aftereffects, and later on involved me in immediate danger.

As soon as the six wounded men were half recovered from their injuries, the Sheik wanted to have them back under his supervision and gave orders, without asking my consent, that they should be brought to his headquarters.

The last time his bandages were renewed, Nimur Tukan pushed an envelope under the bedclothes into my hand.

"Will you look after this letter for me?" he whispered, and added hastily, "I want it delivered to the Brothers in Jaffa."

This last hint seemed to me to suggest a greater danger than the mere request to deliver a letter. If the letter was productive of any action by the Brotherhood, the suspicious Sheik would probably seek to ascertain through what channel the Brotherhood had received information. However, I was quite ready to help my patient, as I had learned to detest the Sheik for his incompetence, his unscrupulousness and his unceasing intrigues.

Perhaps my dislike of the man caused me to lose my sense of caution. Anyhow, I stuck the letter in my sleeve and, when an opportunity offered, I went to look for the address in the old town. My road led me into a winding lane, through a gate like the entrance to a tunnel, across an unlit courtyard, and past a ragged sentry, till at last I found myself in the board room of the local Committee.

As Nimur Tukan had advised, I asked the servant for the chief, Sheik Tewfig Fakhurij.

A tall, thin man in a long caftan came to meet me, his eyes glowing with a zealot's fire. When he had read the letter he said, "By Allah! You have brought us glad tidings. We have been looking for Brother Nimur for three weeks. We and his family believed that he had been abducted by the Haganah. We couldn't guess that the Sheik was holding him prisoner."

He then explained to me that he could not, on his own initiative, take a decision. The matter must be discussed at a secret session of the Executive Committee, but he would forthwith send a messenger to convene the six members to a meeting. He invited me to attend the session, but I refused, promising, however, to come in the evening to find out what had happened.

When I came again, Sheik Tewfig immediately received me. He said in dignified tones, "We talked over the whole question and shall be grateful if you will now inform Brother Nimur that he will soon be free."

Nimur Tukan was set at liberty, and now my neck was in the noose.

Four days later, shortly after noon, just when I happened to be at headquarters attending to the wounded prisoners, three armored cars belonging to the Transjordan Frontier Force disposed themselves around the building with their guns pointing at the windows.

A lieutenant and three soldiers in British uniform, wearing the red and white check headcloth, stepped out of the turret door and walked in through the entrance.

"I want to speak to Hassan Salameh," called the officer to one of the bystanders, who at once pointed to the door of the Sheik's room. The guard in front of the Sheik's door, whose master had just withdrawn to take his siesta, tried to bar the way against the intruders, but the soldiers made it perfectly clear to him that he would do well to stand aside.

The officer walked into the room without knocking. A few minutes later Hassan Salameh appeared, half-dressed and barefoot in the corridor, and, not attempting to conceal his annoyance, gave a surly order that the prisoners were to be handed over to the lieutenant. The language of cannon, even when silent, is understood by men as thick-skinned as Hassan Salameh.

After my patients had been liberated in this manner, I had no more business at headquarters. But one day I received clear and unequivocal orders to report myself to the Sheik at Sarafand.

The prologue to the turbulent little drama that followed was provided by my yellow-haired comrade Said, the most agreeable of my patients, who gave trouble in only one respect.

Whenever I was at leisure, I used to sit with Said. He was not the man for a serious discussion, but he had an inexhaustible fund of wisecracks and anecdotes with which he entertained us generously. The other Germans, the Yugoslavs, as well as the Circassians and Arab volunteers, enjoyed his company just as much as I did. Whenever I tried, as I often did, to get him to tell me about his origin and his past, he simply ignored my questions. He was Said, the mercenary, for me and everybody else. Yesterday and tomorrow meant nothing to him. He lived for today, and only for today. But his enjoyment of today was so thorough that it cost me my whole stock of brandy.

On the day I got my message to go to Sheik Hassan, I had quite a row with Said, whom I found sitting at my writing table with a bottle of brandy three-quarters empty in front of him. I had resolved to save this bottle, my last, for emergencies, and now it was almost finished.

"What do you mean by taking the last bottle out of my cupboard?" I said. I was highly annoyed by his arbitrary behavior, which passed the bounds of pleasantry.

"Don't get excited," he said calmly and took another swig. "It's bad for your blood pressure. In an hour we'll have six bottles here. I've just rung up Hassan, Aly and Kamal and told them to report here with two bottles each. Out of that lot you'll be able to keep one bottle and put it in your larder for special emergencies. Now drink up the rest of this bottle, otherwise you'll see no more of it."

There was a knock at the door.

"Come in," I said, and a soldier from headquarters walked into the room.

"Orders from Sheik Hassan Salameh," he said. "You are to come at once to H.Q."

"What's the matter? Is he ill?" I asked in a routine voice.

"No."

At this Said pricked up his ears and said, "Then why did he send you here instead of telephoning?"

"I was ordered to bring the doctor at once. The Sheik said it was very urgent."

"There's something fishy about this," said Hassan in German. "Don't go. Wait here for a while."

I said to the soldier, "Tell the Sheik that I am busy now. I shall come later."

"But the Sheik said . . ."

"Can't you hear?" bawled Said at the man. "Go back and give your Sheik the doctor's message."

"More than fishy," he continued when the soldier had gone. Then he looked at me searchingly and said, "Now confess, like a good boy, what mischief you've been up to which your daddy doesn't know about."

Up to then, I had said nothing to my comrades about the part I had played in getting the prisoners released. But now I had to make a clean breast of it. Said listened attentively and whistled a few times through his teeth.

"Aha!" said he when I had finished. "It looks as if someone had been blabbing. And the old fox is now capable of really doing something. You see, it isn't merely that a handful of his personal enemies have been snatched away from under his nose, causing him to lose quite a few pounds of ransom money, but now the boys who have been freed will be out for his blood, and how!"

"I wonder who can have given me away?" I said. The Moslem Brotherhood had no interest, any more than the released prisoners themselves, in repaying my co-operation by chattering about it.

After a while Said said, "There are three possibilities. Either there is a spy of one of the other parties in the Moslem Brotherhood, or one of the secret opponents of the Sheik has told him the story out of pure malice in order to irritate him with the news that there are traitors in his corps of officers. Or, thirdly, the released prisoners have recounted the whole incident in detail to their numerous relatives. From them it would spread to friends and neighbors, and within two days several hundred people would know all about it. It would be a miracle if there were not a Judas among them."

"For good or ill, I shall have to go to him," said I, seriously worried. "If he thinks he knows the truth he is capable of sending the whole brigade here to pick me up."

"Yes, and then?" said my comrade with a contemptuous smile. "The hundred and fifty Yugoslavs certainly won't play ball with him. They would sooner come over to our side. The Egyptians and Iraqis will think twice before they do anything. And the others— bah!" He dismissed them with a gesture of contempt. "In any case, I'll tell Ahmed to come too." He took off the receiver, saying as he did so, "The others will be arriving any moment with the bottles, and then all six of us will be here."

Said had just finished talking to Ahmed, when a jeep drove into the courtyard. A Palestinian lieutenant and three soldiers got out, all carrying carbines. They came into the house and up the stairs. Said grasped his stick and hobbled to the door.

There was a knock and I said, "Come in." The four men came in, looking unsure of themselves, and halted hesitantly. The lieutenant cleared his throat and spoke, "I have instructions to bring you to H.Q., Salameh." He said this with every sign of embarrassment. He was obviously uncomfortable about his mission. "Well, what's all this fuss about?" I asked pointing to the three armed soldiers. "I have already sent word to say that I am still busy and will come later."

"But Sheik Hassan insists on your coming at once. . . . "

"Now listen to me, young man," said Said, as he walked right up to the officer, leaning on his stick and looking down from his great height at the four undersized Arabs. "If the doctor says he's coming later, then he will come later. Got it?"

The officer saluted and turned around. One of the three men followed him into the corridor. But the two others remained stubbornly where they stood, and glared at us angrily.

"Can't you hear, you sons of dogs? Get out, I told you." And his walking stick came down on the head of one of the tin soldiers. "Out you go! Out!" And each time he said "Out," he underlined his meaning with a blow with his stick. The soldiers gave way before the strength and fury of the Hun. "That's that!" said Said as he slammed the door behind the two men. "And now if my medicine doesn't come soon, I shall be really ill."

I watched the party who had been sent to arrest me climb into their jeep and drive away.

Soon the four Germans arrived, one after another, bringing the promised six bottles of brandy with them. "Here's your emergency reserve, you hoarder!" said Said, handing me one of the bottles.

While the drink was going around, Aly and I sat by the window to get an early view of the approach of the next cutting-out party.

We had some time to wait; in fact it took the Sheik two hours to organize a large-scale action.

When Said captured armored car Number 466, he had not reckoned that it would be employed to arrest me, but it seemed that since the Frontier Force's armored car had come and carried off the prisoners the Sheik had tumbled to the utility of such vehicles. Number 466 must have been patched up since the affair on the road, for here it came, followed by three trucks full of soldiers.

"Get out the machine-guns," called Said. Hassan and I pulled them out of the cupboard, loaded them and placed them on the window seat. Kamal dragged up the box of hand grenades, opened the lid, and placed it between us.

"Someone get me my tunic and belt," said Said quietly. While the cars were drawing up in the courtyard, Said, who was wearing nothing but a pair of underpants with a tear in the seat, and sandals, got into his tunic and buckled on his belt, with a pistol in the holster. If things hadn't been so damned serious, we should have burst with laughter looking at him.

The armored car stood immediately under the window. The soldiers jumped out of the trucks and stood around. They seemed unwilling to obey the orders of their officer, who was trying to get them into some sort of battle order. Finally, he gave it up and let them stand where they were. Then he advanced to the door of the house.

Nothing could be serious enough to wipe the grin off Said's face. He stepped onto the balcony and looked round the scene with an impudent smile.

"Attention!" he thundered. The soldiers stiffened at the order and looked upward at the blond giant. Even the officer forgot that he wanted to go into the house.

"If any of you moves, we'll shoot him to pieces so that his own mother wouldn't recognize him." He took a deep breath, swelling out his chest, and stood with his clenched fists on his hips. "Is that understood? Very good. Now I've got something else to say to you. If you sheep were now manning your posts at the front, the war would be half won. But you're not soldiers at all. You're just a thieving mob. The Mufti sent us here to help you, but instead of being grateful to us for helping to win your war, which as a matter of fact doesn't interest us worth a damn, you come along here and want to arrest the doctor. All this time you might have been learning a whole lot of useful things, but you're so conceited that you won't listen to what you're told."

He made a studied pause to let his words sink in. "Now then! Go back home and tell your little brigand chief that the doctor will come when it suits him and not when he is ordered to. Dismiss!"

And so it was. They climbed silently into the cars and drove away.

"Well done," said Hassan gratefully. "That was a proper rocket."

"Don't go shooting your mouth off, but open the last two bottles," and Said let himself down into a chair with a groan.

The effect of the alcohol was to rouse me to such a pitch of anger that I didn't care what I did, and as the cork was pushed into the last bottle, I said, "I'd sooner go now to H.Q. and ask that bastard what he wants me for."

"Why not?" said Said drily. "I'll come with you."

As his doctor, I ought long ago to have sent him to bed, but as his comrade, I nodded gratefully.

Said looked around at the others.

"What about you, Hassan?"

Hassan nodded assent.

"Three are enough," decided Said, and hobbled into his room to clothe his lower half.

Meanwhile I got the jeep ready. We buckled our pistols on and hung machine pistols over our shoulders, and Hassan provided for emergencies by stowing a couple of grenades into his trouser pockets.

When we reached headquarters, we didn't give the Sheik any time to think over his next move. We pushed past the sentinel at his door and marched into his room without knocking.

Three pairs of eyes looked at us with an expression of surprise mixed with annoyance. Our commander, dressed in a galabia, was lying barefoot on his bed smoking a narghile. By him on chairs sat a couple of gloomy Bedouin sheiks, who were doubtless discussing an awkward deal with him.

"You wanted to speak to me, Hassan," I said, as I came and stood, in a challenging attitude, close behind the bed.

"But my dear Salameh, the matter was really not so urgent as all that. And you needn't have brought a bodyguard with you." The bulky creature then pulled himself up, got out of bed, and shook hands with each of us, as if we were good old friends whom he hadn't seen for a long time.

I repeated: "You wanted to speak to me."

"Come, come. How can you be so impatient? You must not deprive me of the pleasure of seeing my dear German friends under my roof. I am not going to neglect my duties as a host for a bagatelle like this."

He rang for coffee and asked us how we were, what news we had from home, how Said's wound was progressing, how things were at the front and in the hospital.

"And for what reason. . . " I persisted obstinately, bored by his play acting.

"Oh, yes. A mere trifle. Of course I know it's all nonsense, but there is so much malicious gossip among ill-natured people who wish to undermine our mutual confidence, and thereby to shatter our glorious Arab unity."

He laid his fat flipper confidentially on my knee and looked at me keenly out of his small, watery, blue eyes.

"I'll tell you," he continued with a sigh. "Some one has reported that you had something to do with the release of the criminals. As I told you, I never believed a word of it. It's of course absurd, ridiculous. I asked myself, how could you be mixed up in such a business? What good could it do you to betray your Sheik who takes care of you like your own father. Haven't I always done this, my friends?" He looked around for confirmation at the two Bedouins, who agreed with eloquent gestures.

"How did you come to hear such a statement?" I asked, wishing to find out if he had any precise information or had just been listening to rumors.

"Someone saw you in the darkness going into the house of the Moslem Brotherhood, who were responsible for the cowardly attack on me." He put his head on one side and fixed his fat-cushioned eyes on me, as he waited for my answer.

I was not going to tell the truth to this arch liar.

"As you know, my dear Hassan," I said, suiting my tone to his, "I was engaged by the Moslem Brotherhood in Cairo to join in your struggle for freedom. Some of the members of the Cairo Center commissioned me to give messages of greeting to the Brothers in Jaffa and I carried out my mission."

This explanation was palpably and transparently false, but, sticking to the rules of Oriental intercourse, which allows every lie to pass unchallenged—if it saves face or does no harm—the Sheik accepted it with a sigh of relief.

"You see, my friends. Didn't I tell you that my friend Salameh would immediately clear up the misunderstanding. By Allah and the Prophet, I never believed a word of the story—not a word, my dear Salameh."

Chapter XIX

FLIGHT FROM JAFFA

THINGS happened as they were bound to happen under such leadership.

By the end of April, the Jaffa front was completely disintegrated. The town was almost deserted. Less than a tenth of the 80,000 inhabitants remained in their homes, and even this remnant was trying by all possible means to get out of the town. Fear of their own bullying and cruel compatriots spurred them to leave home and property, not less than the imminent occupation of the town by the Jewish besiegers. Moreover bandits, more dangerous than any occupying force, were roaming through the town singly and in groups robbing and murdering.

The helplessness, disunity and jealousy of the Arab leaders had been cleverly exploited by the Jews amid the general disorder. The latter had systematically occupied and fortified the whole of the hinterland of Jaffa. Now they were pressing forward southward into the town. A singular feature of this half-war assisted the spies of the other side to collect and transmit information quickly and safely. During all this period the telephone system was functioning throughout the whole of Palestine, under the control of the Mandatory Power. There was no difficulty whatsoever about carrying on a conversation between Tel Aviv and Jaffa. For weeks the fire-power of the Jewish forces had been continuously increasing. They had a notable superiority in machine guns, and their heavy mortars, with which they bombarded Jaffa sometimes for hours together, had a demoralizing effect.

To counter them, rocket batteries had been installed on our side. "Give a German a tin box and he will make a cannon out of it" was a catchword in France after the First World War, when there was a move to demolish the whole of German industry. Our Lieutenant

Kamal, who in civil life had been a chemist with a firm that manufactured explosives—and had been mentally disturbed by the loss
of his family in Vienna—had, on his own initiative, organized a
sort of witches' kitchen. With the help of a few Arab workmen, he
made rockets out of old German flak shells propelled by explosives prepared by himself. For a time he made effective use of
these against Tel Aviv, but when his stock of shells and chemicals
was exhausted our schizophrenic genius could manufacture no
more rockets.

Apart from the bandits, there were hardly any men in Jaffa
capable of bearing arms. Before they withdrew, the British police
administration had armed the eighty Arab town policemen with
automatic rifles. This would have meant a badly needed reinforce-
ment for the disintegrating brigade, if the newly armed policemen
and their weapons had not immediately vanished.

Late as it was, an attempt was made to check the flow of deserters and fugitives, by forbidding the population to leave Jaffa. Exceptions were permitted only in urgent cases and had to be authorized by the Higher Arab Committee. In itself, this was a workable
measure, as there was only a single road leading out of the town,
which could easily have been controlled. But the stream of fugitives continued to flow. Some members of the Committee sold
passes, the price of which was assessed according to the means of
the applicant, and sometimes reached two hundred pounds. And
people without passes often got through the guards at the control
station by paying much smaller sums.

It was clear that the depopulated and demoralized town must
soon be overrun by the Jews.

We Germans, who met almost daily in my room in the hospital,
found ourselves in a very precarious situation. As representatives of
law and order, we could to some extent check the depredations of
the bandits and looters, which did not make us popular with them.
At the same time, we felt that we were hated by the embittered
citizens because we could not save their town. If we managed to
survive the final chaos, we could look forward to no prospect or
future but captivity.

The Arabs themselves no longer showed any keenness to fight

for their country. Sheik Hassan had removed himself out of the devil's caldron to Ramle, and from there exhorted us by telephone to stand firm. There was no longer any reason for us not to think of our own skins. We devised many plans for escape, but they were all turned down as too risky. Once we thought of grabbing the armored car and driving through the road controls. A more fantastic suggestion was that we should get hold of a sailing boat and head for the coast of Asia Minor.

One morning, I think it was the twenty-ninth of April, Said dashed into the hospital shouting, "I have it." Our calamitous situation had got us down so badly that he found me and Hassan engaged in drinking whiskey, though the hour was early.

"Well, what is it this time?"

"Listen, boys. There's a ship in the harbor."

Said was tremendously excited about the idea that had come to him and threw his machine pistol noisily on the table.

"And what have we to do with someone else's ship?" asked Hassan.

"We can get away on it."

Even a cool, sober intelligence like Said's became disordered, once hope was abandoned.

"Where is the boat going to?" I asked, just for the sake of saying something.

"Haven't a clue. But that doesn't matter. The point is that she's going away from this hell-broth."

Said had already picked up the telephone and was giving the news to the two other Germans. He wouldn't listen to any arguments or take no for an answer.

"Get cracking, boys." he said, "we meet in half an hour at the harbor."

We had to try, whether we succeeded or failed. I went to my cupboard and got out my soap and toothbrush. My two good suits —no. And my new underwear and my few other belongings—they must all be left behind. Once more, nothing but soap and a toothbrush and the clothes on my back. "My dear fellow, do you mean to say you are leaving the medicine behind?" said Said excitedly as I closed the cupboard door. He took the remaining three bottles of what he called "the medicine" and stuck one of them in his trouser pocket.

"Here, you take one," said he and forced a bottle on Hassan, who had more room in his pockets than we had.

"And now helmets off for prayer."

You could count on Said always to be himself. He drove the cork into the neck of the bottle, which we passed round till we had emptied it. When we had done, Said smashed the bottle against the wall. I thought of our New Year's Eve party.

"To our exodus from the Holy Land."

The road to the harbor took us by shell-torn and burned-out houses, pillaged shops and overturned cars. As we walked together in a bunch, we came upon the dead body of a mule lying in a narrow lane, its belly inflated with gas like a balloon. For once, we Germans did not rage against the countless flies feeding on the carrion, across which we had to step and which no one had thought of removing. Suddenly we heard a deep, hollow booming overhead. "Cover," growled Said and pushed me against the wall of the nearest house. A second later, a mortar bomb crashed into a house ten yards ahead of us. The walls opened outward like a breathing lung and then collapsed. A yellow-gray cloud filled the lane and through the dust and smoke we heard loud shrieks.

"Come on, forward," said Said, driving us through the cloud of dust till we could no longer hear the cries behind us.

Another mortar bomb fell just in front of us. It was as if the enemy meant to prevent us from getting to the port.

"Damnation!" cursed Said. "We must go by another street. They've got the range exactly, and every shot falls about thirty yards short of the last one."

Said knew what he was talking about. We had only just gotten back to the house which the first shell had struck, when the third shell crashed down about a hundred yards down the street. The mortar was clearly ranged onto this area and the gunners tilted it up a little after each shot.

Our detour was worth while. We reached the harbor a little later, but undamaged; there we found our two other comrades waiting for us. One of them pointed a finger toward the vessel we were making for, and his gesture revealed a hopeless situation. The ship—a two-masted sailing vessel with an auxiliary motor and flying no flag—lay at anchor some five hundred yards from the quay, but her decks were so thronged with refugees that there clearly was not room for any more passengers.

"We shan't be able to get away on her," said Hassan in deep disappointment. One of our two companions who had been running around, looking and listening, had learned that the Committee had closed the access to the harbor half an hour before we arrived, in order to prevent more people from running away.

We stood about, thoroughly disheartened, all except Said, who still held his head up confidently.

"Well, let's be going down," he said and started for the port gates.

We looked at him as he strode off. When he had gone twenty yards, he stopped and looked round.

"Aren't you coming?" he asked.

"Would you perhaps have the goodness to tell us where you propose to take us?" I said, bursting with irritation, which always had the effect of making me use very formal language.

"Onto the ship, of course," called Said, just as if he were simply going for a bath.

"No doubt you propose to knock out the sentries and blow down the gate with a grenade, what?"

"Not quite," drawled Said with a grin. "We are just going to play at being military policemen. Does that suit you, my hearties?"

As, in fact, we were ready to follow him wherever his impudent resourcefulness led him, we marched off at a brisk pace toward the gate.

"Why don't you open?" blustered Said.

"We have orders. . . ."

"So have we. Our orders are to search the ship for deserters."

The guards looked at one another helplessly, each trying to place the responsibility on one of the others.

"Come along! Hurry up! Or shall I have to open the gate myself?"

When he had to, Said could roar like a bull. And what he said

and did carried such conviction that even we were almost persuaded to believe that we were there on an important mission.
The door swung open and we marched onto the quay.

Here we found a rowing boat on a chain. Said wasted no time:
he shot the lock off. Then we all climbed into the little craft, which,
not being designed for so many passengers, subsided unpleasantly
low in the water. Said and Aly, who was a sailor by trade, each took
an oar and we started on our course.

"What if the skipper panics when he sees us, and sails off!"
whispered Kamal excitedly.

It wasn't likely, but it was conceivable. We had to hurry. With
the experienced Aly on one side and Said, who knew nothing about
rowing, on the other, our boat kept slewing over to the right; and
Said, who tried to rectify the difference in skill by the force of his
muscles, managed to break an oar, so he pulled out one of the
seats and paddled furiously with it.

We had now come so near the ship that if the skipper took it
into his head to move off, we could compel him with our machine
pistols to wait till we got alongside.

At last we struck against the side of the vessel and climbed up a
rope ladder onto the deck, leaving our boat, for which we had no
more use, to drift away.

"What do you want here?" said a gray-haired man, barring
our way.

"Are you the owner?" asked Said.

"Why do you ask?" The man, who was wearing an oil-stained
vest, which hung over his waistband, looked at him with a hostile
and distrustful expression.

"That depends," said Said, as he rubbed his forefinger against
his thumb in an universally familiar gesture.

The man understood.

"You want a passage?"

We nodded.

"Where are you sailing to?" I asked.

"Beirut. That will cost you thirty pounds a head."

We had money and thirty pounds was not too high a price for

carrying us to safety. But when all was said and done, we had to have something to live on when we arrived, and it was not likely that the skipper would be prepared to come down.

Said offered him a better currency.

"What do you say to half a dozen machine pistols?"

"Come into my cabin," said the man with the oily vest and pushed a way for us through the crowd.

As far as we were concerned, our machine pistols had lost their value and importance once we had left Jaffa. But for the skipper they represented a brilliant bargain, being worth perhaps five times as much as the cost of the fare. He hoped, no doubt, in the privacy of the cabin to diddle us out of a few of the other objects with which our pockets were bulging. We were quite prepared to trade the hand grenades: he could have them, but he got a sharp setback when he tried to get our whiskey as well.

The cabin was small, and we sat in cramped discomfort on a wooden bench. However, our freedom of movement was not so hampered as to prevent us from passing the bottle around and drinking to the success of our voyage. The skipper left and soon we heard the diesel throbbing. Our vessel moved slowly toward the open sea.

We went up the companionway and pressed against the rail. All around people were standing in a dense mass. Poor devils, they were gazing, perhaps for the last time, at their home town, and had each paid a small fortune to get away. Children were screaming, without understanding what was happening to them. Women sobbed, and as the ship carried them farther and farther from land, broke out into wild lamentations. Men, too, were not ashamed to shed tears, when they began to realize that it might be a last farewell.

For us this was no occasion for shedding tears, but we remained silent as we looked back at the town. The droning of mortar bombs became gradually fainter, and the white houses smaller and smaller till the town seemed a distant blur swimming in the midday sunlight out of which the spiky steeple of the Nesher Brewery pointed upward, looking higher than the reality.

What we had to expect was certainly not freedom. After all we had gone through, it was a question whether we still had the grace to feel perfectly free—even if we achieved freedom.

Our ship, overburdened with passengers, ploughed her way slowly northward for a day and a night. On the afternoon of the next day we came to land, but not in Beirut as promised and paid for. Instead, we were landed in boats at the biblical city of Tyre in the south of Lebanon. No one insisted on traveling farther. The skipper's idea was to get rid of his pitiful cargo as soon as possible, and to return at once to the beleaguered city of Jaffa, where he might hope to embark another shipload of frightened and richly paying passengers. We had nothing to complain of. We were completely indifferent as to where we landed.

from Egon E. Schleinitz

". . . a police patrol had
found the dead body of an
unknown man at a water-
hole. . . . ."

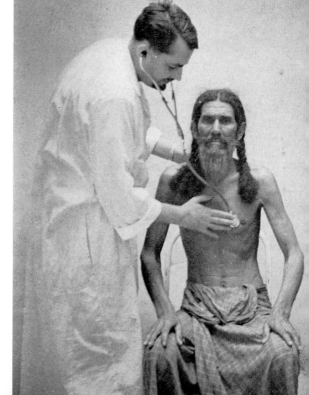

Dr. Pritzke with the slave
dealer of the Tribe of Beni
Hajjar from whose knee he
extracted a bullet fifteen
years old ⟫⟫⟫⟫

الاسم: الدكتور سليم كابلان ساكم

محل الولادة: بابنا طـر سعيد

التاريخ : ١٩٥٨/٥/١٤

مدة الصلاحية لغاية: ١٩٥٨/٥/١٨

A page from the author's Lebanese
identity card

Dr. Pritzke with his son Wolf-
Dietrich at Beirut

Photos from Egon E. Schleinitz

Dr. Pritzke's new practice at Beirut: "In my waiting room sit Bedouins in flowing robes . . . Sometimes I find among my patients one of my friends from Saudi Arabia . . . or a bravo from the hills, who leans his rifle against my instrument cupboard before stripping to be examined."

Photo from Ullstein Verlag

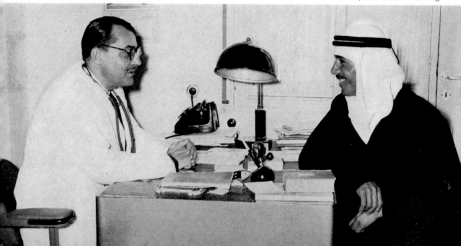

Chapter XX

BACK TO THE DESERT

WE six non-Arabs, who possessed no travel documents, were, as we might have expected, invited to enjoy the hospitality of the police at their headquarters as soon as we landed. It is fair to say that we were not put in prison, but interned in an empty summer villa. However, a police guard at the door saw to it that we did not leave our hospitable refuge.

Next morning a police officer came and took down particulars relating to our persons and our military services—how often had we gone through these formalities!—but our precautionary detention in fact implied only a conditional loss of freedom. The officer informed us that as members of the Mufti's army, we had to report at his headquarters which had, in the meanwhile, been transferred from Cairo to Damascus.

However, when we learned that our glorious leader, Hassan Salameh, was here, we begged the officer to lead us to him, before we set out for Damascus.

Our meeting at the police headquarters was short but dramatic.

"What are you doing here?" snorted the fat man as soon as he had got over his surprise at seeing us. "Why aren't you at the front at Jaffa?"

"And what are *you* doing here?" we replied impudently.

An experienced crook like Hassan was able to recover almost instantaneously from his first moment of fear and was ready with a very plausible answer.

"I am here for an important conference."

Said grinned and said, "And we have found a site for 200 machine guns and have come here to get the guns."

Hassan pretended to believe this grotesque fiction and said,

"But one would have been enough to come and make the arrangements. Why have you all come?"

"I can only carry thirty-five machine guns at a time," said Said mockingly. "The others must take their share of the rest."

The fat man then perceived that he was being made a fool of.

"I'll close your insolent mouth for you," he bellowed at Said. "You are a pack of deserters, traitors and cowards . . ." He would have continued in this strain as he possessed a rich store of invectives, but in his rage he swallowed the wrong way and had a coughing fit.

"Listen to me, you fat pig," said Said, white with anger, as he walked a step nearer to Hassan. "You know very well—better than we do—which of us here is a traitor and a coward." He had raised his voice so that it must have been heard all through the house. "You are a low, common bandit, you son of a whore and sixty fathers!"

Hassan felt for his pistol, but couldn't make up his mind to use it. Then he turned on his heel and left the room. We were never to see him again.

In the afternoon of the same day we drove to Damascus.

The Eminence Grise of the Orient received us immediately after our arrival at his headquarters and questioned us about our experiences and impressions of the front.

Said told him the truth, holding nothing back.

He gave the Mufti a frank account of the untenable conditions in Sheik Hassan Salameh's command, and described the Sheik's despotic behavior and his misuse of his position to feather his nest financially.

It seemed that the Mufti knew nothing of all this. The fat Sheik must have found a way to keep all information disadvantageous to himself from the ears of the Mufti. These revelations roused the Mufti to a pitch of fury, and he insisted that we should submit a written report embodying our verbal statements.

Not long afterward, Hassan Salameh fell during an engagement in Palestine, killed by machine-gun fire in the back. It has never been known whether this upstart was killed by the enemy or executed by his own men.

Meantime, fresh decisions were taken regarding our future. On the whole everyone was satisfied, though there was never any question of releasing us to go home. We were detailed to new commands. Said, Hassan, Aly and Ahmed all insisted on returning to the front, although the Mufti offered each of them a job on the lines of communication. Only Kamal, the chemist, and I preferred to remain in the Lebanon. Kamal occupied himself thenceforward in making mines and Molotov cocktails in a little village in the mountains, while I was transferred to Military Hospital No. 3 in Beirut.

This international metropolis of the Middle East—in which Arabs, Druses, Kurds, Turks and Westerners of all nationalities live peaceably together in a region once famous for Phoenician culture—has now a special economic significance as a free port and a free market for gold and currency. Like Hong Kong and Tangier, it is a central exchange for the transaction of all kinds of important international business both legitimate and otherwise.

I slowly came under the spell of this fascinatingly beautiful city, which affected me all the more, perhaps, because for the first time for years I was now a respected citizen without fear of arrest or attack, living a normal life among my fellow townsmen. I soon got to know my way about and fitted into the easygoing, unregimented life of the Lebanese and, needless to say, I never tired of the improbably beautiful landscape.

During my years of captivity, I had seen neither the mountains nor the sea; and now, here I was, transferred by military order to a sort of Garden of Eden, one of the beauty spots that attracted visitors from all parts of the world and provided a fascinating background for the romance of the Orient. The beauty of the well-watered and fruitful landscape is so overwhelming that even the austere Arabs in the early days of the Islamic invasions were constrained to disobey the Prophet's injunction to abstain from copying the likeness of living things—strictly applicable to plants as well as animals—with the result that flowers, trees and rivers soon formed part of normal ornamentation in Moslem art.

Nevertheless, in spite of these newly won joys, my life was not spent dreaming in the sunlight. My service in the hospital lasted from the summer of 1948 to the summer of 1949. On May 15, 1948, the armies of the Arab League invaded Palestine, and many sick and wounded persons were evacuated from the confused theater of war and sent to us for treatment. Hostilities did not finally cease till the summer of 1949, but before then I had already begun to take an active part in dealing with the endless stream of refugees, numbering 700,000, homeless, penniless and uncared for, housed in improvised camps with tents for shelter. I had been spared the German version of this terrible tragedy in 1945, but now my days were devoted to the relief of this accumulation of human suffering.

An impersonal mass of humanity passed through our hands. We doctors were like factory workers on conveyer belts, with no time for personal contacts with the sick, debilitated and aged persons who passed through our hands. The preventive measures we had to take—in order to avoid epidemics—made us into sanitary policemen, and the pressure of our routine duties left us no leisure to treat our patients as other than impersonal cases.

It gave me a shock to think that I, in the middle of this Garden of Eden, was beginning to long for life in the desert, as for a lost paradise. I remembered that there I had lived the contemplative life of a village doctor among individualistic Bedouins; interrupted, no doubt, by occasional disturbances but still a personal, individual life.

I reproached myself with ingratitude at finding life in a civilized milieu so uncongenial, but desert life had unfitted me for many things. For instance, after I had been sitting for a long time on a chair my legs went to sleep, because I had gotten accustomed to squatting on my heels. My colleagues and acquaintances used to laugh at me for choosing my seat in a restaurant or café in a place where I could see the door and for staring suspiciously at everyone who came in by it. Without the familiar weight of a pistol in my pocket, I felt only half dressed; while the pressure of collar and tie, which every decent man had to wear in Beirut, used to make me feel ill.

An Arab proverb says, "Only in the desert is a man really free." One day I received an invitation from the Saudi Arabian government to take charge of a hospital belonging to the Health Office at Hofuf. I jumped at it in my eagerness to exchange the vortex of civilization for the freedom of the wilderness.

I had forgotten that I had slipped through the barbed wire of my prison camp, out of impatience to return to my home in Berlin. Anyhow, I deferred my hopes as I looked out of my airplane on this new world of mine.

A two-engined plane carried me to Jidda, the Saudi-Arabian port on the Red Sea. Here I transferred to another machine and flew to Riyadh, the capital of the great desert state, whose area equals that of half the continent of Europe. My third stage carried me eastward to Hofuf.

The distance covered on my long journey was not so much to be estimated by the great stretches of blue sea and yellow sand over which we flew, as by the variety of my fellow travelers. Very few Saudi Arabians emplaned at Beirut, and most of the passengers were European and Levantine businessmen on their way to Jidda. They were a lively crowd, talking business most of the time. From Jidda to the capital, which no foreigner is permitted to visit without a personal invitation from the King or by very special authorization, half of the passengers were Arabians and the rest American oil experts on their way to the east coast. On the third lap of my journey, my only companions were a couple of local inhabitants, who slept the whole time. The empty space in the plane was filled with crates, bales and sacks. No American, European or Levantine would want to travel to Hofuf, from which there were no communications by road or rail with any civilized region.

In front of the new airport buildings, I found a Cadillac waiting for me. The driver was a dark-skinned Arab in a blue galabia, with a revolver in his well-filled cartridge belt.

"Are you the doctor?" he asked.

I nodded. He said no more, but started up the engine and drove me through one of the four towered gateways to my destination, the Health Office of Hofuf. This was a new, whitewashed building with a flat roof, like all the houses here, and a courtyard surrounded by arcades for protection against the summer sun and the winter rains.

The Director of the Office was a Syrian named Dr. Fuad, a small, dried-up man with an unhealthy, yellow complexion. When I had introduced myself, he informed me that the Emir wished to see me at eleven o'clock.

"At eleven?" I said, looking at my watch, and observing that it wanted only five minutes to that hour. "How are we to manage that?" I asked anxiously.

"Oh, of course," he said with the superiority of an old hand, "you don't yet know how the people here reckon the time. Our reckoning is based on the sunset. Every evening, when the sun goes down, you must set your watch at twelve o'clock. That means about 7 P.M. in summer and 5 P.M. in winter."

He gazed at me like a teacher, who is not quite sure whether his pupil has understood or not.

I nodded to show that I had.

"Well, by your watch it is now eleven o'clock, but the right time is"—he looked at his wristwatch—"ten minutes past six. Your audience with the Emir then is at eleven o'clock local time and ten minutes past five by your watch."

This system of timekeeping struck me as difficult, but not much use was made of it. Most appointments were made for an hour after sunrise, or immediately after the midday prayer, when the town gates were shut.

At precisely eleven o'clock, local time, I was ushered into the presence of the Emir. After the Syrian had presented me, the Emir, a heavily built man, with a coal-black, full beard which he had allower to grow to a monstrous length, looked at me as critically as if I had been a car he had just bought, whose productivity for all purposes he was estimating. Then he said, "Why are you not wearing a galabia like a reasonable man?"

I explained that I had only just arrived and had not had time to buy a local outfit, but he did not find my excuse acceptable.

"The fellow looks like a woman," he said censoriously. "Don't let me see you again without a beard." That was all he had to say about my duties in Hofuf. Then he dismissed me with an ungracious wave of the hand.

It looked as though I had not passed my test with distinction.

CHAPTER XXI

DOCTOR IN HOFUF

I STOWED away my suit and my shaving tackle, both now useless, at the bottom of my trunk, and treated myself to three galabias, a pair of sandals, some white silk headcloths and an agal.

After I had spent my first night in Hofuf on the roof of the Health Office, for there was no hotel in the town, I had to occupy myself next day in looking for a house to live in, which was as necessary to me as suitable clothes.

The dispenser at the Health Office, a Lebanese from Tripoli, offered to put his local experience at my disposal. The first steps in my education were not too easy. Directly in front of the Health Office was the market place, which during the forenoon teemed with dealers, customers and loafers. Special types of shops were allotted, as in the time of the mediaeval guilds, to special streets or portions of streets. Here you had the carpet dealers, and beyond them the booths of the fruiterers and greengrocers. Then came the money changers, tailors and dealers in arms, while in the spaces between the different pitches were chaffering hawkers with trays full of knickknacks. The temperature was about 98 degrees, but this in no way subdued the activity of the busy crowds. "That is a Sunni woman," explained my companion, as a thickly veiled figure walked by us. From under her woolen cloak protruded a train, trailing dust, straw and thornbush twigs behind her. My guide told me that among these people no woman with less than two and a quarter yards of stuff in her skirt to trail through the dust would be accounted as anything but a pauper—or else the wife of a miser.

"You have to worry about the fashion even in the desert. Only the fashion in shoes is uniform," I said, pointing to the bare feet of a Shirte woman, whose calf-length skirt exposed her barefootedness more clearly than the longer dresses of other women. It was explained to me that it was considered a sin for women to wear shoes. There were, too, other taboos for women, such as carrying fowls or buying eggs and milk.

A dark-skinned Arab was standing in front of a hawker and bargaining with him about the price of a flashlight. His wide sleeves hung down over his bent elbow almost to the ground.

"That's a Bedouin from Oman," said my guide. Instead of advertisements in the newspapers there was a town crier whose ambition was to outshout all the buyers and sellers in the market place. "A goat to sell! Sueylim el Keyashi has a goat to sell! Someone has lost a blue belt! A young girl slave for sale!"

"Have you got that here too?" I asked when I heard the unusual offer.

"Oh, yes. But, look, over there is a man whose acquaintance you had better not make." My companion pointed to a robust man clad in blue, who carried a long curved scimitar suspended on a leather strap from his shoulder. "That's one of the Emir's personal slaves— the Executioner."

The man walked up to a booth and looked appraisingly at a silk headcloth. The dealer stood by him in a submissive attitude praising the article inordinately.

"How much do you want for it?" asked the black man.

"Only twenty-five riyals, as you are a friend."

"Cut my head off, would you!" said the executioner and turned on his heel.

"Do not go away! Don't make me unhappy," said the trader, beginning to yammer, as he caught hold of his customer's sleeve. "If you find the price too high, do me a favor and accept it as a present."

The black man graciously nodded assent, put the kaffiyeh in his pocket and moved away.

I was quite ready to accept my companion's friendly advice not to cultivate the acquaintance of this individual. But half a year had not passed before Yehya, the Emir's Executioner, came one night to fetch me from my house.

It was not long before I had accustomed myself to living and working in Hofuf.

Relying on the advice of the dispenser, I found a suitable house, which I rented at a reasonable price. It was a single-storyed building, long, but not precisely spacious, containing two good-sized rooms, one of which I used for my consultations and the other as a living room. I did not need a bedroom, for I slept on the roof, which was surrounded by a low parapet. During the cooler season, when it sometimes rained, I slept in a small, isolated building, connected with my house by an open-air passage, which had formerly been the women's quarters. The whole modest complex of buildings was enclosed by a high wall, as was every house and farm in Hofuf. I had entered the town through a gate in the city wall, which carried a number of towers for purposes of defense. The *kut*, or inner city, was likewise enclosed by a wall. Within it was the palace where the Emir lived with his family, as well as the great mosque, the barracks with the garrison of 400 men, and the other buildings belonging to the administration. Every evening at nine o'clock, the great gates of the inner city were closed and could only be opened by special order of the Emir.

The first time that I passed through this wall into the inner city it was long after midnight. I had as my companion the public executioner. I had now been six months in the service of the state and was confident that I had performed my duties satisfactorily.

This is what happened. A loud knock on my house door roused me from my slumbers. Dazed with sleep, I went down to open the door where I found Yehya, the executioner, leaning lazily on his great curved sword in its leather scabbard.

He said, "The Emir wants to speak to you at once." I flung on my clothes and set out with the black man. I had a sinking feeling caused by the rough manner in which I had been summoned by the executioner, who marched silently at my side lighting our way with the narrow beam of his flashlight, which every now and then lit up the eyes of one of the great, gray dogs that roamed about the city.

My sinister companion did not take me through one of the main gates leading into the inner city. He stopped and knocked at a low side door, which was immediately opened. We had to bend almost double to get in, as the door was not four feet high. Then we found ourselves in an arched corridor, at the end of which we came to a circular stairway with deeply worn steps. Here a veiled slave lighted us up the tumbled-down stairs with a stable lantern till we reached the flat roof of the palace. Crossing it, we descended a flight of wooden steps which led into the upper story of the Emir's dwelling.

The fluttering in my stomach got worse as the black man led me up to a high double door. Supposing it was a court of judgment—with the judge sitting so late in the night—what could they want me for? Had I violated one of their many taboos unbeknownst to myself?

I remembered that a few days back, I had been treating a concubine belonging to a relative of the Emir and that I had made a remark to her which might well have got me into a bed of nettles. The woman had a thickish skin, which the needle did not penetrate at the first attempt. "You have a skin like a crocodile," I said jokingly and the lady had gone off in a huff.

But even if I had offended seriously against the local code of manners, that would hardly have justified them in summoning me from my house in the dead of night, with the public executioner for their messenger. People in Europe would be inclined to laugh at my misgivings, but anyone knowing the conditions of life in Saudi Arabia will realize that the arbitrary powers of tribal chiefs and rulers in that country render possible any act of capricious tyranny.

An armed sentry in a blue galabia opened one of the wings of the high double door. I walked into a large hall followed by the executioner. At the far end was a kind of dais covered with valuable carpets, skins and cushions, in the middle of which the Emir Saud Ibn Abdallah Ibn Jilawi was sitting. His feet were bare, and he wore a white galabia and a headcloth without an agal. He was reading a newspaper.

My companion bowed before his master and in a quiet voice announced, "The German doctor."

I laid my right hand on my breast in greeting and remained standing before the Emir.

The Emir made a couple of movements with his hand. The first was a gesture with his fingers as if he were brushing crumbs from a table. That was a sign to the executioner to remove himself. I could not quite suppress a sigh of relief when I saw the man walk away with his sword sloped over his shoulder. Then, turning the palms of his hands outward, he made a downward motion, inviting me to sit down.

I squatted on my heels on the steps to the dais and waited to see what would happen.

Nothing happened.

During the whole casual ceremony of introduction and greeting, the Emir had not once looked up from his newspaper. He went on reading, occasionally turning over a sheet with a rustling sound or brushing away the swarm of flying insects that had been attracted by the light. Otherwise nothing whatever happened. I gradually became persuaded that my head was not in danger, whatever the motive for this nocturnal summons may have been. In my relief, I began to look round me, slightly bored, and made an ocular inventory of everything in this great, bare room, counting the cracks in the walls and scanning the patterns of the carpets.

But I was not so pleasantly impressed by the presence of the two bodyguards, black slaves, crouching against the wall behind the Emir in a singular posture. Each was sitting on one heel with the other leg extended, prepared for a sudden spring. Their automatics were tucked between their thighs, and their eyes were mostly fixed on me with an expression of curiosity and suspicion. A third bodyguard stood by the great door.

The Emir rustled his paper once more, as he turned over a sheet. Then he said quietly, "*Qahwa!*"

"*Qahwa!*" echoed one of the guards behind him. The guard by the door opened it and called "*Qahwa*" into the corridor. The word was echoed by the sentry outside, and again by a distant voice.

About half a minute after the first "*Qahwa*" there appeared a small Negro boy carrying a long-spouted copper vessel. The boy took a small, handleless cup from a bag which he carried slung round his neck and poured coffee into it in a practiced curve. Then he stood waiting in silence, with the coffeepot in one hand and the cup in the other. He had to wait for five minutes, till the Emir, still reading his paper, put out his hand with thumb and forefinger spread out toward the boy. The little fellow carefully placed the cup in the hand of his master, who retired once more behind his newspaper. I heard a sip. Then the Emir, whose head was now half visible, nodded in my direction and the boy poured me out a cup of coffee.

A silence followed. The boy went out. The Emir went on reading. And I waited.

A huge cockroach moved lazily across the carpet with flickering antennae, passing close by the Emir's foot. It stopped for a moment, as if to see whether there was anything of value in this big toe, but when its feelers had given it to understand that this obstacle was a piece of living flesh, it ran forward in alarm, for a short distance, before resuming its quiet, lazy gait. But now the two guards had seen it and seemed right glad of this small diversion, which the appearance of a brown insect had brought to relieve the boredom of their watch. Carefully, without switching his eyes from the Emir's back, one of them drew his dagger from its silver-studded sheath and began to drive the cockroach hither and thither with the point. His companion, with a grin on his face, watched the beast trying to escape.

Their little game was interrupted by the voice of the Emir from behind his journal.

"How is your health?" he said to me.

The guards drew nearer to one another, and the cockroach seized the opportunity to get away.

"I am well, praise to God," I answered, "and how is Your Highness?"

"*Elhamdulillah!*" said the Emir nodding graciously. Then he folded his paper and looked at me for the first time.

"I have heard good things of you," he said. "The sick are satisfied with you."

"I am happy that my service is appreciated," I replied.

The Emir looked at me for a moment searchingly.

"Tell me now," he said, "do you think the Americans or the English are better?"

"The Americans," I said, without thinking. I had been too long in English camps and had never been a prisoner of the Americans.

"That is also my opinion," said the black-bearded man, pleased with my answer.

"The Americans fetch oil out of the earth and we receive half the profits. But the English first send missionaries to convert the people to their faith, and then traders and advisers to control the country's economy, and last come the soldiers to occupy the land."

I nodded. It was not clear to me what he was getting at.

"You were a soldier, weren't you?" asked the Emir.

When I said I had been one, he wanted to know what my opinion was of British, American and Russian soldiers. Like a ropedancer, I had to walk gingerly to avoid the dangers of this conversation, and I did my best to make my answers conform to what I surmised were the views of the Emir. I gathered that he did not like the Russians, because they denied the existence of God and opposed the God-given institution of slavery, and that he regarded the English with hatred born of fear.

I calculated that this preliminary conversation was merely by way of introduction to the real subject which had caused the Emir to send for me so late at night. But as a matter of fact, the Emir talked of nothing but politics and kindred subjects, and that in a very casual and desultory manner. Our talk lasted for about half an hour, and then he dismissed me—and picked up his newspaper again.

One of the bodyguard accompanied me as far as the little gate in the wall through which I had entered the palace. As neither the executioner nor any other person was detailed to see me home, I had to grope my way back through the darkness.

I was now left to myself and at the mercy of the pariah dogs, as big as wolves, that slept all day on the housetops around the market place and spent the night scavenging among the offal and refuse thrown out into the streets. They sidled up, noiseless and surly, and my fear of these nocturnal companions was by no means unjustified. As I could not find a stone or anything else to throw, I threw one of my slippers at them and missed. My second shot, with the other slipper, was more successful, and the pack retired to a safe distance. However, I had to reckon that they soon would be after me again. I took to my heels and ran off at full speed, but I hadn't covered 200 yards before the dogs were just behind me. Weaponless as I was, I now planted myself with my back to a wall and waited for the brutes to attack.

"Who is there?" said a voice suddenly out of the darkness. The ray of a flashlight began to look for me.

"Here I am, my friend."

The flashlight was aimed at the direction of my voice, and then I heard powerful blows of a stick on the backs of the dogs, who ran yowling away.

"What are you doing here at this time of night?" asked the man with the flashlight, who had suddenly turned up to deliver me.

"I am the German doctor. I was sent for by the palace."

With a long-barreled gun slung over his shoulder and a cudgel in his right hand, the night watchman came up to me and bent forward, aiming his flashlight at my face to assure himself that I was really the man I claimed to be.

"But you ought to carry a light," he said reproachfully. "You know that it is forbidden to walk in the streets at night without a light."

I belonged to the small privileged class of persons who could be expected to have business at night and who, therefore, were entitled to be in the streets after the evening prayer. But even doctors, government officials, the Emir's body servants or citizens engaged in particular jobs were supposed to carry lights by night to disclose their identity.

Ibn Saud had formerly captured both Riyadh and Hofuf by a *coup de main*. He had smuggled a handful of men into the town by day and, when darkness fell, these men had surprised the guards and overpowered the garrison. The new rulers knew, from their own experience, that it was possible to capture even a well-fortified town by means of a handful of resolute men. And that is why, since Ibn Saud conquered the country, no one is allowed to be out of doors between the hour of evening prayer, one hour after sunset, and dawn.

"I had no opportunity to take a light," I said, to excuse my negligence.

"Well, you ought to buy a little light, like this one," said the watchman with possessive pride in his flashlight, with which he lighted me to my door.

Next day I bought a flashlight and a stout stick. For I wished neither to expose myself to the vagabond dogs a second time, nor to risk falling into the hands of justice for contravening the law.

As a disinterested party I learned something about local justice, but the acquisition of experience in this field, even from a safe distance, was a hard trial for European nerves.

Chapter XXII

SAUDI ARABIAN JUSTICE

ONE day I was informed that I had been appointed doctor to the Court of Justice. There was no formal investiture.

It seems that on the occasion when I was first brought to the palace by the public executioner, I had employed the correct tactics in my conversation with the Emir. From that time onward, he frequently called me to the palace to treat him or some member of his family professionally.

On those occasions I was always drawn into conversation by the Emir about a hundred and one subjects, and he made me talk for hours together about Germany and other European countries.

There was obviously no point in my telling him about our theaters, concerts or museums. The realistic mind of the Emir was interested solely in the practical aspects of Western life—military organization, industry, medicine, the family or the influence of the Church upon public life.

Whenever the Emir felt the need to have a talk with me, he would send for me from the hospital or from my bed. His desire for such conversations overtook him at the most unlikely times. But the inconveniences which I suffered through his capricious summonses strengthened my position; and the guarantee of security which I thus acquired really meant something in a country where position, freedom and even life are at the mercy of the ruler's caprice.

Once we got talking about the medico-legal system in Germany. I explained to him that we had special prison doctors as well as medico-legal experts, whose duty it was to establish the cause of death whenever a murder was suspected.

Before I left the palace after this conversation, I found myself appointed doctor to the Court of Justice in Hofuf. If I had foreseen what duties this function would entail, I would rather have bitten through my tongue than talked about the German relations between medicine and the law.

In Arabia the punishment for each separate offense is prescribed by the Koran, which contains far more in the way of social and criminal legislation than the Bible does. At the time when the Koran was committed to writing, there were very few established towns in Arabia and no prisons for evildoers. Consequently, all the penalties laid down in the Koran are different forms of corporal punishment, extending from whipping for minor crimes to stoning for adultery and decapitation for capital offenses, such as murder and blasphemy, as well as incitement to rebellion and subversive action against the state. Thieves were flogged for the first and second offenses. The third offense was punished by amputation of the right hand, and if the criminal was so contumacious as to go on stealing with his remaining hand, his left foot was cut off.

Every Thursday the sentences pronounced during the past week were carried out. For this purpose, a detachment of police cleared the center of the market place and formed a square into which condemned persons were led to undergo their sentence.

Minor crimes were dealt with first by flogging. Six persons were necessary to carry out the sentence. Four of the Emir's slaves threw the condemned man to the ground and held him fast. The fifth member of the party was the whipping master, a sturdy Negro, whose duty it was to inflict the prescribed number of strokes on the delinquent's bare back with a palm branch. The last person to collaborate in this ceremony was the clerk of the court, who checked the number of strokes against a copy of the judgment and counted each stroke as it left a bloody weal on the victim's back. The clerk stood looking on with a seven-lashed whip in his hand, which he was quite prepared to use on the back of the Negro if he thought the latter was not laying on with sufficient vigor.

Recidivists, with two convictions for theft, had their right arm bound up with leather straps and a tourniquet, in order to stop the circulation of the blood and so to lessen the pain of the operation. The executioner's assistants then held out the delinquent's arm horizontally at full stretch, and the headsman, my nocturnal guide, made a superficial cut on the victim's wrist, to mark the place where he meant to strike. Then he stepped back a pace and severed the hand with a mighty blow of his scimitar delivered with hair-breadth accuracy. The severed hand fell onto the dusty ground before the victim's feet. Meantime a canister full of fat had been set to boil on a fire of brushwood, beside the place of execution. The handless stump was plunged into this to prevent excessive hemorrhage, and not till then was the tourniquet taken off. The severed hand was tied round the neck of the delinquent, who was ordered to leave the town forthwith.

One of the public advantages of this barbarous form of punishment was that everyone could leave his house door unlocked at night. It would have been easy to steal, but the risk was not worth taking. The fear of incurring even the slightest suspicion of planning a theft was such that patients who had knocked at my door without producing any reaction from me, used often to leave the house in haste for fear of being found there and suspected of burglarious intent.

The police prison in which delinquents were lodged from the time of their arrest till the execution of their sentence was always open to me; in fact, I was responsible for the health of the prisoners. I was not, however, allowed to enter the prison of the slaves, in which persons guilty of offenses against the state were detained. The Emir turned a deaf ear when I—partly I admit from curiosity—suggested that I should be allowed to treat the persons confined in this prison. I appreciated the reason for the Emir's deafness, when I learned that these prisoners were all detained by the personal orders of the ruler.

The prison of the slaves, often called the Citadel, reared its head on the edge of the town like a sinister threat. It had acquired its name, harmless in itself, from the fact that in times of peace it had been used as a prison for runaway slaves, who were kept there and subjected to a softening process until their masters came to fetch them away. The high walls with heavy towers at the four corners reminded one of a feudal castle. During the Turkish regime, this building was reckoned to be the last point of resistance in the system of fortifications; and it was anticipated that even if an attacker had succeeded in occupying the outer tower, the defenders would first withdraw into the inner city; and then, if that were stormed, would be able to hold out in the prison buildings, each tower of which was a fortress in itself.

One night the clerk of the court fetched me from my bed. An order had come from the Emir that I was to undertake the treatment of one of the prisoners in the Citadel. Equipped with flashlights and staves, we set out for the Sign el Abeed.

The clerk of the court knew all about the prison. When we arrived, we found ourselves facing a single iron-studded door, so low that one had to bend down to pass through it. The clerk knocked boldly on the door with the butt of his pistol. After a while, an aperture the size of a man's hand was pulled open.

"I am Hassan, the clerk," said my companion, turning his light on his own face. "I have brought the doctor with me."

The lid came down and keys rattled. There was a sound of chains and bolts, and then the door turned groaning on its hinges.

"You are welcome," croaked a husky voice.

By the light of a lamp in the guardhouse, we saw the chief warder of the prison waiting for us. He had a crutch under his left arm and carried a carbine in his right hand. He looked greasy, subservient and humble. This guardian of the underworld limped since the day when the Emir, making a surprise visit to the prison, had caught him in a misdemeanor. In return for a handsome baksheesh, he had given one of the prisoners a leg of mutton for his dinner. The Emir, apprised of this, had lost his temper, snatched a sword from one of the slaves and crippled the corrupt guardian's knee joint with a fierce thrust.

They led me over a courtyard by the light of a stable lantern. At the entrance to an arched corridor, the lame man first drew three heavy iron bolts and then stuck a foot-long key into an old-fashioned lock. Two Negro slaves, as powerful as bears, were sitting on their hunkers inside. The guard was locked in with the prisoners.

I was then taken down a stone stairway into the casemates of the Citadel. The upper floor of the cellars lay, I should judge, about fifteen feet below ground level, and the door by which alone air could penetrate into these subterranean vaults was kept continuously shut. The quality of the air can be guessed.

Passing a second staircase, which led down into still deeper regions, we came on a vaulted chamber, lying crosswise to our line of approach, which was shut off by an iron grille. Again our guide had to draw bolts and turn locks, but eventually we found ourselves in a great, cross-shaped vault.

In a niche in the wall there was a sort of lamp, consisting of an oil-filled jampot with a floating wick, which illuminated the horrors of the scene with its flickering light. Eight men lay in two rows on the ground, their feet facing one another and protruding from the circular holes in a long line of stocks fastened over their ankles.

Offenders against the state had no right to see the sun, and even the darkness was forbidden to them. They languished in the flickering light of the oil lamp, with their ankles rubbed raw by the stocks. Twice daily, before dawn and after sunset, they were led, chained together, into the small inner court to pray, wash and feed. Rice and dates were thrown to them as if they were beasts, and like beasts they fought over their food.

Eight pairs of eyes stared at us out of dirt-encrusted, wasted faces.

The clerk of the court ran his light over the line of prostrate figures and pointed to a man wearing a blue silk robe, drenched with blood at the shoulder.

A slave opened the lock of the stocks, and the lame warder saw to it that none of the other prisoners profited by the temporary freedom of their feet to try to escape.

My patient raised his feet out of the contrivance, which was immediately closed down again, but he was then manacled with a pair of handcuffs and a cannon ball was chained to his foot. The warder then ordered him to lift the cannon ball and carry it with him, but with only one sound hand he was not strong enough to do this, so one of the Negro guards had to carry it behind the prisoner.

In the courtyard of the Citadel, I examined my patient and bandaged his wounded shoulder. He had received a bullet through the muscle, which looked as though it would soon heal. I also gave him an antitetanus injection and some sulfa tablets, and when I had finished my task, the clerk came into action. He squatted down beside the prisoner and began to interrogate him in a whisper, and the man whispered his replies.

I could not catch a word that might have given me a clue to the identity of the mysterious captive, who looked so different from the others.

About twenty minutes later, the clerk got up and the prisoner was led back to the underworld. The lame warder opened the creaking door, but not till the bolts were shot behind us and the key turned in the lock did I feel able to breathe a sigh of relief.

I determined never again to be curious and ask for permission to look into hell.

Pleasanter experiences awaited me, although my hospital duties, my growing private practice and my often animated conversations with the Emir did not leave me much time to myself.

Chapter XXIII

THE FIGHT AT THE WATERHOLE

IN MY capacity as doctor to the Court of Justice, I was frequently consulted by the police.

One morning the Commandant, Major Abdallah, sent for me and informed me that a police patrol had found the dead body of an unknown man at a waterhole some thirty miles away.

The major told me that another patrol had been ordered to drive to the spot, and that the Emir had given orders that I should accompany the party and make an investigation at the scene of the crime.

"Did you say thirty miles? You know I'm very busy."

"The Emir's orders."

"Supposing you bring the body here. I can make a much more satisfactory investigation here than there."

"The Emir's orders."

An order from the Emir ranked as law. Major Abdallah had always obeyed the law and seen that it was carried out. He was already a police officer in Arabia in the days of the Turkish Empire, and he had remained in the local police when the new regime took over. This white-haired old Turk was now sixty-five, but he seemed to be irreplaceable both on account of his expert knowledge of his profession and his loyalty toward the dynasty, which was so intense that he could not understand my daring to question the Emir's order.

I still found unquestioning obedience somewhat difficult to achieve, although I had had ample time to accustom myself to the notion of it. Anyhow, I was soon climbing into a jeep as the fifth man of a party bound for a spot in the southern desert. By the driver sat the patrol leader, Sergeant Mahmoud, while I shared the back seat with a policeman and Omar the tracker.

Like the major, Omar al Manassir was a survivor from the time of the Turks. From his youth he had been employed as a tracker by the Turkish police, and he was now so old that he could remember the times when the Arabs of the Peninsula possessed very few pistols and rifles and when tribal warfare over women, water, camels and grazing grounds was still waged with curved swords, throwing clubs, daggers, spears and shields. It is true that in the days of his youth some of the tribesmen carried muzzle-loaders, mostly homemade, often beautifully decorated with inlay of ivory, silver and mother-of-pearl, but Omar had never liked them nor had he later got accustomed to the use of automatic weapons. He had finally decided to carry a sword as his only weapon. Nevertheless this almost unarmed man was a redoubtable antagonist, and not solely on account of his great physical strength.

When we came in sight of the Cisterns, I thought we were approaching the ruins of some ancient temple. What looked like tall stone columns were standing amid a chaos of granite slabs, looking exactly like the architecture of vanished millenniums. But nature alone was responsible for the shapes we saw. The winter torrents had, in the course of thousands of years, hollowed out the rocky hillside, leaving pillar-like forms, and then, rushing down the steep slope, had dug out a trough. Around the pool thus created some vegetation always grew.

We found the body hidden between two thick bushes, lying on its back with head and arms in the water. Over our heads two vultures were wheeling, waiting for us to go away and leave them to the feast they had already begun. The blood-soaked clothes of the dead man were torn, but the flesh wounds, I noticed at first sight, were the work of the vultures. The policemen pulled the body out of the water.

"The man has no belt," remarked one of them immediately. The local Arabs always carry their money in their belts, and the inference that the victim had been murdered for his money was obvious.

By bending the limbs, I was able to confirm that the rigor mortis was in an early stage, and I also observed that the body was not quite cold. Death could not have taken place before the early hours of the morning.

"What did he die of?" asked Sergeant Mahmoud, who was following my examination with interest. It was difficult to answer the question. I doubted if it would be possible to recognize the signs of illness or human violence on a body stripped of most of its flesh by birds of prey. In Saudi Arabia it was forbidden to open up a dead body, with the result that murders by poisoning were almost never cleared up. This method of investigation was therefore closed to me. I could not find on the head, breast, or belly of the corpse any wounds not inflicted by the beaks or claws of the vultures. However, when I had almost given up hope of establishing the cause of death, I discovered two narrow, deep perforations which could not have been made by the teeth of a beast or the beak of a vulture. Round one of these there was a purple edge, and I concluded that a knife or dagger must have been driven in up to the hilt, bruising the flesh at the entrance to the wound.

I got up from my knees saying, "The man was stabbed."

"Yes, I know," said a deep voice behind me. It was Omar the tracker, who had been scouting around during my examination of the body. "I know. The tracks have shown me what happened."

While the two policemen were burying the dead man, Omar led the sergeant and me up the stony slope, which commanded the waterhole, till we reached the sandy surface of the desert. There he stopped and pointed to three tracks of walking men. Two of these led toward the waterhole and one in the opposite direction.

Then he knelt down and measured the length and breadth of the footprints with a thin, wooden measure which he took out of his pocket.

"The man with the smaller feet came back," he said. "He has a patch on the sole of his right sandal," and he pointed to a slight irregularity in the print.

We followed the footmarks till we came to two large, flat hollows in the sand.

"That is where the camels were barracked." The tracks of two baggage camels had come from the east to this spot and afterward led in a southerly direction.

Omar continued, "Two men came here in the early morning. They were either acquaintances or had gotten to know one another on the road and had ridden on together. The tracks are parallel and never cross one another. Both of the camels knelt down here, and the men dismounted and went down together to the waterhole. There one killed the other. The killer returned alone and rode off with two camels."

Sergeant Mahmoud called to the driver to get ready. Then he said to the old man, "Do you think we can still catch up with the killer?"

"Why don't you wait till you get news of him from one of the villages, instead of chasing after him?" asked Omar.

"Then I'll have to make two journeys into the desert, for I shall have to go and pick him up," argued the sergeant, taking a perfectly logical view. Both he and the tracker were sure that one of the village omdehs or sheiks would sooner or later send word that the murderer had turned up in his village. If he went after him now, he would save himself the trouble of driving out a second time to arrest him. "With those camels," he went on, "he cannot be more than twenty-five miles away."

Omar went to examine the tracks again. He knelt down beside those leading south. "Both of the beasts are old baggage camels," he said, "and, besides, they have been ridden through the night and must be pretty well exhausted by now." He pointed to their prints and showed how the beasts must have been shuffling along. "We shall come up with him in three hours," he concluded.

So we drove on in pursuit. Omar sat next to the driver and watched the spoor intently. For a good stretch it was easy to follow, but then we came on hard ground covered with tufts of tough desert grass, till we eventually found ourselves in the middle of a huge flock of grazing camels.

"Now we shall have to give it up," I said disappointed. "Even if we get onto his tracks again, we shall not be able to recognize them, as the fellow will certainly have exchanged his tired beasts for one of these fresh, fast-riding camels."

The sergeant shook his head. "You can depend on it," he said, "that the man has not made off on one of these animals. He has a slight chance of lying low with his old crocks, but with a good *hejin,* bearing the Emir's brand, he would certainly be arrested by any omdeh. You know this herd belongs to our governor."

We drove as fast as we could through the herd, but lost time dodging the ruminating beasts. Then Omar looked up at the sun.

"Time to pray, *ya Muslimeen!*" he called. "Pull up, Hassan."

It seemed strange to me that while we were hunting a fleeing murderer, whose tracks we had lost and might take hours to find again, we should call a halt for prayer. If we did not come up with him soon, the fugitive, with his long start, might well find an opportunity to get clean away.

"Can you not postpone your prayers?" I said, all worked up. "Allah will certainly understand that the capture of a murderer is more important than praying?"

The four men had already got out of the jeep and were rolling out a straw praying mat on the ground.

Omar said to me with contempt in his voice, "That is something you do not understand. If God wills, we shall catch the murderer even if he is mounted on a flying camel."

With that he turned around, removed his sandals and faced toward Mecca, and they all began to prostrate themselves in prayer.

When we resumed the pursuit, we found the pasture beginning to thin out and at last came out onto sandy ground. Then Omar made the driver halt, while he got out and began to hunt about for the lost tracks. We drove slowly behind him and had plenty of time to talk.

"Tell me," I said to the sergeant, "why did Omar advise you to wait for a report from an omdeh, instead of going after the killer? If he has had time enough before the pursuit starts and if, into the bargain, his way leads over stony country, where even Omar can't follow him, I don't see how anyone can know where he is in this unending desert."

"No one can hide in Saudi Arabia," said the sergeant categorically.

"Why not? The desert is enormous, practically boundless."

"You must not forget," he replied, "that men need food and

water. Most of the waterholes are in inhabited oases. And the smaller ones, even the secret springs which have to be dug out, are known to the police. The murderer has got to go to water."

"Yes, and then he goes on farther."

"The people here do not move about much, and every member of a tribe knows the other members. A stranger is at once remarked, though he receives as a matter of course the customary hospitality, for in the desert no one is refused food, water and shelter. But it is the duty of the omdeh to ask every stranger where he comes from, whither he is going and to what tribe he belongs."

It sounded like the identification system we have at home! Even in the desert there must be order.

"Persons fleeing from justice have often tried to deceive the omdehs. But, you know, a Bedouin who knows only about horses, camels, sheep, weapons and the dialects of the desert will not easily deceive a native of the Hedjaz into thinking that he is a merchant from the Yemen. The omdeh can detect such false pretenses not only by a man's dialect and clothing, but by the brand, color and hide of the camel he rides. Moreover, there are in every region different breeds of camel which, to the expert, are as easily distinguishable as the different makes and models of cars to a townsman."

"But if an omdeh fails to report or to arrest a suspicious person?"

Mahmoud smiled. "With very few exceptions we can rely on the omdehs. A few weeks ago we had a case of that kind. A Bedouin of the Shammar, whom we had arrested, admitted that he had managed to hide himself for some days in the oasis of El Hani. The omdeh had not reported his presence. We were able to prove that he had neglected his duty, and he received a flogging. Over and above, the village had to pay a fine of 2,000 riyals, and to raise this sum the villagers had to pledge their date crop and to sell camels and sheep. It will be long before an omdeh will take such a chance again, merely to help a fugitive."

I thought to myself that in a modern state it is much easier for a criminal to go to cover in a great city provided with a highly trained police force, than it is in the desert.

Omar put up his hand and called "Halt!" He had found a track and gone down on his knees to test it.

"We are onto him again," he said, as he resumed his seat in the jeep. "Both of the beasts are dead-beat and in an hour we shall have him."

"Yes," said Mahmoud evenly, "the waterhole at Ain Nigm is only an hour's ride from here. We shall find our man there."

The matter was perfectly clear. We should run into him at the waterhole. He couldn't be anywhere else.

A short distance before the waterhole we found a high sand dune barring our way. In order not to be obliged to drive around it, we got out and plodded laboriously up to the top of the dune, from which we could see the waterhole directly below us. There were a few thornbushes in a shallow depression and a pool of muddy water reflected the sunlight. Beside it lay a pair of camels sleeping, with their necks stretched out on the ground. We could not see the rider.

Our next move was a tactical mistake. We slid down through the loose sand toward the waterhole, when a bullet which passed just over our heads, warned us that we were no safer than targets on a range. There was a second shot, and one of the policemen dropped his rifle with a cry and clapped his hand to his shoulder. "Keep away from the edge," I called to the sergeant, and let myself roll crosswise down the steep slope till I fetched up behind a boulder.

Running, sliding and rolling, the others came after me. Mahmoud crawled along to share my boulder, as two more shots were fired at us.

"He is sitting in the bush to the right of the water," said the sergeant, who then aimed his carbine from the side of our cover and fired several shots at the thornbush, apparently without hitting.

Meantime, we were held in check by the fugitive in his hiding place. Mahmoud reloaded and missed again, but before he could fire once more we heard a loud cry from the bush. The sergeant laid down his rifle and peered out to see what was happening.

"Come out!" called a deep voice from the bush. "I have him." Then out strode Omar, with matted hair and shaggy beard, looking like a primitive man, and beckoned to us to come across to him.

While we had been exposing ourselves directly to the enemy's fire as we came down the face of the dune, the old man had slipped around on the other side and, coming from behind, had overpowered the runaway in a hand-to-hand struggle. Omar was irresistible.

The sergeant was annoyed. "Why didn't you tell me what you meant to do?" he said. "I could have come to give you a hand."

"You would have only been in the way. Two men make more noise than one."

"And supposing he had heard you, and shot you down before you could jump on him?"

"Who told you I jumped on him? I threw a stone at him from up there," he pointed to the dune, "and hit him on the head. A well-aimed stone is as good as a bullet from a gun—or so I was taught."

But the stone had not killed him. He lay unconscious with a bloody head, and when he came to he was glad to accept a cup of tea from the man who had knocked him out. Unbound, he was glad to sit with his captors drinking tea around a fire of sticks, and he made no further attempt to escape. He looked at it like this: he had committed a murder and then done everything in his power to escape. In the last extremity, he had engaged in a hopeless battle. But now that he was captured and disarmed, he resigned himself with Oriental fatalism to his destiny.

"Up to prayer! Comrades, up to prayer!" called Omar once again, and the little group rose and disposed themselves for worship. Omar represented the Imam, and the others stood in line behind him, their faces turned toward Mecca—Sergeant Mahmoud, the murderer, the wounded policeman and his comrade.

"There is no God but God and Mohammed is his Prophet!"

It seemed that Allah had not wished the killer to escape.

A few weeks later I saw the man again. His appearance was unchanged.

I was ordered to attend his trial, and to give evidence regarding the discovery of the dead man. The hearing took place at the palace. The murder of the man at the waterhole was just one of the cases on the roll, and when I reached the judgment hall with German punctuality, another suit was being tried. The Emir Saud, Ruler and Chief Justice of the Province of Al Hassa, was the Dispenser of Justice, according to the precepts of the Koran, in all civil litigation, as well as being the Supreme Judge in all criminal processes, great and small. The Emir looked up crossly when the door opened, and I pressed through the throng of interested spectators.

When he recognized me, his face lit up and he beckoned to me to come and sit by him on the dais, where he sat surrounded by an armed bodyguard and attended by a few of the notables of Hofuf.

But he immediately concentrated his attention on the case he was trying. He gazed stonily at a small, voluble Bedouin whose hawklike face had assumed an ill-used expression and who, as I came into the court, was proclaiming his innocence with eloquent words and sweeping gestures. The plaintiff, an obese mulatto, easily recognizable as a merchant, was standing a little behind him to one side.

Hardly had I sat down when the defendant, who seemed to have been put out of his stride by my entry, began his speech in his own defense all over again. However, a gesture from the Emir cut him short.

"*Qahwa!*" said the Emir to one of the guards and, just as it had happened when I came to the palace for the first time, the word "*Qahwa!*" was passed on by the clerk to the doorkeeper, and by the doorkeeper to the sentry in the corridor, till finally it reached the coffee pantry. And in came the black boy with his coffeepot and cups for the Emir and all his guests on the dais.

"I swear by Allah and the life of my children . . ." said the defendant, trying his luck one more, but an ungracious gesture silenced him again.

"Now listen to me," said the Emir, turning toward the defendant, as he held his cup in his right hand and pointed at the man with his left forefinger. "You have signed a paper to the effect that you have received a loan of 3,000 riyals. You have not yet paid back the money. If you do not repay the loan within thirty days, you will go to prison and stay there until your family has paid your debt."

"But . . ." began the man.

"There is no 'but'," said the Emir. "And now be off with you. Clerk," he said, turning to a man sitting on the ground at his feet with a writing block and a pencil, "That fellow is to get thirty strokes for perjuring himself. Have you got that down? Thirty, I said."

Then he turned to me saying, "And how are you, my dear doctor?"

We talked for about a quarter of an hour about all manner of subjects, till the Emir suddenly remembered that he had to try a man accused of murder.

The accused, now loaded with chains, was brought into the Court at the order of the Emir. The sergeant and I gave evidence regarding the finding of the body and the circumstances in which the accused was arrested. The latter made a frank confession of his crime and submitted himself to the judgment of the Emir, who, in accordance with Koranic law, condemned him to death by the sword.

The sentence was executed on the following day. According to custom the police cleared a space in the market place. The condemned man was led to the place of execution by slaves of the Emir. There he found the executioner waiting for him with his sword unsheathed. Also present was an official of the administration, whose duty it was to supervise the proceedings.

With his hands bound behind his back, the condemned man knelt on the ground and bent his head. Yehya, the executioner, came up to his side and raised his sword to strike, but his victim instinctively drew back his head between his shoulders. Whereupon the headsman, instead of striking, stabbed him in the side with the point of the sword, which caused him to writhe with pain and stretch out his neck. At once, the headsman delivered a sweeping blow which severed the head from the trunk.

Chapter XXIV

SLAVES

MY patients came to me afflicted with the strangest aches and pains, and, like patients all over the world, they had preconceived ideas about the cause of their sufferings.

"I think I have rheumatism in the knee," said a small, haggard man of fifty who came to consult me.

He looked as though he had had no contact with soap and water for years. His long black hair hung in tangled skeins down his back. But this insignificant little fellow showed me with what fortitude a true man can bear pain.

"Let me have a look," I said.

I took my patient into the clinic and began to examine him. I felt his knee carefully in an attempt to localize the pain and, as I did so, I came upon a hard round lump. When I touched it my patient groaned. The thing felt like a bullet, but I could find no entry scar in the region of the knee. I asked him if he had had a bullet wound.

"One?" said the man contemptuously. "My son, my body is covered with the scars a man should bear. I am Sheik Fahed Abiari of the Tribe of Beni Hajjar."

I pulled up Sheik Fahed's drawers higher, as I wanted to see if his thigh bore any trace of an old bullet wound. Sure enough, I found an old scar about two handbreadths above the knee, with no exit mark, from which I could deduce that the bullet was still in his leg and had moved in the course of years down to his knee. That was the rheumatism of which he complained.

"I have no procaine in the house," I said. "Come to the hospital tomorrow, and I'll take the bullet out."

"Tomorrow? No, do it now. We of the Beni Hajjar are not afraid of pain," he declared proudly.

As I had no operating table in my house, I had to get him to lie down on the floor. I disinfected the part on which I had to work, and then cut back the skin above the bullet. I had to exercise some lateral pressure, but finally managed to extract the ball with a forceps.

All the while, my patient lay perfectly still. Only now and then he twitched a little or gave a faint groan. When it was over, he was feeling somewhat weak and asked permission to rest for a time before he went on his way. I prepared coffee and kept him company.

The bullet which he held thoughtfully in his hand had a caliber of about 11 mm. It was too short for a rifle bullet and too long for a pistol.

I asked him if he knew from what weapon the bullet had been fired.

"A Martini-Stutzen," he said. This short-barreled breechloader, caliber 11 mm,. was originally meant for a cavalry carbine.

"But the Martini-Stutzen has been long out of use, hasn't it?"

"This bullet wound of mine," he said, pointing to his bandaged knee, "is already fifteen years old. In those days the Martini was practically the only rifle we had. Only since this last war have we had modern weapons."

"If it is already fifteen years ago . . ." I began.

But he interrupted me in tones of professional pride. "You must know," he said, "that I was the official slave dealer for the Courts of the East Coast. Every governor was obliged to supply yearly a fixed number of slaves for the King's use. In addition, the Emir had to keep up his establishment and the rich merchants had to be supplied. I can tell you, I had my hands full."

"You were going to tell me how you got that wound," I put in.

I was now so familiar with the customs of the country that the practice of slave trading seemed to me almost normal.

"Patience, my friend!" said the Sheik. "I am going to tell you a story which will enable you to understand."

He took a cup of coffee and lit a cigarette. "Well then: at that time I was accustomed to make many journeys, in company with my worthy uncle, to Oman and Qatar for the purpose of buying slaves. This was just at the time when the oil began to pay. People

became rich overnight and wanted to have new slaves. The prices
rose. We were happy. But suddenly there was a shortage, and all
at once it seemed as though there were no purchasable slaves to
be had. We could not go out of business, so we had to kidnap children and sell them as slaves." It seemed as though there were
many things of which I was ignorant.

"One day we were again in Qatar. My respected uncle, who is
now enjoying the bliss of Paradise after the labors of this earthly
life, had been spying out the land and had discovered a favorable
opportunity of improving our business.

"During the night, while my uncle was watching the camels, I
entered a house and took two ten-year-old girls from their beds. I
must have been clumsy, because one of them started screaming,
and two slaves came rushing in. I dropped the girls, swung myself
out of the window and ran to the wall which surrounded the house.
With one leap I was on the top, but the slaves had already spied
me and began to shoot. They shot very badly. The moon was bright
and the range short, and if I had been in their place, the intruder
would not have had a chance. They fired at least six rounds of
which only one hit me—that one there. I remained lying on the
ground outside the wall, where luckily I was picked up by a police
patrol."

"How do you mean, luckily?"

"My friend, you don't know the people of Qatar. If the police had
not come, the two black slaves would have killed me—not on the
spot, but slowly, for their pleasure."

"Yes, but being arrested is only a modified form of happiness."

"Of course, you are right. They put chains on me and tied cannon balls to my legs and, believe me, Doctor, they weighed at
least twice as much as I do. They took me to the frontier and
handed me over to the Saudi Arabian police, who naturally put
me in prison."

I knew that the abduction of children was a capital offense. But
the Sheik was there, before me, fully alive, and chuckling as he
drank his coffee. He had escaped the headsman's sword, so he
must clearly have got out of prison.

"How did you break out?" I asked.

"Break out?" he repeated. "They had to let me go. After all, I am one of the Beni Hajjar, as I told you."

"I know, but what had that to do with your release?"

"Don't you know? Our tribe did more than all others to help King Abdul Aziz Ibn Saud, may God preserve him, to conquer Arabia. In gratitude for our support, the King decreed that no tribesman of the Beni Hajjar shall ever be condemned to death. And, as kidnaping is not one of the punishable crimes mentioned in the Koran, they were obliged to let me go."

He got up and walked for a few steps to see how his knee felt.

"All right," he said and smiled with satisfaction.

"Where are you going now?" I asked as he took his leave.

"To the palace," he said. "I have to talk business with the Emir."

Limping slightly, he disappeared into the evening shadows.

Our Emir had to supply seventy slaves every year to his liege lord, the King, and we doctors of the Health Office had from time to time to report on the health of the convoys coming to Hofuf and leaving for the capital. The business which my friend of the Beni-Hajjar was going to discuss with the Emir was clearly concerned with the trade in black ivory, the price of which had been rising all the time since the profits from oil had enriched so many people and increased the demand for slaves.

And what about the fate of these black slaves, whose life, like that described in *Uncle Tom's Cabin,* was one of miserable monotony!

During the course of the year, I saw many hundreds of these people and treated a few hundred medically. They were sent for treatment at the slightest excuse, not for humane considerations, but because they represented property worth up to $1,000 apiece. And it was not out of pure humanity that slaves were almost always treated better than free workers or employees. Slaves always looked better nourished and better clothed than free members of the lower order, because, in a sense, they represented their owners. Just as in Western countries—though I don't like the analogy—a man is judged to some extent by the appearance and upkeep of his car, so in Arabia an ill-fed, badly clad or sickly slave redounds to the discredit of his master. That was one of the reasons that in my practice I had to treat so many slaves as free patients.

Each of the slaves in the Emir's palace, numbering in all over two hundred, had a well-defined task to perform. The duties incidental to making coffee were distributed among three adolescent Negro boys—one to roast and grind the beans, one to boil the coffee and one to serve it. And so it was in other occupations. Each slave had his allotted task in the subdivision of duties and, as a result, most of them had next to nothing to do. Free workers had to toil to keep themselves alive. The slave was well provided for, without any obligation to work hard. One seldom heard slaves complaining of their lot. They were mostly contented and wished for no other life. In my early days in Arabia, I could not see a slave without a deep feeling of pity, but as I acquired knowledge and experience I became convinced that one could inflict no severer punishment on a slave than by releasing him from his carefree, irresponsible existence to a life of liberty. I knew of cases where freed slaves had come knocking at the doors of their former masters and begging with tears in their eyes to be taken back.

That is, of course, no proof that freedom from anxiety is a proper substitute for real freedom, but life in slavery renders a person incapable of a free life. The desire to return to slavery may be compared with the attitude of many ex-convicts in Western lands, who find themselves so little at home in freedom that they will take any opportunity to get back to prison. So, in Arabia, the child of slaves has little or no longing to be free, and passes automatically and without suffering into a life of slavery.

In former times, slaves were procured almost exclusively from the East Coast of Africa by traders or raiders. But now this trade has practically ceased. Most of the slaves in Arabia are the descendants of slaves, and therefore born in captivity, or else were sold into slavery as children by impoverished parents. But there is still an import trade in slaves from Qatar, Oman, Hadramaut and Abyssinia.

The traffic in girls from Europe and the Near East hardly exists today, but it does just exist, otherwise I would not one day have become the owner of a female slave.

One winter evening in 1951, I was summoned to the house of Ibrahim the merchant to visit a sick slave girl. As usual, I was received on my arrival by my host in his great salon and offered coffee amid the formal ceremonies of welcome. Ibrahim sat on a circular cushioned seat, because owing to the size of his belly he could not cross his legs like the clerk sitting on the floor in a far corner of the room, writing in beautiful *rigga* in his account book. Half sitting, half lying, Ibrahim made himself as comfortable as he could on his seat and jested with the slave boy who brought us coffee.

At last the formalities of politeness were satisfied, and I was able to devote myself to my patient.

Great, black eyes stared at me out of a pale, somewhat sunken face, as I felt for my patient's pulse. Wishing to lighten the oppressive atmosphere by a little friendly talk, I asked the slave her name.

"Nadia," she said and looked at me with a frightened expression.

"Surely you're no Arabian?"

Her white skin and the shape of her face made the question superfluous.

"No. I am from Homs in Syria."

I finished my examination and concluded that she had no organic disorder. The troubles she complained of were probably induced by nervous causes. While I was writing her a prescription for a sedative and another for a tonic, she sat up and looked at me intently. Then she said, "You are not an Arab either."

"No. I am an *Alemani*."

"Are you a slave too?" She apparently had got it into her head that all foreigners in Arabia were slaves.

"No," I explained, "I work here of my own free will. But how do you come to be here? Did some one buy you in Homs?"

"No," she said, looking in front of her as though reflecting, "that is to say, I suppose that is what happened." Then she paused again before saying, "Ah, I don't know."

Her obscure and hesitating words aroused my curiosity. I

pressed her to tell me her story and, though at first reluctant, she finally consented.

She was the fourth daughter of a casual laborer living near Homs. One day, she said, her father told her that he had made the acquaintance of a man from Damascus, who was looking for a wife. He showed her a photo of the man, and it was agreed that she should be given to this stranger.

"A few days later," she continued, "my father went with the man from Damascus to the Qadi. The marriage contract was signed, and on the next day a man appeared in our house and told me I was now his wife. He drove with me and the little bundle in which I carried my things to Aleppo, where we got into an airplane.

"Where are you taking me?" I asked.

"To Damascus."

"But one doesn't need a plane to go to Damascus."

"Of course not," he said, but as he knew that I had never flown he wanted to give me a treat. I had not realized that it was such a long way to Damascus, with so much desert and an immense blue sea lying below us."

"And then instead of Damascus you found yourself at Jidda?" I understood.

"That may be," she said, "I can't read and I had never seen Damascus."

She went on to tell me the rest of her story. In Jidda they took a room at a hotel. Soon after they arrived, her husband told her that he had to go out to keep an urgent business appointment. When he left the room he turned the key in the lock. Many Arab men are so concerned about preserving the virtue of their wives that they never leave them unguarded—and Nadia suspected no harm till three hours later the door was unlocked and, instead of her husband, a Saudi-Arabian merchant walked in and informed her that he had just bought her.

So she found that she was a slave and this man's legal concubine. After a while, the merchant got tired of her and exchanged her for another girl, who belonged to one of his business friends in Riyadh. Her new master made a present of her to his son, who sold her to a cultivator in Hofuf, who in turn passed her on to Ibrahim, the merchant, as security for a debt, and so it was that I came to find her in Ibrahim's harem.

By this time, I had got to know hundreds of slaves and my viewpoint in regard to slavery was approximating that of the Arabs. I was beginning to regard the institution as something natural, self-evident and ordained by Providence. But now I caught myself sympathizing with the girl, perhaps not so much on account of her white skin as because Nadia was the first and only slave I had met who could not reconcile herself to her lot.

My sympathy was, however, completely academic. Nature has not cast me for the part of the hero of romance, who, carrying a lovely maiden enveloped in a mantle, climbs down the wall with the aid of a convenient creeper after laying out a couple of harem guards and, braving countless hazards, brings his beautiful prize to home and safety.

Several weeks later, shortly before the Birthday of the Prophet, which shares some of the characteristics of our Christmas, this particular problem was solved in a perfectly unromantic, businesslike manner. During one of our nocturnal conversations, the Emir asked me if he could gratify any wish of mine on the occasion of the feast.

There were many things I could have mentioned, but of course I could not think of the most important ones at the right moment and something very out-of-the-way occurred to me. The memory of Nadia's sad, expressive eyes rose into my mind, so I began to relate the long and complicated story of the girl's betrayal. The Emir listened to me attentively.

When I had finished I said, "Give this girl her freedom."

"Is she pretty?"

"Yes."

"That's bad," said the Emir with a sour expression, obviously hoping that his "Birthday" present would not cost him too much. "But is she a virgin?"

"Not very likely."

"That's better," he said with a nod. "And who is her present master?"

"Ibrahim Muhanna, the merchant."

The Emir burst into a ringing laugh. "Why didn't you say so at once? You can buy a female slave from him for a mere song. You must know that he has no interest in girls."

I remembered how he had looked at the coffee boy.

"Very good, then," went on the Emir, "I shall buy her for you."

"But I don't want her as a present, I want you to give her her freedom."

I could not see my way out of this tangle.

"Only her master can free her," insisted the Emir, shaking his head. "I won't buy her for myself, but as a present for you. Then you can keep her or set her free as you will."

There was no place for abductions in this sober land with its oil fields and airlines and a market price for everything from camels to female slaves. So, a few days later, I was saying good-by to Nadia at the airport. Her eyes were full of tears as she bade me farewell, saying, "I shall never forget your goodness, Doctor."

I said, "Now remember. Your plane will take you to Dharan. There a friend of mine will meet you and accompany you farther on your way to Damascus. See that you really arrive there this time."

A year ago we met again. She had married an honest bookseller in Damascus. I found her standing by a pile of washing. Twins were crawling about the floor at her feet and a third infant was chortling in his cradle.

"Now I am a real slave," laughed Nadia and pointed to the three tyrants for whom she was drudging. "But, believe me, Doctor, I like it."

Chapter XXV

THE EXPEDITION TO BARAIMI

"*MAL ma andina, mal ma andina.*"

"No goods have we: no lovely women either."

It sounds desperately sad when the Bedouins, squatting round the campfire, sing their endless refrain about the things they do not have. I have heard them sing this mournful lament in Palestine too, chanting with guttural tones into the darkness.

"*Mal ma andina. . . .*"

I had sent the lovely woman away to Damascus, where she belonged. My goods consisted of a modest chest of medicine and surgical instruments. My home was Hofuf. Truer to say that my home was nowhere, not even in a life of adventure, unless it was fair to call this life of mine under the all-powerful law of the Wahabis an adventure. Maybe it was, for even though I enjoyed the favor of the Emir, I never knew when the fires of the desert would burn me up.

I ought now to have been thinking about returning to my native land, as my contract was up, but the overwhelming heat was too much for me.

"*Mal ma andina. . . .*"

There were no longer any exciting incidents in the life of a Public Health official in the desert. The summer heat of the Persian Gulf was too great to allow of incidents. No one who was not obliged to do so would walk a yard unless it was absolutely necessary. I had not even the energy to walk from my office over the burning sand of the market place to my house to get my lunch.

When a truck drove into the market place below the office, the banner of yellow dust it threw up remained motionless in the air.

As we watched the vehicle arrive, I heard my colleague Dr. Nagy say, "Aha! The hounds of Paradise." A Syrian, Dr. Nagy had been assigned to Hofuf after being employed in the health department in the mountainous region of Abha in southwestern Arabia. He was sitting by me at the window, as weary and listless as I, staring down at the market square.

The dust banner remained stationary when the truck drew up. The door of the driver's cab was opened, and the heat came steaming out as if from a baker's oven. Then the driver and his mate climbed down and let down the backboard.

The driver picked up a long pole and started poking about under the awning. His mate slapped his hands against the sides of the truck and shouted at the top of his voice. Then I saw the extraordinary cargo they had been carrying. Ten, twenty, thirty dogs jumped down into the market place, looked around, whining undecidedly, and then disappeared like a pack of gray phantoms between the houses.

"I suppose these are reinforcements," I said, "to prevent the pied dogs of Hofuf from dying out."

Dr. Nagy smiled. "Do you mean to say that after all this time you don't know the story of the dogs?"

"Don't torment me. It is too hot to think and especially about dogs."

"Well, it won't tire you to listen to a fairy tale."

"Go on," I said, "tell me your tale if you have a mind to."

"There was once a king," began Dr. Nagy smiling, "who wished to conquer a great desert land. But there were some tribes who objected to being conquered. One night, while the king and his soldiers were lying fast asleep in the city, a band of enemies succeeded in slipping into the town, meaning to murder the king. But in the town there were many dogs and the dogs began to bark furiously as soon as they became aware of the intruders. The king and his men awoke and put the enemy to flight. Then the grateful ruler promised that in his capital no dog should be killed any more. He gave orders to his chamberlain to pay a pension to the dogs consisting of a daily meal of meat and rice."

"Well, and then . . . ?"

"That's the end of my story. The capital city, if you wish to know, is called Riyadh and the King Abdul Aziz Ibn Saud. And if those particular dogs have not yet died of senile decay, they must be alive today. I expect you want to know what the truck down there has to do with my story. I'll tell you. As all dogs are under the King's protection and as no one is allowed to kill them, there seems to be nothing to check the increase in the canine population, at least there was nothing until the authorities had the happy idea of rounding up a few dozen dogs in the different towns and deporting them to other places. As you can hear, the local dogs do not approve." The first battle between the dogs of Hofuf and the intruders from Riyadh was now in progress and the noise was tremendous.

Dr. Nagy went on with his explanations. "Within a week the immigrants are nothing but skin and bones, as the indigenous dogs will not allow them a bite of food. Then it is only a question of days before the newcomers are bitten to death or die of hunger. But a promise is a promise and in Riyadh no dog may die of hunger."

It was growing no cooler as my colleague rambled on. The yellow dust banner, grown paler now, still floated above the square. And there were many more weeks of heat before us. The date was the twenty-ninth of August of the year 1952.

One of the Emir's personal slaves, recognizable by his blue galabia, came hurrying over the square through the sweltering heat with a message that we were to report to the Emir immediately—yes, both of us.

As was our custom when we went into the town, we took a case of instruments with us. We arrived at the palace, dripping with sweat, and found the Emir awaiting us in his audience room. Together with him were a couple of Bedouins and Omar the tracker. Omar's presence suggested some such incident as the murder at the waterhole.

The Emir wasted no time. He told us that we two doctors must immediately set out, in company with Omar and the two Bedouins, to treat some persons who had been injured in an accident somewhere outside the town.

"I shall hold you responsible with your life for the safety of the two doctors," he said to Omar impressively. "If anything happens to them, it will be better for you not to show yourself here again."

He was in deadly earnest. Then he dismissed us without further explanations. A car picked us up outside the palace and drove us to the south gate of the town. There we found a police officer who had commandeered all incoming trucks and parked them in a row.

"Pick out the one you would like to take," he said, pointing to the trucks. "I suggest the red one, the Ford. It is still pretty new and besides the color is attractive."

Whereupon a voice groaned in protest.

"The car is not new and the engine is ready to fall to pieces." The man was allowed to speak, but there was no resisting the Emir's order.

"We want a second car," said Omar, looking keenly at the four other trucks, whose owners had begun to sigh with relief. Omar was right, for a long journey in the desert would tax the engine very severely. The owners declared in chorus that all the trucks were only fit to be broken up, but Omar, unmoved and expert, chose a Chevrolet. Then he and one of the Bedouins climbed into the driving seat of the red Ford, while two other men took their places in the back of the truck. My colleague and I sat by the driver in the Chevrolet. We got a bit of a shock when we were driven to the military garage to fill up with tins of gasoline and waterskins before we left the town.

The houses thinned out as we approached the desert. We drove through the date plantations, passing garages and the slaughter-house, till we finally left behind us the stinking refuse pits on the rim of the town, full of dead donkeys, cows and camels in all stages of decomposition. Packs of curs and a few vultures were rummaging in the horrid heaps.

By evening, we had still not arrived at the scene of the accident. We reached Abqaiq, on the Persian Gulf, where there was an oil refinery. There we reported to the Omdeh, who invited us to take a short rest in his house. The respected lord of this small domain was, characteristically, a slave of the Emir's.

"Is it far to the place of the accident?" I asked Omar before we set off again.

"Oh," he said, "I don't suppose we shall need more than two days to get there."

"Are we going to China, then?"

"No . . . the place is a bit behind Salwa," said the old man calmly, as though he were taking us for a picnic in the neighborhood.

I told Dr. Nagy that Omar had said our destination was behind Salwa.

"So that's the way the wind blows," he said and whistled through his teeth. "They must be taking the Baraimi business seriously."

"What business?"

"It's a complicated story," he said. "The Oasis of Baraimi, now situated in the territory of Oman, was formerly one of the possessions of the family of Saud. Now it is a wretched, poverty-stricken spot of ground which has cost the government much more than the taxes the people pay. Finally the Saudi government abandoned it and left the inhabitants to fend for themselves."

"And why should anyone be interested in it now?"

"I give you three guesses."

"Oil," I said with some confidence.

"Clever boy," said my colleague approvingly. "And that is why this comfortless piece of desert has suddenly become a precious possession. Oman and Saudi Arabia are disputing about the possession of the oil underground. King Saud claims that he is the original owner of the property, and the Sultan of Oman takes the line that the region legally belongs to him, having been abandoned by Saud. Now it appears as though King Saud meant to settle the question by force."

"You mean that he has simply sent an expedition to Baraimi and occupied the oasis?"

Nagy nodded. "I should not be surprised if this so-called 'traffic accident' turns out to have been an armed collision between the local inhabitants and the Saudi forces. The local people may not wish to return to their old allegiance."

"I can't help wondering how the Emir obtained such early news of the traffic accident."

"Well, you know, Saudi Arabia is a modern country and it isn't difficult to carry a transmitting set in a trunk."

If we had not been so much interested in talking politics, we should have noticed that our driver was crouching lower and lower

BEDOUIN DOCTOR • 238

over the steering wheel and that he was, in fact, driving in his sleep and had deviated a long way from the track. We could no longer see the taillight of the leading car. We damned the driver and he, doubtless, silently returned our reproaches with interest. After a good deal of zigzagging, we got back to the track, but saw no sign of the other car. We had to keep nudging our chauffeur in the ribs, when his head slumped forward. About midnight Nagy fell asleep, and I was not long in following him.

I was awakened by a violent jolt and a severe blow on the head, as well as by the resounding curses of my colleague, who had a remarkable command of Arabic swear words. We found ourselves bogged up to the axles in a sand drift, and we both had knocked our heads against the windshield when we came to a sudden stop.

We had to get out somehow. The driver stepped on the gas, but the wheels merely revolved in the sand and bedded themselves more deeply in.

I told the driver to fetch the spade and the sacks out of the truck. He had got out and was leaning against the car, still half-asleep, and staring at the back axle.

"I haven't got a spade," he said surlily, as he lay down in the sand by the car to see what could be done.

We certainly could not extricate ourselves without help, but we were very tired and decided to sleep until the others missed us and came back to find us. I took the first watch.

It was bitterly cold. In the hurry of starting, we had taken no blankets, imagining that we were called to treat victims of an accident that had taken place not far from Hofuf. I walked up and down to keep myself warm. Dr. Nagy and the chauffeur, who had lain down at a little distance from one another, had snuggled up together like sheep.

Then I climbed into the driver's seat and turned on the parking lights, so that we should be visible when they came to look for us. A jackal barked in the night and another jackal answered him. I heard the deeper note of a wolf. The cold had penetrated into the driving cab and had become unbearable. So I got out again to warm myself by walking, but as I jumped down, I kicked off a sandal and had to crawl under the truck in search of it. This made me so furious that I began to curse and swear at everything, and especially at the carelessness of the authorities who had sent us out without arms, without blankets or spades, and wearing thin leather sandals, on an adventure that smelled of war.

Hearing a shot in the distance, I started and bruised my head against the bottom of the truck as I crept out—my second head wound that night!

"The other car!" cried the driver as he jumped into his seat and started blinking the headlights.

The car lights in the distance came off and on. They were answering our signals. Before long the rescue party arrived and, by good luck, they actually had with them a tow rope with which they pulled us out of our sand drift.

Omar was awake as usual. He changed places with Dr. Nagy and sat next to me for the rest of the way, but I fell asleep as soon as we got going. It was nearly midday when I awoke with a burning thirst. My head ached terribly from my bruises and the merciless heat of the sun, even though Omar had thrown his linen cloak over me.

"Careful with the water!" warned Omar. "We haven't much left."

I was drinking greedily out of the half-empty waterskin, when Omar, as an object lesson in the meaning of empty waterskins, pointed out of the window, where the dead bodies of five camels lay near the road. Their riders had not even carried off their valuable pack saddles, when they had marched on with their last supplies of water in the vague hope of finding a waterhole somewhere.

"This year the waterholes near Fouka dried up very early," said Omar. "The desert is full of corpses. Round about here you don't even find wolves or jackals, as the nearest water is 125 miles away."

If even camels, which can go for three or four days without water, died of thirst here, it wouldn't do for our engine to break down as it ploughed through the soft sand in first or second gear. The dark specks we saw in the desert always turned out, when we got near them, to be vultures feasting on bodies. During the afternoon, we ran into the remains of a little caravan in the middle of the road. The drivers had cut the throats of their beasts to drink their blood, before going forward alone. We found their bodies on the track an hour farther on.

The track vanished on a rubbly slope. On our right we could see the blue outlines of mountains on the hazy horizon. We drove over stony ground almost until sunset. Then we came to sand once more. A wolf ran off in front of us and then we saw sheep's droppings in the sand.

Water! There must be water somewhere near. Sheep are never more than a day's march away from water.

It was already almost dark when we at last reached Salwa, the Saudi frontier post on the Persian Gulf—a collection of ragged tents and some reed huts. But it contained a few dwarf palms and a well of brackish water which saved our lives.

Fish were hanging up in long lines to dry. After all the sand we had seen and the thirst we had suffered, it was wonderful to see once again the element in which fish can live. In the Omdeh's house we were able to recuperate to some extent after the fatigue of our journey. There we learned, as we drank cups of tea flavored with cinnamon, that the expeditionary force for which we were seeking had set out two days ago from the frontier post for the Baraimi Oasis. Omar, with characteristic circumspection, had observed a government-owned truck with a four-wheel drive in front of the Omdeh's hut and had requisitioned it for our use. The Omdeh's son, after some argument, had agreed to come with us and drive it.

We continued our journey by night. I was in the second car. From time to time our headlights shone on the back of the Ford, which led the convoy, and showed us the Bedouins, who had taken the corks out of the muzzles of their rifles and were keeping both sides of the road under observation.

The stern laws of the Saudi state protected us no longer. We were now enemies and intruders. We had a short glimpse of a small Bedouin encampment, looking more wretched and poverty-stricken than the poorest settlements in Egypt or Saudi Arabia. Two slender riding camels, tethered in front of a tent, fitted strangely into the picture. I wondered who were the visitors. It didn't matter. We drove on.

When the first light of dawn disclosed the landscape, we found that the face of the desert had undergone a change. The fine sand through which we ploughed was now brick-red. We were in the Rub'al Khali, the Empty Quarter, an immense and lonely region devoid of all vegetation.

The road had long ago faded out. Each of the trucks steered its own course between or over the dunes, which sometimes rose to a height of 600 feet. But we kept more or less together, so as to be able to help one another in case of a breakdown. The danger into which we were running was emphasized by the attitude of the Omdeh's son, whose all-purpose car with its balloon tires, suitable for driving through soft sand, ought to have led the convoy, but, in fact, lagged consistently behind. It was clear that the fellow preferred to have us in the lead in the event of our coming under fire from the Bedouins. Omar put a stop to this method of life insurance by sitting beside the young man and insisting on his taking the lead, while I got my colleague Nagy to come and sit by me.

About noon a wind came up, light at first, but then streamers of dust began to blow off the crests of the sand hills and spread over the rolling desert like a red veil. But the wind caused no drop in the temperature. It poured through the open windows in a scorching stream, and soon the heat inside the car was unbearable. "Sandstorm!" said our driver, screwing up his face and pointing to the sun, which looked like a glowing red ball behind the curtain of sand.

Then it disappeared altogether and a reddish-brown wave, as high as a house, swept down on us. We had just time to pull our headcloths over our faces, before we were in the thick of it. It was as dark as night. The hurricane picked up the sand as it howled along and whirled it into the air, which was so thick with sand grains that we felt as if we had driven into the side of a dune. We pulled up the windows, but the fine sand blew in through all the cracks and penetrated our garments and headcloths, and coated our sweat-covered bodies. In a few seconds my eyes were gummed up, and the pain forced me to bury my head in the hollow of my elbow.

The driver laid his head on the steering wheel and kept on driving blindly into the darkness, for though the headlights were on, there was nothing to be seen.

Suddenly the bumping and jolting of the vehicle stopped.

"Don't stop, you idiot," I shouted. "If we get silted up here, we shall never get out."

He shouted back at me, "The engine has stopped."

The gasoline pipe was choked. We huddled up together and let the storm do its worst, but after a while we felt we could not simply submit to its rage. Nostrils and larynx filled up with sand. I could no longer breathe and pulled the door open, giving access to a blast from hell. As I tried in desperation to shut it again, I was all but whirled out of the car.

For about an hour we were in purgatory, and then it all ended as suddenly as it had begun.

Slowly the light began to return, as though day was dawning. With burning eyes, we stared out on the scene. Nagy began to scoop the sand out of the driver's cab, while the driver and I tried to get the engine going. First we had to find the engine, hidden under a thick layer of sand which, laced with oil and gasoline, had formed into an almost solid, pitchlike coating. We shoveled the sand away with our hands—the only tools we had—and at the end of a couple of hours had managed to free the engine and the wheels. To our astonishment, the wheels began to grip as soon as we got the engine started.

But we had not gotten very far on our way to safety. We were completely alone. There was no sign of the other cars. We zig-zagged to right and left to no purpose, and then tried to fix our course by the position of the sun and drove laboriously over the dunes.

At one point our driver swerved violently, causing me to knock my head again, and I shouted to him to take care. But he had seen, quicker than I had, that the summit of the dune fell away almost vertically, and but for his presence of mind we should have somersaulted down the slope.

Then Nagy caught hold of my arm and pointed at a figure outlined on the top of a dune.

"Look there," he said.

"Perhaps it is one of our people."

"Or one from the other side."

We kept moving toward him.

"Anyhow, it's a Bedouin," put in the driver.

"Why, did you expect to see an Eskimo?" said Nagy maliciously.

"He is waving to us."

"Yes, he's waving all right, but perhaps he is signaling to his comrades."

The man on the top of the dune had taken his white cloak from his shoulders and was waving it to and fro. After such a journey, I was glad enough to see a human being and wishfully believed he must be one of our men.

I told the chauffeur to drive up to him. He was not one of our people but was, nevertheless, a Saudi-Arabian.

"God be praised that you have arrived safely!" said the man, smiling all over his face as he climbed up into our truck. "We were afraid that you had lost your way. That's why we posted sentries on all the dunes to give you your direction."

In front of us lay a long flat depression in which eight trucks were parked in a square. There were a dozen long tents beside a shallow, dug-out waterhole. Ain Dahr, our stopping place, was one of the many secret sources of water, where the water did not rise to the surface but had to be dug out. It was an unwritten law that every user must carefully cover the waterhole with sand before going away.

The tents had been left open on all sides, owing to the great heat, and were being used solely for the purposes of shade.

Bundles of rifles in their leather cases were tied to the tent poles.

We arrived just at the hour of the afternoon prayer, and found forty Bedouins prostrating themselves in the direction of Mecca.

"*La ilaha il'Allah wa Muhammadun Rasul ullah.*"

Nagy and I sat down in the shade of the tent till the prayer was over.

Chapter XXVI

THE "TRAFFIC ACCIDENT"

EMIR Turki, a relative of our Emir, who commanded the expedition against Baraimi, shook us all warmly by the hand as he greeted us on arrival with the customary "*marhaba*," after which he presented three influential citizens of the Oasis of Baraimi to us. They were Mahmud er Rumi, Khaled er Riwayis and Matlak Abdurraziq.

Before accepting his invitation to tea, Nagy and I asked to see the injured persons on whose account we had been ordered into this unknown region. We had already surmised the nature of the "traffic accident," which had resulted in a couple of casualties from gunshot wounds, neither of them dangerous. Both of the wounded men were fit to be moved, and I at once recommended that preparations for the return journey should be made.

Omar, thereupon, undertook the task of filling up the cars from the gasoline containers we had brought with us. He employed the old-fashioned method of inserting a length of rubber hose into the bung hole of the container and drawing the gasoline off into the tank of the car. During the operation one of the drivers and a couple of Bedouins gave him a hand, but none of them thought of removing the cigarette from his mouth.

"*Maaleysh*," said one of them, when I told him off; and Omar said, "If it is God's will that the benzine should explode . . ." I did not wait to listen to the end of his sentence but hurried off to the tent. It appeared that it was not God's will that the benzine should go up. However, when I got back to Emir Turki's tent, I found an explosive atmosphere prevailing. The three men from Baraimi were far from being unanimous. For my part, I was dead tired from the journey and was completely indifferent to the problem of the ownership of the oasis. But I was not too tired to notice that each of the three notables was wearing a brand-new black mantle with a gold-lace border, an inlaid dirk and a gold wrist watch with a green enameled monogram, an embroidered silk headcloth and new sandals. These identical trappings were obviously gifts from the Saudi Arabian monarch.

It was evident that these three trusty citizens had already visited the old King in Riyadh, and had there made their kowtow to him. Without any undue exercise of intelligence, one could guess that they had begged, in the name of their fellow citizens for protection and help against . . . yes, against whom?

It looked like a desert version of *Anschluss* politics.

"Will you have some more tea, Doctor?" said Turki.

I handed my glass to the servant.

"Suppose we ask the doctor for his opinion," suggested Mahmud er Rumi, a haggard ascetic with the glowing eyes of a fanatic in a corpse-pale face. "The doctor's views on this question will surely be unbiased."

"What do you want to ask me about?" I said, though I knew very well the subject of their question.

"Well, do you think that the annexation of our oasis to Saudi Arabia would be an advantage for us or not?"

I couldn't tell them how little I cared. The years I had spent in the East had long ago taught me to observe the rule of safety first. On this occasion, I found it expedient to hunt with the hounds and accordingly expressed the view that union with the powerful kingdom of Saudi Arabia could only bring benefits to the inhabitants of Baraimi—the benefits of peace, freedom and prosperity.

"Well spoken, Doctor!" said Turki with a nod of approval and a friendly smile. "We must never forget that the people of the oasis have always felt that they belong to our house, and that they stand loyally by us in the struggle against the British colonizers and are resolved to shake off the rule of the puppet government of Oman. Peace, Freedom and Prosperity shall now return to Baraimi."

Freedom announced herself by a dull report from the distance.

"Muzzle-loaders," said Turki smiling. Then he added, turning down the corners of his mouth, "A pack of bandits."

For a while we could hear the sharper reports of the rifles of our troops, and then the shooting ceased.

"They have emptied their barrels and must load again," said Turki, commenting on the lull, "but I expect they have had enough and are now withdrawing."

It appeared that he was not quite right about the muzzle-loaders, as the firing began afresh and the sharp reports we heard clearly came from the discharge of modern repeating rifles.

"It sounds as though there were a lot of bandits in the neighborhood," said I crossly, as the Bedouins, reviving from their fatigue, listened wakefully to the noise of fighting, which could not be more than a mile away. The rifles were untied from the tent poles and pulled out of their leather cases.

Two Bedouins came stumbling down the dune in front of us, dragging a wounded man between them and shouting, "They have attacked. Imam has fallen."

Nagy and I took charge of the wounded man, and the Bedouins hastily reported what had happened. In a moment the whole camp was alive, like a disturbed ant heap. Turki certainly couldn't complain of any lack of fighting spirit among his men. Snatching up their arms and waiting for no orders, they all rushed up the steep slope.

"Halt! Stay here, stay here! You sons of dogs," shouted Turki after them, but the town-bred Emir had none of the qualities of a military leader. He was able to restrain only three men from running forward, and these he formally adjured to remain and guard the camp. Then he seized his rifle and ran after his troops.

The wounded man had been shot through the lung, and his condition was serious. We could do little except relieve the pain. Without much hope of saving him, we laid him on the sand in the shade of a truck. Nagy wiped the blood off his hands on his galabia and, looking around the camp, said, "Three guards, two unarmed doctors and three wounded men! If our friends now try the old ruse and, after feinting at our outposts, attack the camp, that will be the end of us."

I expressed my doubts. "That sort of tactics is only employed in desert battles to lure the enemy out of the camp, with a view to plundering the stores and carrying off women and camels. The people who are attacking us know perfectly well that there is nothing worth plundering in the camp. Their object is to annihilate our expedition."

"If they want to do that," said Nagy, "they have only to set fire to the cars. They couldn't choose a more effective method. Let us hope it won't occur to them."

As a precaution, I ordered the three guards to collect all the arms and ammunition available. I found that, counting the weapons of the wounded men, we had five Mauser rifles and one pistol with thirty rounds for each rifle and a magazine with six cartridges for the pistol. Very little, but better than nothing.

Meanwhile, Nagy drove some of the cars closer together so as to restrict the area we had to defend. We disposed our slender defense force under the trucks and, lying in the red sand, stared at the slopes surrounding us. I and my colleague kept our eyes on the southern slope. Our lung casualty lay between us, so that, if need be, we could attend to him. He lay silent on his back, his face contorted with fear and his breath rattling in and out of his lungs, as he stared at the differential of the car above his head.

"I hope we shan't both stop one," said Nagy quietly, without turning his head. "So long as one of us is all right, we both have a chance of getting through. But who is going to help us, if we both are wounded?"

Had he really got to conjure up such an unpleasant picture at a moment like this? I felt in my pockets for a cigarette, but couldn't find one.

"Have you a cigarette on you?" I ask Nagy.

Without a word he threw me one.

"I've got nothing to light it with."

He threw his lighter across to me.

I never got as far as lighting it, for at that moment a bullet pierced the metal side of the truck with a sharp crack. Immediately afterward, we heard the echo of the shot from the dunes behind us. I threw down my cigarette and the lighter in the sand, pushed back the safety catch of my rifle and watched the hostile Bedouins streaming down the slope toward us, uttering piercing cries. They were still about 300 yards away, and as they ran they fired wildly at the car park. The bullets whistled over our heads, struck the cars or threw up spurts of sand in front of us. One of our people fired a couple of shots at the attackers.

"Hold your fire, you camel!" I yelled. "Let them come nearer." That meant only twenty-eight more cartridges.

The attackers numbered some twenty men, if in the excitement of the moment I counted correctly. They were opposed by the five of us, with twenty-eight shots to fire. Now they were within 150 yards of us. Some of their shots came unpleasantly near, though they were still firing without aiming. Damnation. That shot must have struck a gasoline tank on one of the cars. A thin stream of gasoline spurted out onto the man with the lung wound and Dr. Nagy dragged him a few yards toward him. "Pull him behind the wheel," I shouted to Nagy. A ricochet struck the back tire of the truck under which we were lying. The air hissed out, kicking up a spurt of red sand. Then I crawled behind the other wheel of the truck.

From the other side I heard someone crying, "Doctor, Doctor! Saad is wounded."

Holding my rifle in front of me, as I had learned in my infantry training, I crept around to the other side. The injured man was bleeding profusely from a scalp wound. While I was winding a bandage around his head, I had to keep my eyes on the attacking Bedouins who, now split up into little groups, were not more than fifty yards away.

Near enough. I shouted the order to fire into the screaming attackers, and instantly heard the discharge of our rifles.

"Give me your rifle, Doctor," begged the man I was dressing. "I can shoot while you are tying me up."

I put my carbine into his hands and went on trying to stop the flow of blood from his head. Saad fired, wiped the blood out of his eyes and fired again. I saw dark bodies lying in the sand in front of the car park. One of the attackers who had gotten to within ten yards of us threw his head back and then collapsed at the knees.

"Keep shooting, Saad," I cried, as a tall muscular mulatto came running at us, shooting from the hip. In his belt was a broad-bladed, curved dagger, and a throwing club hung at his side.

Saad did not answer. He had slumped forward unconscious into the sand with my carbine under him. I struggled vainly to pull it out from under his body. It was caught somewhere.

The mulatto had halted a few yards from the truck and was watching my frantic efforts with a scornful smile. Then he slowly raised his rifle and took aim. Still tugging at the carbine, I stared like a hypnotized rabbit into the black circle at the end of his rifle barrel.

He pressed the trigger. *Click* went the firing pin.

The fellow looked at his rifle and then pulled the breech open. The magazine was empty. In a fury he hurled the weapon at me.

Then he went for me with a roar, swinging his club in his hand. I debated for a moment whether to remain under the truck or to get out and meet him in the open. I concluded to jump out of cover, and as I did so his throwing club flew over my head and struck the side of the truck. I ducked instinctively and before I could right myself, the brute sprang on my back.

The momentum and weight of his heavy body brought me down, and it was lucky for me that I had not the force to stand up to his attack, for then he would surely have stabbed me in the back with his dagger. As it was, we both rolled on the sand, in which his dagger was buried up to the hilt.

However, he soon got over his surprise and was on his feet again before I had pulled myself together.

As he flung himself down on me again, his dagger in his hand ready to strike, I rolled over like lightning. I was not quite quick enough, for though the dagger missed me and stuck into the sand, I received the full weight of this powerful man on top of me.

Panting and struggling in deadly silence, we fought for our lives. I saw the vein in my enemy's forehead swelling. He raised the dagger once more to strike. There was no taking of prisoners in the desert. One of us was for it, and I was the one if the dagger struck home. I gripped his wrist with both hands and managed to arrest the point a few inches from my throat. Then he took hold of the handle of the dagger with his other hand in order to overcome the resistance of my straining arms, and pressed downward with all his force. I saw the blade trembling not a handbreadth from my neck. I felt my strength ebbing away. My enemy—a bundle of muscles—was stronger. In despair I tried to get my legs around him, but he only bent lower over the hilt of the dagger.

Then an idea came to me, and I let go with my left hand and with my right pushed the weapon across to the left. My action took the mulatto by surprise, and the dagger ran deep into the sand by the side of my neck. In the certainty that I could not save myself otherwise, I had done the right thing.

Before my antagonist could pull himself up and deliver another blow, I managed to pick up a handful of sand with my left hand and threw it into his eyes. He roared with pain and began to scrape out the sand with the fingers of one hand, while the hand that held the dagger waved in the air. Then I seized his wrist with both hands and tore the dagger from him. Then I stabbed blindly, without aiming, three or four times into his massive body, which collapsed on top of me.

It took minutes before I had gathered enough strength to roll the body off me. The ashen face of the mulatto, with its bluish lips, had not lost in death the desperate expression which it had worn during the combat.

A thin trickle of blood seeped from his half-open mouth into his beard, sticky with sand and sweat.

I was not yet able to get on my feet. Sparks danced before my eyes. I cared nothing for what was happening around me. I heard no sounds. After a while, when I was somewhat recovered I obeyed the rule of the desert and stripped the dead man of his broad girdle and picked up his weapons—dagger, club and rifle.

Everything was curiously still. The shooting had stopped.

A long line of men was marching down the dunes toward the camp. This time it was our army, carrying their wounded with them. With laughter and raised voices, they told the story of their adventures and proudly showed us the booty they had captured.

While the Bedouins buried the dead, quickly and without ceremony, we two doctors looked after the wounded.

When it was dark the campfire was lit. Above us curved the star-spangled dome of the southern sky. The Bedouins sat by the fireside singing, "No goods have we, no lovely women either: nought but a cackling hen and a cock withal."

Nagy and I had settled down some way from the others in order to be nearer the casualties. The scene on which we gazed was worthy of a painter—the Bedouins in their flowing robes, with their weapons in their hands or at least within reach, their dark, bearded faces lit up by the flickering flames of the campfire. On the horizon the full moon was climbing, red as blood.

Mal ma andina, mal ma andina." I had not even a name. To what purpose would I have died, if my enemy's dagger had pierced my throat? In this red desert, the trace of blood was not visible for more than a day.

Now again, I dreamed of a land where the brightness of moon and stars was tempered by a veil of mist. I dreamed and I wondered.

A hand was laid on my shoulder. It was old Omar. "Shall we be going home, Doctor?"

"Yes," I said, "let us go home."

Chapter XXVII

I FIND A HOME

ON the day after our return from the expedition to Baraimi, I found on my office table a letter from a former colleague with whom I had served in the military hospital at Beirut and with whom I had kept up a desultory correspondence.

After I had read the letter, I reflected that if I had not come back it would probably have been thrown away, and the sender would have been annoyed at not receiving an answer. Or it might have been returned with the notice "Addressee dead," in which case my colleague would have passed on the news regretfully to my few acquaintances in Beirut, and I should soon have been forgotten like the Bedouin soldiers whom we buried in the red sand by the car park in Baraimi. No one would have made a fuss about a man without a passport or a registration certificate, who for practical purposes did not exist.

However, I did come back and did read the letter, which began with a brief summary of the news from Beirut, as far as it was likely to interest me, and continued in these terms:

"Our lazaretto has now become a proper hospital for the refugees from Palestine under the auspices of UNRRA. The work is still very strenuous, but much better organized than in your time. As a matter of fact, I have more work than I can cope with, and we have no children's specialist, so I am obliged to look after that branch. If only you were here, the problem could be easily solved, but I can't help thinking that we have lost you forever in the desert . . ."

"If only you were here!"

The only paper I possessed regarding my service in the war hospital at Beirut was an identity card, and Lebanon was the only country to which I had legal access.

The letter had come exactly at the right moment, for I had come to the conclusion that it was not worth my while to continue living in the desert till someone cut my throat or brought me to some equally violent end and I disappeared without a sign, *ad majorem Saudi Regis gloriam*. It did not take me long to reach a decision. I hurried to the post office and cabled to my colleague in Beirut.

"Accept post. Wire confirmation."

Two weeks later, I took up my new assignment as children's doctor in the only country in which I was welcome.

I found quarters on the outskirts of Beirut quite close to the blue expanse of the Mediterranean. I was no longer lodged in a mud-brick house with the roof for my bedroom, but in a solid modern building with bath, central heating and elevator—in fact, the same amenities I should have had in Berlin or Hamburg.

Three weeks after I had settled down in my new home, I received the visit of a little old man wearing the turban of a Hadji. He leaned on a stout cane to support his faltering steps and wheezed as he talked.

"*Ahlan wa Sahlan!*" I said. "You are welcome. Come in and be seated."

Over coffee and cigarettes and sweet cakes, which my maid brought from the kitchen, we sat for a while in silence. After his third cigarette my visitor, with the polite curiosity which characterizes so many Arabs, began to question me about my life and experiences, and I answered his questions without reticence. In return, he recounted to me at great length the story of his family and drew a complicated picture of the genealogical tree of the Haidar family, starting almost with our first parents in the garden of Eden. From time to time, he laid his left hand on my knee to emphasize his words. The shape of this hand was not particularly elegant. Old age had diminished its beauty. Nor was it particularly clean. It was, in fact, the pitch-stained hand of a shoemaker, who carried on his business in the cellar of the next-door house. But this shoemaker was a person of the very highest importance. He was my first private patient.

In November, 1952, I passed the Lebanon State Examination for doctors and was now free to engage in private practice. But I acquired yet another privilege. I was now entitled to regard myself as a citizen of Lebanon and was authorized to travel as a Lebanese through all the frontiers and customs barriers of the world—a right hitherto denied to the German Dr. Pritzke, a physician of Berlin.

There was no longer anything to prevent me from flying to Berlin to visit my parents and my son by my first marriage, who lived with them.

I had not seen them since my departure for the Italian front in 1944, when my boy was only eighteen months old. After all the trials and sufferings that I had endured with stoicism during my eight years in the Orient, I am not ashamed to admit that I wept for joy to hear the familiar speech of Berlin at the Tempelhof air-field and to see a ten-year-old youngster looking shyly at the man who, they told him, was his father.

Wolf-Dietrich did not know me, and I could hardly recognize Germany. I had hoped to find everything as I remembered it, but I could not find the land I had known. Germany was for me a foreign country—Frankfurt am Main an unknown city. Only in Berlin did I have any feeling that I was safe in the shelter of my own home town. But all the time I was in Berlin I was wading through a slough of troubles. My apartment had been plundered at the end of the war. My boy had been born in the Warthegau, which now belonged to Poland, and I possessed no papers of any sort to show that he was my son or that I, as his father, had any authority over him. Morever, my parents were living in the Eastern Zone, where the authorities refused all permission to leave the territory. In a desperate struggle to get possession of my own child, I used every imaginable artifice to defend my rights, but it was only when the Occupying Powers came to my help that I finally succeeded in obtaining the custody of the boy and taking him back with me to Beirut. That was the end of December, 1952.

Today Wolf-Dietrich talks and writes Arabic and chaffs his schoolmates like a regular young Lebanese. His only complaint is that his father comes home from work too late and too tired to play with him.

Soon after midday I come home after my work in the UNRRA hospital, and when I arrive I find my waiting room full of patients who hardly leave me time for a hurried luncheon. The last of them may not leave till seven or eight, and then I must go on a round of visits which may keep me busy far into the night. I have no time for any private life, but I wonder if I have ever really cared much for anything except my professional work.

I suppose I might long ago have returned to Germany to live there, but in the meantime I have settled down and taken root in Beirut, which now I feel is my home, and a lovely home too.

Here I have friends and a reputation. I have my work, and professional possibilities which I shall strive to develop in my new surroundings. Moreover, after so many years of adventure, involuntary if you will, in which my recent life has been spent, where in the world could I lead such an interesting life as here in Beirut, the Hong Kong of the Middle East, with the Switzerland of the Arab lands as my background?

In my waiting room sit Bedouins in flowing robes, veiled women and Druzes from the Jebel, with their secret religion. Sometimes I find among my patients a Syrian politician or one of my friends from Saudi Arabia, who has come here to spend his easily earned oil money in high living, or a bravo from the hills, who leans his rifle against my instrument cupboard before stripping to be examined.

And I think that here I can serve, not only the country I live in, but Europe and Germany as well, by the work I do in my new home where all call me El Hakim el Alemani.

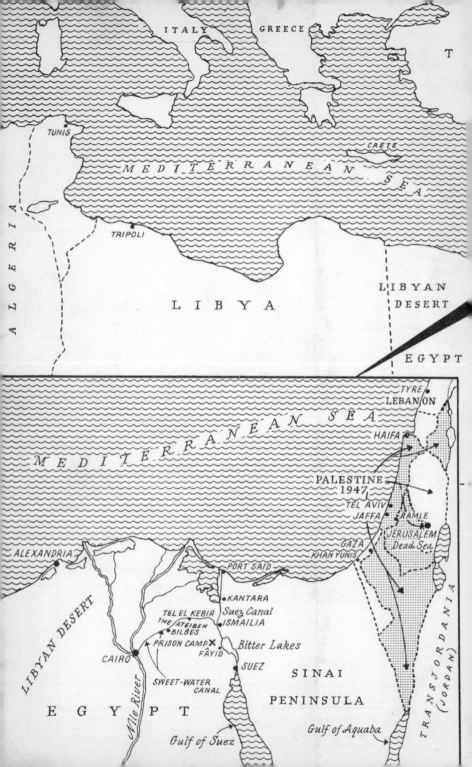